Non-Photorealistic Rendering

Non-Photorealistic Rendering

Bruce Gooch

Amy Gooch

University of Utah
School of Computing

A K Peters
Natick, Massachusetts

Editorial, Sales, and Customer Service Office

A K Peters, Ltd.
63 South Avenue
Natick, MA 01760
www.akpeters.com

Library of Congress Cataloging-in-Publication Data

Gooch, Bruce, 1966–
    Non-photorealistic rendering / Bruce Gooch, Amy Gooch.
        p. cm.
    Includes bibliographical references and index.
    ISBN 1-56881-133-0
    1. Computer graphics. I. Gooch, Amy, 1973– II. Title.

    T385 .G656 2001
    006.6–dc21   2001019893

Printed in Canada
05 04 03 02 01   10 9 8 7 6 5 4 3 2 1

Photorealism, like pornography,
leaves nothing to the imagination.
–Cassidy Curtis

Contents

Preface

Our intent in writing this book is to bring together in a single reference all of the research to date in the field. We also attempt to categorize and comment on this research in order to aid the reader in understanding the state of the art. Each chapter includes an artistic reference section; while conducting NPR research ourselves, we have often spent long days in libraries and book stores pouring over art books.

The major problem we faced in the writing of this book was when to stop. Because NPR is a new field, new work is constantly being published. We therefore made the decision to limit this book to published works before and including SIGGRAPH 2000. We will be maintaining an NPR web page at (http://www.cs.utah.edu/npr) which can be used as a resource to find new NPR-related papers.

Acknowledgments

We would like to thank our families for their love, support, and patience. We are also indebted to our advisors, Peter Shirley, Rich Riesenfeld, and Elaine Cohen, as well as the graduate students, faculty, and researchers in the graphics research groups at the University of Utah. Thanks to A K Peters for believing we could pull all of this together, and particularly to Ariel Jaffee for actually making it happen. Thanks to all of those who helped us with edits on the final draft: William Martin, Kristi Potter, Shawn Ramsey, Eric Reinhard, Charles Schmidt, Mike Stark, Chris Wyman, Sandy

Hiskey, Karen Feinhauer, Matt Kaplan and John McCorquodale. Special thanks to all of the NPR researchers, especially those whose imagery is presented in this book.

Amy Gooch
Bruce Gooch
June 5th, 2001

Chapter 1

Introduction

The ubiquity of computer-generated imagery around us, in movies, advertising, or on the Internet, is already being taken for granted. What impresses most people is the photorealistic quality of the images. Pictures, as we have often been told, are worth a thousand words and the information transported by an image can take many different forms. Imagine a photograph of a sailboat out on the water on a fall day. From such a photograph a viewer can infer a vast amount of information such as the time of day, the weather, wind direction and speed, relationships between people on the boat, and the like. However, such an image would be of little use to someone attempting to build a sailboat. A sailboat builder would certainly prefer technical drawings or blueprints, while someone who simply wanted to communicate the idea sailboat may only need to draw a shape representing the boat and a triangle representing the sail. In the past, imagery generated by artists has been used to provide information that may not be readily apparent in photographs or real life. Applying a similar goal to computer-generated images is the motivation for a new field of research in computer graphics called non-photorealistic rendering (NPR).

The driving force behind computer graphics for the past 35 years has been photorealism. The quality of images created using a computer is judged by how closely they resemble a photograph. Images are rendered by running a physics-simulation which emulates the behavior of light inside the modeled scene. The term photorealistic rendering is used to describe this type of computer graphics technique.

In NPR images are instead judged by how effectively they communicate. When using images to communicate the essence of a scene, simulating reality is not as important as creating the illusion of reality. NPR

1

involves stylization and communication, usually driven by human perception. Knowledge and techniques long used by artists are now being applied to computer graphics to emphasize specific features of a scene, expose subtle attributes, and omit extraneous information to give rise to a new field.

NPR brings together art and science, concentrating less on the process and more on the communication content of an image. In photorealistic rendering, it is hard to neglect detail; in fact the highest level of detail is generally preferred, even if this high level of detail makes the image cluttered and confusing. The level of detail in NPR varies between images and can be adapted across a single image to focus the viewer's attention. This level-of-detail change in an image is called a modification in the "level of abstraction" of the image. NPR is now being acknowledged for its ability to communicate serious ideas. For example an X-ray or MRI scan of an injured knee is difficult for a non-expert to decipher, while an embellished computer-generated medical illustration of the injury which is more abstract will help a patient understand the problem and the treatment.

Research in NPR can be separated into three general categories; artistic media simulation, user-assisted image creation, and automatic image creation. NPR research in media simulation attempts to model the physical properties of an artistic medium such as watercolor, pen and ink, or pencil drawing. Research in user-assisted image creation is aimed at guiding a software user in creating artistic images. This type of research attempts to incorporate the skills and techniques of human artists into expert systems enabling non-artists to produce images with a hand-crafted look and feel. Automatic image creation research aims to automatically create artistic images with a previously defined communication goal.

When an artist sets out to paint an image, he must have three types of physical tools. The first is a medium such as oil paint, acrylic, or watercolor with which to construct the image. The second is some type of applicator or brush to apply the media. The third is a substrate such as paper or canvas on which to apply the media. NPR researchers have built computer systems that physically simulate artists' tools and the interaction of the tools. Examples include systems that model water color painting using dynamic fluid flow calculations, pencil drawing systems based on electron microscope observations and procedurally-modeled pen and ink drawing systems.

Sutherland's paradigm, the idea that a keyboard is not the optimal form of human-computer interaction, is the basis for all interactive computer input techniques. NPR research in this area focuses on using novel computer input devices and virtual reality to create images, animations and virtual worlds. Examples include: the SKETCH system where simple gestures are used to create three-dimensional models, and the Harold system where a user draws and can interact with an entire virtual world like Harold in the children's story "Harold and the Purple Crayon."

Not everyone has the time or ability to produce great works of art. Methods have been explored for automatically creating artistic imagery. Computer scientists research the methods and techniques of an artistic form such as technical illustration. They then compile a list of rules that artists follow in order to produce images using the artistic form. Finally, computer algorithms are developed which automatically render images according to the artistic rules. For example, the process of creating operation and repair manuals can be automated by extracting technical illustrations during the design process. Another example is automatic painting techniques used as special effects in movies such as *What Dreams May Come*.

Non-photorealistic rendering is a field in its infancy, consequently fundamental questions tend to arise quickly in any discussion of NPR. For example: Is it difficult to imitate the decisions of a real artist? Can computer programs have artistic inventiveness? Can computer programs be expressive? Can creativity be automated? One observation is that computers can attend to fine detail and repetitive tasks, but without a user, simulating artistic expression is difficult and, some researchers argue, impossible.

One key idea that is often overlooked when scientists try to codify art is that a non-photorealistic rendering method cannot be applied to any image or scene and produce a work of art. The benefits of NPR are maximized when one thinks about the subject matter, the scene composition, and the purpose of the image. NPR algorithms cannot make a bad image good. However, as images produced by the results of non-photorealistic rendering research show, NPR algorithms can significantly enhance good images.

The complexity of the research we are reporting on varies by orders of magnitude—from programs that can be implemented in a single afternoon to large systems that have taken teams of programmers years to encode. For some of the simple methods we provide pseudo code, while for the large systems we can only explain the process in the space allowed. For some of the research reviewed in this book, it is left to the interested reader to get the implementation details from the paper. However, in all cases, we provide images which result from the research discussed.

Part I
Simulating Artistic Media

Chapter 2

Simulating Artistic Media: Drawing

We begin this chapter by reviewing digital drawing strategies, then provide in-depth coverage of algorithms designed to simulate charcoal pencil, colored pencil, and pen-and-ink drawing. We discuss four systems in depth in this chapter: graphite pencil drawing, colored pencil drawing, and two methods for pen-and-ink drawing.

2.1 Background

The first algorithms to be considered are standard computer line-drawing algorithms. These are modified by researchers in NPR to produce lines with a hand-drawn effect. Appel et al. [Appel et al. 79] describe a method for hidden line removal using the haloed line effect. Tomihisa Kamada and Satoru Kawai [Kamada, Kawai 87] give an enhanced treatment of hidden line algorithms. Finkelstein and Salesin [Finkelstein, Salesin 94] describe a multi-resolution curve representation based on wavelets that supports global smoothing and editing functions, but preserves local detail.

Modified line-drawing algorithms are incorporated into higher level tools as primitives. Allan Vermeulen and Peter Tanner [Vermeulen, Tanner 89] presented "PencilSketch," a standard computer drawing system with the goal of making lines that simulate the look of hand-drawn pencil lines. Mario Costa Sousa and John Buchanan [Sousa, Buchanan 99a] [Sousa, Buchanan 99b][Sousa, Buchanan 00] built a system to simulate graphite pencil drawing based on an observational model. They model the micro-interactions of pencils with paper, as well as the effects of blenders and erasers. Takagi et al. [Takagi et al. 99] have built a volumetric model for colored pencil drawing. Their system models the interaction of pencil and substrate, and the effects of a water-wash over the completed drawing. Salisbury et al. [Salisbury et al. 94][Salisbury et al. 96][Salisbury et al. 97] present an interactive system for creating pen-and-ink illustrations. Their system gives the user high-level interactive tools with which to produce illustrations based on a source image. Georges Winkenbach and David Salesin present algorithms and techniques for rendering polygonal models and free-form surfaces in simulated pen-and-ink [Winkenbach, Salesin 94] [Winkenbach, Salesin 96].

2.2   Simulating Pencil

2.2.1   Observational Models of Graphite Pencil Materials

Mario Costa Sousa and John Buchanan designed a system for simulating graphite pencil-drawing based on electron microscope observations [Sousa, Buchanan 99a][Sousa, Buchanan 99b] [Sousa, Buchanan 00]. They observed the interaction among physical pencil drawing materials (pencil, paper, eraser, blender), with the goal of producing algorithms that simulate these interactions. An example of the type of electron microscope image used is shown in Figure 2.1. Sousa and Buchanan break the problem of simulating graphite pencil drawing into four fundamental subproblems:

1. Drawing materials—These are algorithms that simulate, at a low level, graphite pencils, drawing paper, blenders, and kneaded erasers.

2. Drawing primitives—These algorithms build up tones and textures using the drawing-material algorithms.

3. Rendering methods—These algorithms use the drawing primitives to outline, shade, shadow, or texture images based on reference images or three-dimensional objects, in a manner that emulates hand-drawn pencil renderings.

4. High level tools—These tools allow interactive user control of the drawing process by ordering and repeating lower-level drawing processes.

The following set of artistic references are mentioned by the researchers whose work we cover in this chapter.

For charcoal pencil drawing:

- *Art of the Pencil: A Revolutionary Look at Drawing, Painting, and the Pencil* by S.W. Camhy [Camhy 97].

- *The Drawing Process: Rendering* by D. Douglas and D. van Wyk [Douglas, van Wyk 93].

- *Pencil Drawing* by G. Franks [Franks 88].

- *Rendering in Pencil* by A.L. Guptill [Guptill 97].

- *An Introduction to Drawing* by J. Horton [Horton 94].

- *Pencil Drawing Techniques* by D. Lewis [Lewis 84a].

- *An Introduction to Pencil Techniques: Easy Start Guide* by H. Misawa [Misawa 93].

- *Barron's Art Handbooks: Drawing* by the Parramon Editorial Team [Parramon 97].

- *The Art of Drawing in Lead Pencil* by J. Salwey [Salwey 25].

- *Pencil Drawing (from the Art Is... Video Series)* G. Price [Price 93].

- *Course in Pencil Sketching, Four Books in One* by E.W. Watson [Watson 78].

For colored pencil drawing:

- *Colored Pencil Drawing Techniques* by I. Hutton-Jamieson [Hutton-Jamieson 86].

- *The Encyclopedia of Colored Pencil Techniques* by J. Martin [Martin 97].

For pen-and-ink drawing:

- *Pen and Ink Techniques* by F. Lohan [Lohan 78b].

- *Rendering in Pen and Ink* by A. Guptill [Guptill 76].

- *Ink Drawing Techniques* by H. Pitz [Pitz 57].

- *The Technical Pen* by G. Simmons [Simmons 92].

Graphite pencils are modeled by taking into account two factors: the hardness of the pencil "lead" and the shape of the sharpened pencil point. Drawing pencils are made up of a wooden shell surrounding a "lead" where the lead (the writing core of the pencil) is composed of a combination of graphite, wax, and clay. The relative percentages of lead and clay determine

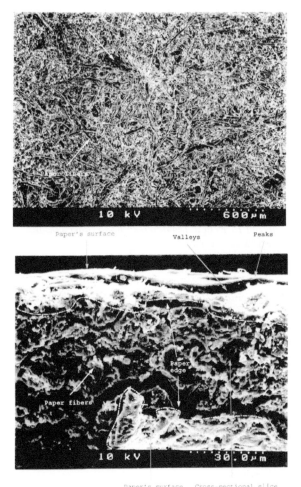

Figure 2.1.   Aerial and cross-sectional views (left and right images respectively) from real drawing paper (medium weight, moderate tooth) generated by a scanning electron microscope (SEM) at 10kv acceleration voltage, with different magnifications (50 times on the left image and 1000 times on the right image) and with scale resolution in microns (600 microns and 30 microns for the left and right images respectively). Paper roughness results from the clustering of paper fibers which form peaks and valleys across the paper surface. Copyright 2000 Sousa and Buchanan [Sousa, Buchanan 00]. Used by permission.

the hardness of the pencil, and the wax is included to lubricate the pencil tip as it moves across the paper. Pencils with a higher percentage of clay than graphite are harder, and therefore deposit less lead on the paper when used. Changing the manner in which a pencil is sharpened will effect the manner in which graphite is deposited on the paper's surface. Sousa and Buchanan use a three-dimensional polygon to define the pencil tip shape. From the lead type, polygon tip shape, and a pressure distribution, a lead distribution is computed for each mark on the paper's surface. The lead distribution determines the number of graphite particles deposited on the paper's surface. Examples of pencil marks generated with Sousa's algorithms are shown in Figure 2.2.

The drawing paper is simulated using a three-dimensional height field. The grain of the paper is defined as the smallest feature of a particular paper simulation. The paper to be simulated is then gridded off according to the grain of the simulation and each grid point is assigned a height. The height of each cell represents the maxium local lead volume. The amount of lead, wax, and clay contained in the cell is computed at runtime for those cells which interact with the pencil's tip. Sousa and Buchanan call these grid cells grains. By using pseudo-random textures in the manner of Curtis et al. [Curtis et al. 97] or by thresholding scanned drawing paper, Sousa and Buchanan compute the grain size and the height field.

The core of Sousa and Buchanan's algorithm is the interaction between the paper and a pencil. The paper reacts to the hardness of the pencil and the pressure exerted on it. The pencil's tip shape is changed by these same factors, and pencil strokes are left on the paper due to the interaction. Sousa and Buchanan define 47 variables to describe paper, graphite pencils, and their interaction. Because of the complexity of the system, we provide only an outline of this algorithm for modeling paper and pencil interaction. The interested reader should consult Sousa and Buchanan's papers [Sousa, Buchanan 99a][Sousa, Buchanan 99b][Sousa, Buchanan 00].

- For each new position of the pencil tip over the paper:

    1. Evaluate the polygonal tip shape of the pencil's point.

    2. Compute the local lead-threshold volume of the paper (how much material can a cell hold).

    3. Distribute pressure applied to the pencil across the tip shape.

- For each paper grain interacting with the pencil tip:

    1. Compute the grain-porous threshold volume (how much material does each cell hold).

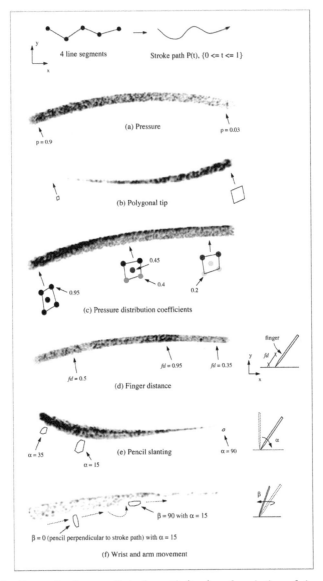

Figure 2.2.   Example of a pencil stroke path (top) and variation of six parameters defining the pencil-stroke primitive, rubbed with soft leads over a rough medium-weight paper. Copyright 1999 Sousa and Buchanan [Sousa, Buchanan 99b]. Used by permission.

2. Process the grain biting the lead.

3. Compute damage caused to the grain by the pencil lead.

Blenders and erasers are modeled using the same basic algorithms; however they are allowed to both absorb and distribute lead particles during the interaction process with the paper. Blenders are used to soften edges and to make smooth transitions between tone values. Erasers remove graphite particles to lighten a drawing. Examples of blending and erasing are shown in Figures 2.3, 2.4, and 2.5.

Sousa and Buchanan simulate artistic shading using a mark-making primitive that renders a collection of strokes. The reason for this primitive is to create areas in screen space with tone and texture. Example methods are illustrated in Figure 2.6.

Sousa and Buchanan's system allows three-dimensional models to be rendered as pencil drawings using two methods. The first method is an outline sketch using silhouette and crease lines extracted from the three-dimensional model. Methods for extracting these lines are covered in Chapter 8. The second method is to render the model using a simulated tonal contrast drawing. Three-dimensional models are rendered in tonal contrast by first producing a grayscale reference image using Phong shading. Then for each visible polygon face and each shadow, a mark-making primitive is constructed to fill that area of screen space with simulated pencil lines. The pencil lines can be clipped to exactly fill the region, or allowed to wander outside the screen space area to create a sketchy feel to the rendering. In addition, the two drawing methods (outline drawing and tonal contrast) can be used together in a single image. The tone-matching work is extensive, and the interested reader should study Sousa's Eurographics 99 paper [Sousa, Buchanan 99b]. Examples of his system for rendering pencil sketches from three-dimensional models are shown in Figure 2.7.

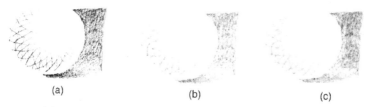

(a)   (b)   (c)

Figure 2.3.   (a) Hand drawing of a sphere drawn using a very soft pencil and using cross hatching to convey tone values. (b) Automatic rendering using a simulated 2B pencil (1.24 sec.). (c) Smudging the cross hatched lines on the sphere (30 sec.). Note the shadow is also smudged to make it softer. Kneaded eraser is used to enhance the highlight and clear a portion of the shadows (8 sec.). Copyright 2000 Sousa and Buchanan [Sousa, Buchanan 00]. Used by permission.

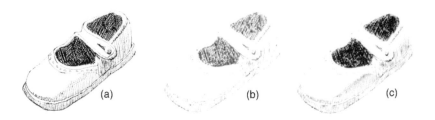

Figure 2.4.   (a) A physical pen-and-ink illustration of a shoe. (b) An automatic pencil rendering using a simulated 3B pencil (2.79 sec.). (c) The lines are smudged (30 sec.) and then a kneaded eraser is applied to the top and inside of the shoe to enhance the tonal contrast (12 sec.). Copyright 2000 Sousa and Buchanan [Sousa, Buchanan 00]. Used by permission.

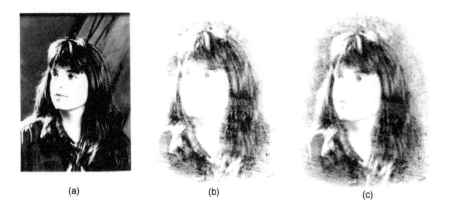

Figure 2.5.   (a) A high contrast photograph of Patricia. (b) An automatic rendering using a 6H pencil (2.18 sec.) followed by interactive rendering with strokes applied using medium-soft pencils applied with light pressure (15 sec.). (c) Smudging the darker tones in the background of the photograph, the shadows, and some of the face lines (40 sec.). Kneaded eraser lightly applied to emphasize the highlights (30 sec.). Copyright 2000 Sousa and Buchanan [Sousa, Buchanan 00]. Used by permission.

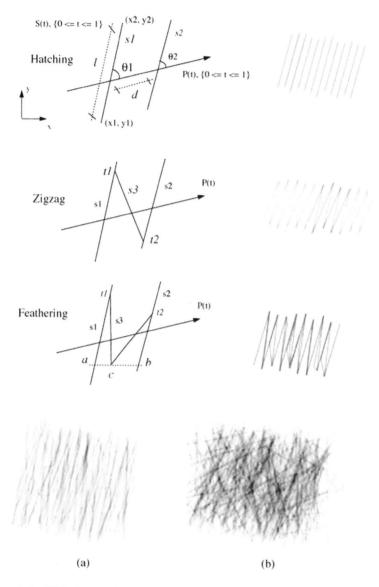

Figure 2.6. This figure illustrates three variations of Sousa's mark-making primitive. The images (a) and (b) in the lower portion of the figure are the result of composing a layer of feathering with a layer of zigzagging. Copyright 1999 Sousa and Buchanan [Sousa, Buchanan 99b]. Used by permission.

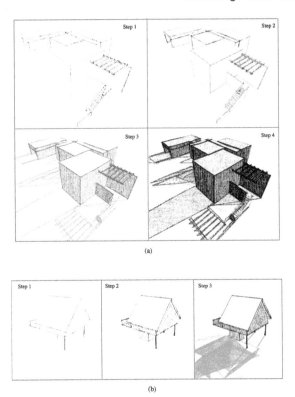

Figure 2.7.   This figure shows the evolution of two pencil drawings using Sousa's system.   The drawings are simulated on semi-rough paper using a variety of pencils.   The upper drawing was rendered in approximately five minutes while the lower image took approximately three minutes.   Copyright 1999 Sousa and Buchanan [Sousa, Buchanan 99b].   Used by permission.

2.2.2   Volumetric Modeling of Colored Pencil Drawing

Saeko Takagi, Masayuki Nakajima, and Issei Fujishiro [Takagi et al. 99] propose a volume graphics model for colored pencil drawing (CPD). Their model uses three volumetric sub-models as building blocks to create a CPD system. They first construct a volumetric model of the micro-structure of drawing paper. They next model the physics that simulates the colored pencil distributing colored lead particles onto the paper. Lastly Takagi et al. model the redistribution of colored lead particles that results when water is brushed over the pencil drawing. Images are then rendered using volume visualization software. A graphic overview of this process is shown in Figure 2.8.

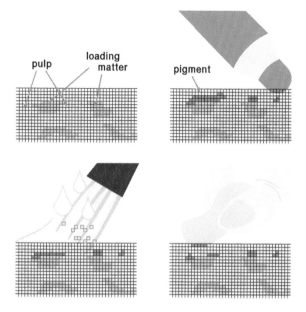

Figure 2.8. This figure shows volumetric diagrams of the paper volume, pigment distribution, and redistribution process concepts in cross section. Copyright 1999 Takagi et al. [Takagi et al. 99]. Used by permission.

Takagi et al. model the micro-structure of drawing paper by first observing that drawing paper is made up of pulp fibers and a binder or talc. Pulp fibers are modeled by long cylinders whose length, radius, orientation, and path are randomly perturbed. The talc binder is simulated at the micro scale by disks of random size. Takagi et al. chose discs because talc tends to form disc-shaped crystals.

Drawing paper is simulated by placing alternating layers of talc and pulp fibers onto each other and then allowing the layers to settle. A voxel field is created by sampling the simulated paper and recording a scaler value for each voxel that represents density of the paper elements. Voxels are updated during the drawing and washing process to reflect the amount of pigment contained in each voxel.

The distribution of colored lead particles that are deposited onto the paper when it comes into contact with a pencil are modeled using a method known as Offset Distance Accessibility (ODA) [Miller 94]. Takagi et al. assume that pencils and brushes have a spherical tips and use ODA to find which paper voxels a pencil or brush can affect during a stroke. Once the

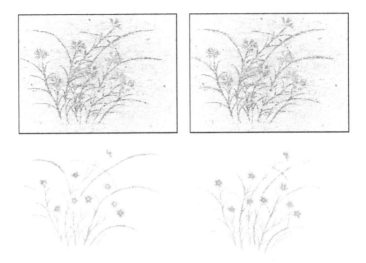

Figure 2.9.   Left: Simulated colored pencil drawings on Japanese paper called "washi." Right: Actual colored pencil drawings. See Color Plate II. Copyright 1999 Takagi et al. [Takagi et al. 99]. Used by permission.

voxels that have been touched during a stroke are found, the distribution of colored lead pigment to those voxels can be computed. Colored lead particles can be distributed in two ways. Particles can be shaved off from the pencil lead by friction and deposited onto a convex region of the paper. Alternatively, particles may adhere to the surface of the paper as the pencil crosses the paper. Brushstrokes and eraser strokes are modeled in a similar manner. Brushstrokes, however, are not allowed to deposit new pigment particles; they may only redistribute existing particles or remove particles. Eraser strokes may only remove particles. An example of a colored pencil drawing simulated with this technique is shown in Figure 2.9.

2.3   Simulating Pen-and-Ink

2.3.1   Pen-and-Ink Illustrations

Georges Winkenbach and David Salesin describe the principles of traditional pen-and-ink illustration, and present algorithms and techniques for rendering polygonal models and free-form surfaces in simulated pen-and-ink [Winkenbach, Salesin 94][Winkenbach, Salesin 96]. They introduce two new ideas for creating tone and texture on three-dimensional models: "stroke textures" for creating tone and texture on polygonal models, and "controlled density hatching" for free-form surfaces. They also demonstrate

Figure 2.10.   Hat and Cane. Both the hat and the cane are modeled with
B-spline surfaces. The ribbon is modeled as a separate B-spline surface. Note
the curved shadow that the hat projects on its rim and the use of crosshatch-
ing on the curved portion of the cane.   Copyright 1996 Winkenbach and
Salesin [Winkenbach, Salesin 96] and ACM. Used by permission.

methods for scale-dependent rendering, generating outlines, clipping, and
casting curved shadows onto curved surfaces. An example of this type of
pen-and-ink illustration is shown in Figure 2.10.

The work of Winkenbach and Salesin is an excellent example of non-
photorealistic rendering research. They research the methods and techniques of an artistic form, compile lists of rules that artists follow in order to produce images using this form, then write computer algorithms to
render images according to the artistic rules. The method employed by
Winkenbach and Salesin also allows them to build systems which encapsu-
late artistic methods, enabling non-artists to produce images with a hand-
crafted look and feel. Readers interested in research in the field of non-
photorealistic rendering are encouraged to read their papers and examine
their research methods more closely, in particular, [Winkenbach, Salesin 94]
and [Winkenbach, Salesin 96].

Pen-and-ink illustrations convey shape information using outlines and
shading. Outline strokes are used to convey the contours of an object and
to delineate the interior regions. In illustration, shaded regions are said
to have a "tone." Tone is a representation of the amount of light that
is reflected toward an observer from a point on the surface of an object.
Pen-and-ink illustrations are made up of strokes and therefore convey an
average of the reflected light in a region. In addition, the character of the
strokes can be manipulated by the artist to convey an idea of the material
properties or "texture" of the surface. Myriad methods exist for combining
outline strokes and shading strokes in an illustration. Winkenbach and
Salesin present some common conventions in their papers. Examples of
outlines, tones, and textures are shown in Figure 2.11.

In standard computer-graphics rendering, tone and texture are separate elements of the rendering pipeline. In illustration, because both

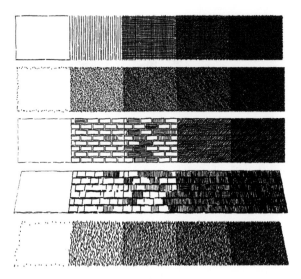

Figure 2.11. Using strokes to indicate both texture and tone. The stroke textures used, from top to bottom, are: "cross-hatching," "stippling," "bricks," "shingles," and "grass". Notice that the outline style of each texture is particular to that texture. Copyright 1994 Winkenbach and Salesin [Winkenbach, Salesin 94] and ACM. Used by permission.

are rendered using strokes, they must be tightly coupled. In addition, three-dimensional information encoded in standard computer renderings of a modeled object or scene does not, beyond projection, need to interact with the two-dimensional image of the object or scene. In illustration, this is not the case, because the outline of an object can be affected by other objects in the scene. Winkenbach and Salesin note that the following changes must be made to the standard graphics pipeline.

Maintaining a two-dimensional spatial subdivision. The need to consider two-dimensional adjacency information in rendering suggests the use of some form of spatial subdivision of the visible surfaces. Winkenbach maintains a planar map using a half-edge data structure [Manyyla 88].

Rendering of texture and tone. Texture and tone are conveyed with stroke hatching instead of scan-converted polygons.

Clipping. Strokes must be clipped to the region they are shading. The algorithm used must be fast because of the large number of strokes involved.

Outlining. Exterior outlines need to be drawn in a way that takes into account both the texture of the enclosed region and the texture of adjacent regions. Interior outlines can be used within shaded regions to suggest shadowed regions or to give view-dependent accents to the stroke texture.

Winkenbach and Salesin's rendering process proceeds as follows:

- First, the visible surface polygons and shadow polygons are computed.

- Next, these polygons are projected to screen space and used to build a two-dimensional BSP tree and the planar map data structure.

- Next, each surface is rendered by invoking the procedural texture attached to it.

- Strokes generated by the procedural texture are clipped using the two-dimensional BSP tree.

- Finally the outline strokes are drawn using the planar map data structure.

As shown in Figure 2.12, simulated pen strokes in a procedural texture are prioritized to enhance the communication of the material properties of the object being textured while allowing variation in tone. In this example, when the shingle texture is viewed from a grazing angle, the vertical lines in the texture are not drawn.

Some additional advantages of prioritized stroke textures are outlining (at no additional expense) and the ability to indicate texture across a surface. Prioritized textures can be built so that the highest-priority strokes are the outline strokes. If the user wishes to draw in outline mode, the textures need only be set to draw the highest-priority strokes. A style often observed in pen-and-ink illustrations is to draw texture details only near

Figure 2.12. The effect of changing the view direction of the outline strokes of a texture. Notice how the vertical edges begin to disappear as the texture is viewed from a more edge-on direction. Copyright 1994 Winkenbach and Salesin [Winkenbach, Salesin 94] and ACM. Used by permission.

Figure 2.13. Indicating texture. The left house is drawn using "indication;" the house on the right is not. Copyright 1994 Winkenbach and Salesin [Winkenbach, Salesin 94] and ACM. Used by permission.

the edges or in the foreground of a surface. Winkenbach and Salesin's system allows the user to interactively edit an outlined version of the model to indicate which edges should have texture drawn near them. An example of texture indication is shown in Figure 2.13.

In order to generate pen-and-ink illustrations of curved objects, such as a panama hat, Winkenbach and Salesin expanded their system to include non-uniform rational B-spline (NURBS) surfaces. NURBS, however, cause a problem when using uniform strokes to texture an illustrated object. A uniform distribution of strokes over a curved surface will change in tone based on the curvature of the surface. The problem is solved by drawing strokes with a non-uniform width using a process called "controlled density hatching." An example of the hatching problem for curved surfaces using Winkenbach and Salesin's solution, is shown in Figure 2.14.

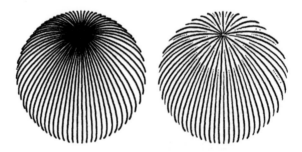

Figure 2.14. Left: Controlled-density hatching for a perspective view of a sphere. Rendering isoparametric curves with constant thickness results in an image with varying tones. Right: Using varying stroke thicknesses keeps the "apparent tone" constant. Copyright 1996 Winkenbach and Salesin [Winkenbach, Salesin 96] and ACM. Used by permission.

Figure 2.15.   Creating a pen-and-ink illustration. The steps involved are not
so different from those required to create an attractive photorealistic rendering. From left to right: constant-density hatching; smooth shading with rough
strokes, using a single light source; smooth shading with straighter, longer strokes
adjusted to depict glass; introducing environment mapping; and finally, the same
image after adjusting the reflection coefficients. Copyright 1996 Winkenbach and
Salesin [Winkenbach, Salesin 96] and ACM. Used by permission.

Controlled-density hatching causes some problems with the current
shadowing algorithm owing to the difficulty of calculating shadow boundaries for curved surfaces. Winkenbach and Salesin solve this problem by
switching to a two-pass system for stroke clipping. In addition to the planar map, which is used to clip strokes based on visibility, a second shadow
planar map is generated. Shadow strokes are generated for every surface
and first clipped by the planar map to be sure that they are visible from
the eye point. Then the shadow strokes are clipped by the shadow planar
map if they are not visible from the light source.

The advantage of using controlled-density hatching is the fine-grained
control of the generated hatching. This allows the software user to generate
hatching based on standard texturing algorithms such as bump mapping
and environment mapping. Some results of this expanded texturing palette
are shown in Figure 2.15.

2.3.2   An Interactive System for Pen-and-Ink Illustrations

Michael P. Salisbury, Sean E. Anderson, Ronen Barzel, Corin Anderson,
Dani Lischinski, Michael T. Wong, John F. Hughes, and David H. Salesin
[Salisbury et al. 94][Salisbury et al. 96] [Salisbury et al. 97] present an interactive image-based system for creating pen-and-ink illustrations. The
goal of Salisbury et al.'s research is to provide a non-artist user with high-
level tools that allow the user to create pen and ink illustrations easily,
with the appearance of being hand drawn by a professional artist. An example of a pen-and-ink illustration made using their system is shown in
Figure 2.16.

Salisbury et al.'s system [Salisbury et al. 94] works by having the user
first acquire a grayscale reference image which is used to define shape and

Figure 2.16.   Stacked books (after an illustration by Frank Lohan [Lohan 78b].)
Copyright 1997 Salisbury et al. [Salisbury et al. 97] and ACM. Used by permission.

tone in the illustration. Reference images can either be computer-generated
or scanned photographs. The software user then "paints" areas of the
illustration using high-level brush tools. Stroke textures that are applied
to the illustration by the "brush" are selected by the user from a texture
library. Examples of the stroke textures used by Salisbury et al. are shown
in Figures 2.17 and 2.18.

Users of Salisbury et al.'s original system [Salisbury et al. 94] painted
over a copy of the reference image. The reference image is shown faintly,
as if it lies beneath the surface on which the illustration is being produced.
The software user "traces" the illustration over the reference image. An
example of this process is shown in Figure 2.19. In this original system,
the user is responsible for the choice of the crosshatch texture, the tone or
darkness of the texture, where the textures are applied, the orientation of
the texture, and where the outlines are drawn. The system aids the user by

Figure 2.17.   A single texture drawn with several tone values. Copyright 1994
Salisbury et al. [Salisbury et al. 94] and ACM. Used by permission.

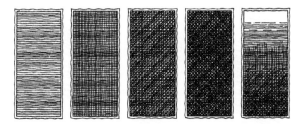

Figure 2.18. A prioritized texture. Only the most significant strokes are drawn for light tone values. Less important strokes are brought in to darken the texture. Copyright 1994 Salisbury et al. [Salisbury et al. 94] and ACM. Used by permission.

extracting edges from the source image, and by defining stencils. Stencils are regions of the illustration where a given texture is to be applied. The software user can interactively specify a range of intensities in the source image, and the corresponding region in the illustration image is marked off as a stencil. Edge extraction allows the user to draw outlines along an edge, or to clip an illustration texture with an edge. Figure 2.20 shows a user-defined region drawn with outlines, and then with the interior stroke texture clipped to the region edges.

In later research, the system of Salisbury et al. [Salisbury et al. 96] was improved in two fundamental ways. The first improvement to the system was to make the resulting illustrations scale-independent. This means that the resulting illustrations have the same tone and similar character when viewed at any size. The second improvement is the introduction of an interactive interface for manipulating the orientation of stroke textures in an illustration.

In order to engineer scale independence into the illustrations resulting

Figure 2.19. An example of using a grayscale reference image. Left to right: original gray scale image; extracted edges; curved hatching across the gradient. Copyright 1994 Salisbury et al. [Salisbury et al. 94] and ACM. Used by permission.

Figure 2.20.   An example of clipping strokes to an outline. Left: The outline and strokes are drawn. Center: The outline has been removed; note the hard edge caused by exact clipping. Left: A small amount of random offset in clipping creates a softer edge. Copyright 1994 Salisbury et al. [Salisbury et al. 94] and ACM. Used by permission.

from their system, Salisbury et al. store a sampled version of the grayscale reference image, pointers to the stroke textures used in the illustration, and a set of discontinuity edges. Discontinuity edges are a set of edges found by processing the source image using an edge-detecting algorithm. The set of discontinuity edges is used by the algorithm that resizes the sampled reference image, and can be used to help the software user place outline strokes in the illustration. In order to render an illustration at a given resolution, the grayscale image is resized and hatched with strokes. An example of the effects of resizing an illustration with and without the discontinuity edge algorithm is shown in Figure 2.21. Salisbury et al. modified their stroke-texture algorithm to compute the local tone of a texture every time a new stroke is added during the rendering phase of the algorithm. If the resulting stroke texture is darker than the tone of the reference image, the stroke is not drawn. This local-tone algorithm also enhances the power of the stencils used during the interactive drawing phase of the illustration process by allowing shape cues to be included in the stroke textures. An example of an illustration rendered at a variety of resolutions is shown in Figure 2.22.

Salisbury et al.'s most recent interface for creating pen-and-ink style illustrations has the user specify an orientation and a stroke type for a region of an illustration. The system then automatically places the strokes in the region and matches the tone of the region in the illustration with the tone of the reference image. This allows stroke directions to communicate the surface orientation of the illustrated objects, and results in more

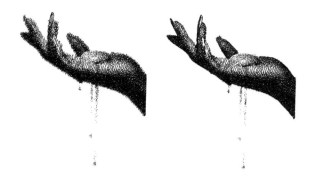

Figure 2.21.   Left: An example of image resizing using a set of discontinuity edges.
Right: An example of the effects of using a resized grayscale image. Copyright
1996 Salisbury et al. [Salisbury et al. 96] and ACM. Used by permission.

compelling illustrations. Figure 2.22 shows examples of illustrations where
the strokes line up with the principle curvature of the surface. An example
of an illustration using a computer-generated image as a reference and a
user-defined set of stroke directions is shown in Figure 2.23.

2.4 Summary

All of the systems described in this chapter are large and required a number of programmers a year or more to complete. In the case of pen-and-ink
many years were spent building the systems. In all four cases, the researchers did more than simulate the physics of the medium. They also

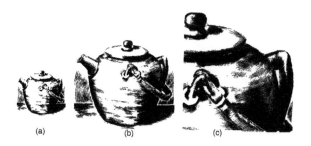

Figure 2.22.   A teapot at three different scales (after illustration by Arthur
Guptill [Guptill 76].) Copyright 1997 Salisbury et al. [Salisbury et al. 97] and
ACM. Used by permission.

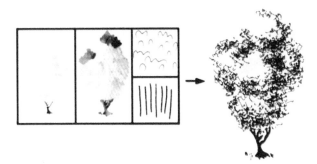

Figure 2.23.   A tree with curved strokes for leaves and straight strokes for the branches and trunk. Copyright 1997 Salisbury et al. [Salisbury et al. 97] and ACM. Used by permission.

provide high-level tools for both artists and non-artists reducing the time and the skills needed to produce a work of art.

Chapter 3

Simulating Artistic Media: Painting

We begin this chapter by reviewing digital painting strategies, then we provide in-depth coverage of algorithms designed to simulate brushstrokes, mediums such as paper or canvas, fluid flow, and pigment distribution. Techniques for both simulated oil painting and water color are discussed.

There are two main tasks involved in the creation of a digital painting. First is the creation of brushstroke positions. The second is the "rendering" of brushstrokes into pixel values. If the brushstroke positions are manually created by a user, the software is a classic "paint" program. Non-photorealistic painting systems of this types are covered in Chapter 4. If the brushstroke positions are computed algorithmically, then this is an "automatic" painting. The topic of automatic paint systems is covered in Chapter 9. In either case, once the brushstroke geometry is known, the brushstrokes must then be rendered, with the best case simulating the physical nature of paint and canvas.

When any artist sets out to paint an image, he or she must have three types of physical tools. The first is a medium, such as oil paint, acrylic, or watercolor, with which to construct the image. The second is some type of applicator or brush with which to apply the medium. The third is a surface, such as paper or canvas, on which to apply the medium. We first discuss methods for modeling brushes and brushstrokes, and then discuss methods for simulating various surfaces or substrates. Physical modeling of the mediums can either be encapsulated into the brush or substrate models, or can be explicitly modeled.

**The following set of artistic references are mentioned by the researchers whose
work we cover in this chapter.**

For sumi-e:

- *The Art of Sumi-e* by S. Sato [Sato 84].

For painting and watercolor:

- *Making Color Sing* by J. Dobie [Dobie 86].
- *Mastering Glazing Techniques in Watercolor* by D. Rankin [Rankin 86].
- *The Artist's Handbook* by R. Smith [Smith 87].
- *Creative Watercolor Techniques* by Zoltan Szabo [Szabo 74].

3.1   Background

Work intended to simulate artistic mediums can be further divided into
those which simulate the physics of a work of art, and those which emulate
the "look and feel" of a particular medium. Whitted made the first attempt
at this latter type of emulation using antialiased brushstrokes [Whitted 83].
Strassmann simulated the look of traditional Japanese painting with poly-
lines and a unique raster algorithm [Strassmann 86]. Strassmann's brushes
are modeled as a collection of bristles which evolve over the course of the
stroke, leaving a realistic image of a sumi-e brushstroke. Pham augmented
Strassmann's technique by modeling brushstrokes based on the offset approximation of uniform cubic B-splines [Pham 91]. The trajectory of a
brushstroke is represented as a three-dimensional cubic B-spline and each
bristle as a three-dimensional offset cubic B-spline of the brushstroke's trajectory. Zhang et al. presented a model of water and ink particles based
on a two-dimensional cellular automaton, and an application of the model
to a Suibokuga-like rendering of three-dimensional trees [Zhang et al. 99].
Pudet described a method for fitting the outline of hand-sketched pressure brushstrokes with Bézier curves [Pudet 94]. His method combined the
brush-trajectory model, in which a stroke is generated by dragging a brush
along a given trajectory, with a fast curve-fitting algorithm. Williams provides a method of merging painting and sculpting by using the raster image
as a height field [Williams 90].

A number of researchers have shown that stroke-based models of
non-photorealistic images have a number of scaling and memory advantages. Smith [Smith 95] points out that by using a scale-invariant primitive for a brushstroke, multi-resolution paintings can be made. Berman et

al. [Berman et al. 94] show that multi-resolution painting methods are efficient in both speed and memory usage. Perlin and Velho [Perlin, Velho 95]
use multi-resolution procedural textures to create realistic detail at any
scale or dimension. Their work emphasizes that digital paintings stored as
strokes may be useful for transmitting stylized images across a network.

Several authors have simulated the interaction of paper/canvas and a
drawing/painting instrument. Cockshott simulated the substrate, diffusion, and gravity in a physically-based paint system [Cockshott 91]. Small
explored the problem of predicting the actions of pigment and water when
applied to paper fibers using cellular automata on a parallel computer ar-
chitecture [Small 91]. Curtis et al. [Curtis et al. 97] expanded this work to
simulate more realistic watercolor effects by using more complex methods
for simulating paper and shallow water, and by using the Kubelka-Munk
method of compositing pigment layers. Takagi et al. [Takagi et al. 99] have
added a volumetric model of paper and fluid flow to their colored pencil
drawing system, in order to simulate the effects of a water wash over a
pencil drawing.

3.2 Simulating Brushes

3.2.1 Hairy Brushes

Steven Strassmann's [Strassmann 86] method for simulating the effect of
ink brushed onto paper produces sumi-e images as in Figure 3.1.

Strassmann breaks the simulation process into four components:

1. Brush—a compound object composed of bristle objects.

2. Stroke—lists of positions and widths.

3. Dip—a description of the initial state of the brush.

4. Paint—a method for rendering the brushstroke.

Strassmann's method works by having a user input lists of positions and
pressures via keyboard. Two cubic B-splines are then computed, one for the
positions and one for the pressure values and distance along the stroke. The
position spline values are used to find smoothly varying positions along the
stroke, while the pressure and distance spline is used to find width values
for each derived position. At each position point along the stroke, unit
normals are found, and the corresponding width value is used to find the
coordinates of the edge of the stroke. An example of a stroke is shown in
Figure 3.2.

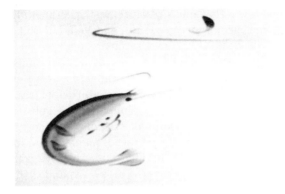

Figure 3.1. Strassmann's "Shrimp and Leaf" image. Copyright 1986 Strassmann [Strassmann 86] and ACM. Used by permission.

This process results in a series of quadrilaterals representing the body of the stroke, and two triangles representing the beginning and end of the stroke. A problem may occur in areas of the stroke with high curvature, when the line in the normal direction crosses back beyond the previous edge-position coordinate. This will cause a "twisted" quad, which Strassmann calls the "bow-tie" case as shown in Figure 3.3. It can be corrected by swapping the closest two edge points in the quad when a crossover is detected, and then recursively checking all prior quads.

Next, the sumi-e brush is modeled by an array of color values and an array of integers. The colors of the color array are perturbed in a preprocess in order to simulate variable pressures on individual brush bristles. The integer array simulates the amount of ink held at each bristle position along the brush. Each element of the integer array is decremented as each quad is drawn during the rendering of the stroke, to simulate the placement of ink onto the substrate. Antialiasing is accomplished by drawing to a frame buffer, then supersampling the frame-buffer image.

Figure 3.2.   A stroke defined by four control points with intervening nodes generated by a cubic spline. The area covered by the stroke is approximated by quadrilaterals. Copyright 1986 Strassmann [Strassmann 86] and ACM. Used by permission.

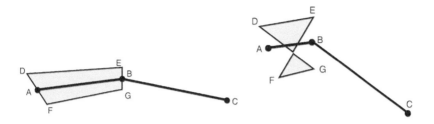

Figure 3.3. Left: Construction of the polygon connecting nodes A and B. Right: The annoying bow-tie case. Copyright 1986 Strassmann [Strassmann 86] and ACM. Used by permission.

Strassmann experimented with various diffusion functions that update the integer array after each quad is drawn. He also texture-mapped images onto brushstrokes. Different techniques for beginning strokes, applying pressure during a stroke, and for stroke completion are simulated using a two-parameter function to perturb the width function. The dry-brush phenomena is simulated by initializing the integer array in a non-uniform manner. Examples of brushstroke effects possible with Strassmann's system are shown in Figure 3.4

The following is pseudo code for an implementation of Strassmann's method. Note that the DrawLine function in the Paint method could be modified to draw texture mapped quads.

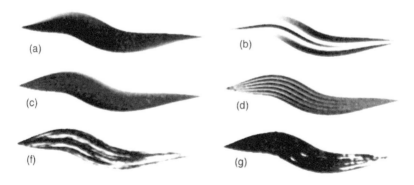

Figure 3.4. Effects: (a) Start/end interpolation from one ramp to another. (b) Interpolation from spike to notch. (c) Fast ink diffusion. (d) Slow diffusion. (e) Random Brownian evolution of ink. (f) "Ink stealing" evolution of stroke quality. Copyright 1986 Strassmann [Strassmann 86] and ACM. Used by permission.

```
Pair{ // an ordered pair class

Data:

 float x, y

Methods:

 void add(Pair); // adds the contents of a Pair to this Pair

 void subtract(Pair); // subtracts the contents of a Pair to this Pair

 void scale(int); // multiplies the contents of this pair by a constant

 void normalize(); // normalizes the contents of this Pair

 Pair NormalPlus(Pair1, Pair2, width); // returns a Pair in the
                                       // positive direction normal to
                                       // Pair1 and Pair2, width units away

 Pair NormalMinus(Pair1, Pair2, width); // returns a Pair in the
                                        // negative direction normal to
                                        // Pair1 and Pair2, width units away

 Pair[MaxWidth] LineValues(Pair1, Pair2); // returns a Pair array of values on
                                          // the line between Pair1 and Pair2
}




Stroke {

Data:

Pair positions[Length]    // a set of screen coordinates that define a stroke
int width[Length]         // stroke width at each coordinate

Methods:

void Paint(Brush)

}




Brush {

Data:

Color BristleColor[MaxWidth]
int HowMuchPaint[MaxWidth]
```

```
Methods:

  void Dip()

}

Dip() {

  for (int i = 0; i < MaxWidth; i++) {
    HowMuchPaint[i] = Length * RandomNumber(0, 1);
  }
}

Paint(Brush) {

Pair LastDrawPositions[MaxWidth];
Pair ThisDrawPositions[MaxWidth];
Pair PlusNormal;
Pair MinusNormal;

  Dip(Brush);
  PlusNormal = Pair.NormalPlus(positions[0], positions[1], width[0]);
  MinusNormal = Pair.NormalMinus(positions[0], positions[1], width[0]);
  LastDrawPositions = LineValues(PlusNormal, MinusNormal);
    for (int i = 1; i < Length-1; i++) {
      PlusNormal = Pair.NormalPlus(positions[i], positions[i+1], width[i]);
      MinusNormal = Pair.NormalMinus(positions[i], positions[i+1], width[i]);
      ThisDrawPositions = LineValues(PlusNormal, MinusNormal);
        for (int j = 0; j < MaxWidth; j++) {
if(Brush.HowMuchPaint[j] > 0) {
  SetColor(BristleColor[j]);
  DrawLine(LastDrawPositions[j], ThisDrawPositions[j]);
  Brush.HowMuchPaint[j]--;
        }
      }
    LastDrawPositions = ThisDrawPositions;
    }
}
```

3.2.2 Expressive Brushstrokes

Binh Pham [Pham 91] also created a sumi-e painting system. Pham designed his system with simplicity in mind and made greater use of B-splines.
His system models brushstrokes based on variable offset approximation of
uniform cubic B-splines. The advantage of Pham's system over Strassmann's is that, by being based on B-splines, Pham's system readily lends
itself to computer animation. An example of his work is shown in Figure 3.5.

Unlike Strassmann, Pham did not attempt to capture the physical nature of the medium or the evolution of brush bristles during a stroke.

Figure 3.5.   Pham's "Flowers and Reeds" image.   Copyright 1989
Pham [Pham 91]. Used by permission.

Pham's representation of a brushstroke consists of three components:

- Trajectory—The path of the brushstroke.

- Thickness—The width of the brushstroke at a point on its path.

- Shade—The color of the brushstroke at a point on its path.

In Pham's system the trajectory of a brushstroke is modeled by a cubic
B-spline. The number of knots the trajectory spline contains is determined
by the user, and depends on the desired brushstroke shape.

Brushstroke thickness is modeled by sweeping a set of bristle points
along the curve of the trajectory. Each bristle point will be used to trace
an offset curve along the trajectory. At each knot on the trajectory spline,
a pressure value is set by the user. As the bristle points are swept along the
trajectory curve, the curve traced by each bristle point is blended based on
the pressure value of the two closest knots of the trajectory curve. A series
of quadrilaterals is formed by connecting points on adjacent bristle paths.
An example of the resulting bristle representation is shown in Figure 3.6.

To achieve realism, Pham allows the shade of the stroke to change
along each bristle curve. For each bristle, the user enters color values at
the beginning and end of the stroke. Quadrilateral regions are formed
by linking the values of adjacent bristle curves at their knot values. A
color value for each quadrilateral region is found by interpolating linearly
between the beginning and end color values for each bristle, based on the
knot values at the vertices of the quadrilateral. Examples of brushstrokes
rendered using Pham's system are shown in Figure 3.7.

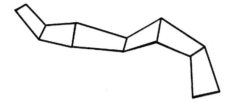

Figure 3.6. Quadrilaterals formed by two adjacent bristles. Copyright 1991 Pham [Pham 91]. Used by permission.

3.2.3 Real-Time Fitting of Hand-Sketched Pressure Brushstrokes

Thierry Pudet [Pudet 94] improved upon Strassmann and Pham by allowing the user to input brushstrokes into his system using a cordless pressure-sensitive stylus on a digitizing tablet. From the trajectory of the stylus across the tablet, the pressure data recorded by the stylus, and the type of software brush chosen, a stroke of variable width is computed and displayed in real time. Figure 3.8 shows an example of an illustration drawn using Pudet's system.

Pudet's method works in three steps. First, the digitized trajectory is fitted to a Bézier curve. Next, a polygonal approximation of the stroke outline is computed from the fitted trajectory and the brush outline. Polygonal approximations are used to reduce the computations to geometric operations and simplify the treatment of the pressure-controlled brushes. Finally, the polygonal approximation of the stroke is fitted to a Bézier curve.

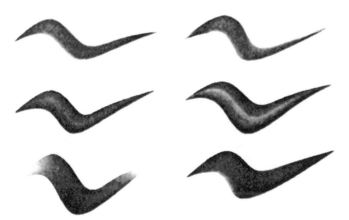

Figure 3.7. Examples of different shading effects made with Pham's system. Copyright 1991 Pham [Pham 91]. Used by permission.

Figure 3.8.   Pudet's "Sans titre" by Serge Ellissade. Copyright 1994 Pudet [Pudet 94]. Used by permission.

Pudet achieved interactive rates by drawing strokes in two modes. While the stylus is in contact with the digitizing tablet, only an echo of the brush-stroke is drawn to the screen. This is done by drawing filled circles to the screen along the trajectory of the stroke with the width of the circle dependent on the pressure applied to the stylus. When the stylus is lifted, the echo is erased and the brushstroke is fitted to a curve and displayed.

Pudet's system allows the user to choose between different types and sizes of brushes. Brushes have the following parameters: width, height, angle, and elasticity. The height, angle, and elasticity determine how the brush shape deforms under pressure. Brush sizes vary between 0.1 mm and 10 mm. Brush types in his system fall into two categories: rigid and dynamic. Brushstrokes made with rigid brushes are only allowed to change in width, based on the angle the stylus makes with the digitizing tablet. Brushstrokes made with dynamic brushes are allowed to change in width based on the pressure applied to the stylus as well as the angle of the stylus with respect to the tablet. Examples of both types of brushstroke are shown in Figure 3.9.

A full treatment of Pudet's method is beyond the scope of this text. Readers interested in implementing this type of system are encouraged to read his Eurographics 94 paper [Pudet 94].

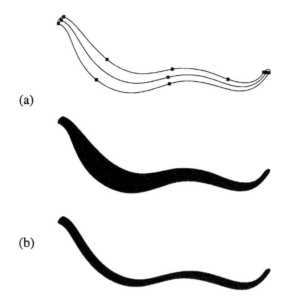

Figure 3.9. (a) Brushstroke from a dynamic elliptical brush. (b) Brushstroke frame the same size elliptical but rigid brush. Copyright 1994 Pudet [Pudet 94]. Used by permission.

3.3 Simulating Substrate

3.3.1 Modeling Watercolor by Simulating Diffusion, Pigment, and Paper Fibers

David Small explored a parallel approach to predicting the actions of pigment and water when applied to paper fibers using complex cellular automata in order to simulate watercolor painting [Small 91]. Small models watercolor paper as a two-dimensional grid of cells. He defines simple rules for the behavior of a cell based on the state of that cell and its immediate neighbors. Realistic behavior of substrate, water, and pigment can be achieved by iterating the computation over all the cells with a large number of discrete time steps.

Small's simulation takes into account the physical parameters of diffusion, surface tension, gravity, humidity, absorbency, and weight of each particle of pigment. At each time step, for each cell in the paper grid, water and pigment gradients as well as surface tension and gravitational forces are computed. The results of these computations are used to determine whether there should be any movement of water or pigment into neighboring cells. Small uses a parallel processing hardware system for his simulation, which models the physics of watercolor at about one-tenth of the time it takes the actual physical process to resolve.

Small uses a four-step process to model the interaction of watercolor with paper:

1. Simulate paper and environmental variables.

2. Apply pigment and water to the paper.

3. Simulate the movement of the pigment and water.

4. Render an image given the state of the simulation.

Physical paper is made up of intertwined fibers which are held together with some type of binder. The length and type of the fibers as well as the amount and type of binder determine the absorbency and diffusion characteristics of a particular type of paper. Small makes the assumption that for small enough cell sizes, the aggregate actions of fibers, adhesives, and cavities in the paper can be expressed by a relatively simple formula.

Each cell contains five parameters which are given initial values at the beginning of the simulation. These parameters are: location, initial color (when using non-white paper), absorbency, water content, and pigment content (cyan, magenta, and yellow). In order to speed up computation, Small uses only three color values for each pigment. In addition, there are the global parameters of humidity, gravity, surface tension of the medium (water), and the weight of the specific pigment. Initial conditions for both the local and global variables are set by the software user prior to the simulation. Pigment and water can be applied or removed using a variety of tools.

After an initial state is described, the simulation can begin. Small's simulation runs in three steps: first, movement of the fluid (pigment and water) on the surface is computed; next, fluid movement through the paper via diffusion is modeled; finally, fluid movement between the surface and the interior of the paper is modeled. The global variables of surface tension and gravity affect the movement of the fluid on the surface. Next, fluid diffusion is modeled based on the absorbency of the modeled paper, gravity, and the local variables: absorbency, water content, and pigment weight. Diffusion is calculated separately for each value of the pigment (cyan, magenta, and yellow).

Rendering an image from the simulation can be done in myriad ways once the pigment value at all of the cells is known. The simplest method is to equate the pixel value with the pigment value per cell. Note that the pigment per pixel value is a subtractive measure of the final color of the pixel, as the pigment absorbs light. In addition, the surface water calculations used in the first step of simulation can be used to render drips on the surface of the paper.

3.3.2 Wet and Sticky

Tunde Cockshott along with David England and John Patterson present the "wet and sticky" method of modeling wet paint on a substrate [Cockshott 91][Cockshott, England 91][Cockshott et al. 92]. Like Small's watercolor system, the "wet and sticky" system is based on cellular automata. However, Cockshott's system has a larger range of parameters that allow it to simulate additional paint medium.

There are three parts to Cockshott's model.

Paint particles. The term *paint particle* is not used as in a particle system, but to describe discrete units of paint. The paint particles are analogous to the fluid (pigment and water) used by Small. In the "wet and sticky" system, parameters exist that describe the color, liquid content, viscosity, drying rate, ability to mix, and transparency of paint. This large range of parameters allows the modeling of watercolor, oil, acrylic, and other types of paint. Cockshott's system also allows a wide variety of paint qualities to be modeled, ranging from thick impasto-type paints to thin glazes. Paint parameters are set by a software user prior to running the simulation phase of the system.

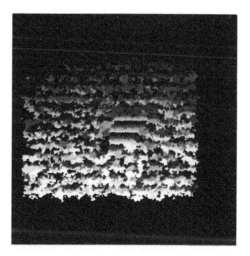

Figure 3.10. An example of the "wet and sticky" system, demonstrating how painted horizontal lines interact with the substrate and each other. Copyright 1991 Cockshott and England [Cockshott, England 91]. Used by permission.

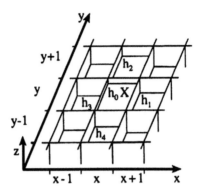

Figure 3.11.   Cell Reservoir Model. Copyright 1992 Cockshott et al. [Cockshott et al. 92]. Used by permission.

The intelligent canvas. The *intelligent canvas* is the name given to the two-dimensional array of cells that represents an artist's canvas. Each cell in the intelligent canvas contains parameters that describe the absorbency, horizontal and vertical orientation, and the type and volume of paint that the cell holds. Cockshott likens the cells to an array of open-topped containers capable of holding paint particles, much like an ice-cube tray. Unlike an ice-cube tray, however, each cell can have a different volume, as seen in Figures 3.11 and 3.12. Parameters of adjacent cells are allowed to vary in order to simulate the surface texture of the canvas and to allow areas of the canvas to have differing absorption abilities.

The painting engine. The *paint engine* is used to simulate the independent behavior of real paint. The paint engine runs continuously throughout the painting process to update the state of the canvas cells. Cells are updated according to the following steps:

1. Age paint.

2. Diffuse paint.

3. Apply gravity.

4. Mix any changes in the paint based upon a cell by cell basis.

The painting engine mimics the passage of time by aging the paint in each cell. Aging the paint reduces the liquid content of the cell, which effects how the paint in the cell responds to environmental factors such as gravity and humidity. Next, the painting engine uses the simulated environmental conditions to affect the state of each cell and its neighboring

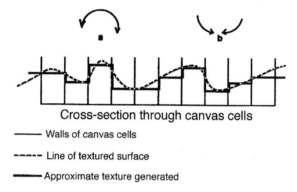

Cross-section through canvas cells

—————— Walls of canvas cells

------ Line of textured surface

━━━━━ Approximate texture generated

Figure 3.12. A two-dimensional cross section of an array of cells. Paint applied to point(a) will tend to flow down to its lower neighbors; conversely paint will tend to accumulate in troughs like point(b). Copyright 1991 Cockshott [Cockshott 91]. Used by permission.

cells. During this stage, the painting engine models gravity acting on the paint, diffusion, and surface tension acting against the movement of the paint. Local models of these effects are shown in Figure 3.13. The painting engine updates the status of each cell based on a set of rules that simulate these effects. If the potential for paint flow exists, and a neighbor cell can accept paint flow, both cells' paint-value parameters are updated.

Finally, the paint engine attempts to mix the paint in any of the cells that have been changed during the diffusion or gravity simulation. The paint engine models paint-mixing by blending each of the parameters of the paint particles contained in the cell, using a weighted average based on the number of each type of paint particle in the current cell.

Rendering the canvas to the screen is accomplished, as in a simple rendering of Small's system, by creating a one-to-one mapping between cells and pixels. A canvas can be treated as a height field by equating the volume of each cell with height. Then the canvas can be lit and rendered as a bumpy surface simulating the substrate texture and brush artifacts. It is interesting to note that although one would expect this one-to-one mapping to cause aliasing artifacts, none were observed in practice. Cockshott believes that this is because of the diffusion and paint mixing steps of the paint engine, which seem to automatically anti-alias the brushstrokes. Cockshott also notes that some of the most interesting effects made possible by this system were discovered when violating the physical rules. For example an "absorbency" brush was implemented, which could be used to make portions of the canvas more or less absorbent at any time during the

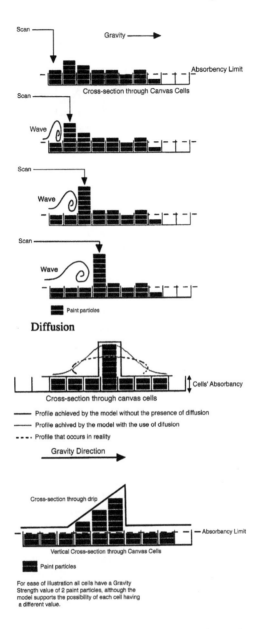

Figure 3.13. Top: The "wiper" effect that results from the painting engine. Middle: Illustrates why the system needs to model diffusion. Bottom: Gravity strength is used to control the trailing slope of drips. Copyright 1991 Cockshott [Cockshott 91]. Used by permission.

painting process. Another example was adding a "gravity" parameter to the paint particles, which would force the particles to a predefined edge of the canvas.

3.4   Simulating Media

3.4.1   Computer-Generated Watercolor

Cassidy J. Curtis, Sean E. Anderson, Joshua E. Seims, Kurt W. Fleischer, and David H. Salesin [Curtis et al. 97] present a system for computer-generated watercolor. Their system starts with Small and Cockshot's work on paper substrate. They then add physically-based methods for computing fluid flow and light interaction. The results of their system are often indistinguishable from physical watercolor, such as the watercolor image in Figure 3.14.

Figure 3.14.   An example of an automatically generated watercolor image, and the source image. See Color Plate III. Copyright 1997 Curtis et al. [Curtis et al. 97] and ACM. Used by permission.

Figure 3.15. An example of the effects possible with the method of Curtis et al. From left to right: dry-brush, edge darkening, back-runs, granulation, flow effects, and glazing. See Color Plate IV. Copyright 1997 Curtis et al. [Curtis et al. 97] and ACM. Used by permission.

In order to demonstrate a faithful simulation of the watercolor medium Curtis et al. show both *wet-in-wet* and *wet-on-dry* simulated watercolor effects, as demonstrated in Figure 3.15. These effects include:

Dry-brush effects—When a brush that is almost dry is applied to dry paper, it will apply pigment only to the raised edges of the paper.

Edge darkening—As the watercolor dries, pigment will migrate to the edge of a stroke, leaving a dark deposit.

Intentional back-runs—Back-runs happen when a puddle of water spreads back over a damp painted area, resulting in branching regions with darkened edges.

Granulation and separation—Granulation yields a grainy texture that emphasizes the texture of the paper. Separation is the splitting of colors that results when heaver pigments settle before light pigments.

Flow patterns—Used for wet-in-wet painting. Flow patterns occur when the wet paper allows pigment to spread freely.

Color glazing—Color glazing is the process of adding thin pale layers, or washes, of watercolor on top of each other.

Curtis et al. expand the substrate models of Small and Cockshott to a three-layer system shown in Figure 3.16. Fluid flow computations are bounded by the use of *wet-area masks*, which represent the areas of the paper that have been touched by water. These masks limit where water is allowed to flow, and provide boundary conditions for the fluid flow computations. Note that all of the quantities describing the fluid simulation are discretized over a two-dimensional grid representing the paper. From top to bottom, the layers that model fluid flow are:

1. The *shallow-water layer*—where water and pigment flow above the surface of the paper.

2. The *pigment-deposition layer*—where pigment is deposited onto and lifted from the paper.

3. The *capillary layer*—where water that is absorbed into the paper is diffused by capillary action.

In the shallow-water layer, water is allowed to flow across the surface but is bounded by the wet-area mask. As the water in this layer flows, it can lift, carry, or deposit pigment on the paper. The parameters used by Curtis et al. to simulate these processes are the velocity of the water in the x- and y-directions, the pressure of the water, the concentration of pigments in the water, the slope of the paper surface, and the physical properties of the watercolor medium (viscosity and viscous drag).

Pigment particles are transfered between the shallow-water layer and the pigment-deposition layer through adsorption and desorption, using a physically-based simulation that depends upon the physical properties of the individual pigments.

The capillary layer functions expand the wet-area mask by simulating capillary flow through the paper. Capillary flow is modeled using the water saturation of the paper (the fraction of the paper volume filled with water) and the fluid holding capacity of the paper (the fraction of the paper volume not occupied by paper fibers).

Curtis et al.'s paper entitled "Computer-Generated Watercolor" contains the necessary equations for implementing the fluid flow simulations and the Kubelka-Monk model, as well as easy-to-understand pseudocode [Curtis et al. 97]. The Kubelka-Monk (KM) model is used to perform the

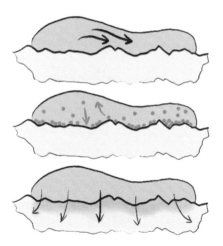

Figure 3.16.   The three-layer fluid model. From top to bottom: The shallow-water layer. The pigment-deposition layer. The capillary layer. Copyright 1997 Curtis et al. [Curtis et al. 97] and ACM. Used by permission.

Figure 3.17.   An example of the automatic watercolorization technique. This example also shows how different layers of watercolor glaze can be built up using the Kubelka-Monk method. See Color Plate V. Copyright 1997 Curtis et al. [Curtis et al. 97] and ACM. Used by permission.

optical compositing of glazing layers. In their use of the KM model, Curtis et al. assign absorption and scattering coefficients to each pigment. The coefficients are functions of light wavelength, and control the amount of light absorbed and scattered from successive layers of pigment. An example of an image being built up in layers is shown in Figure 3.17.

Three software applications of their watercolor simulation work were presented by Curtis et al. These include: interactive painting, automatic image "watercolorization," and three-dimensional non-photorealistic rendering. Interactive painting is accomplished by interfacing their software with a paint program. Automatic watercolor painting is performed by first extracting mattes for key features in the image. Then, for each matte a color separation is performed using a commercial paint program. Next, brushstrokes are planned using an expert system that queries the user for input at set intervals. A straightforward extension of the system renders watercolor images from three-dimensional models. Given a three-dimensional scene, mattes are automatically generated, isolating each object. These mattes are used as input to the "watercolorization" process. Animations can be produced in this manner by manipulating the three-dimensional models and watercoloring successive output frames.

3.5 Summary

In this chapter, we have covered the work of six different researchers in modeling the physics behind the process of painting. Some of the methods, such as Strassmann's sumi-e painting, can be implemented in a single afternoon, while others, such as Cassidy et al.'s water color system, would take a good programmmer a few weeks to implement. In addition, with the exception of Curtis et al., none of the systems mentioned in this chapter attempt to model any sort of high-level tools.

The area of physically-based modeling of traditional artistic materials warrants additional research. In addition, once good physical models of the materials exist, high-level tools that empower the non-artist seem to be of great interest to the graphics community.

Part II

Assisting a User in the Artistic Process

Chapter 4

Assisting a User:
Drawing and Painting Systems

In this chapter we provide an extensive background of painting and drawing systems. We then provide a more in-depth coverage of four systems whose goal is to provide a non-artist user with high-level tools for producing works of art which look as if they were produced by a professional artist.

4.1 Background

Ivan Sutherland's Sketchpad [Sutherland 63] system is the progenitor of all computerized drawing and painting systems. Sutherland's paradigm, that a keyboard is not the optimal form of human-computer interaction, is the basis for interactive techniques. Following Sutherland's work in 1963, interactive painting software continued to evolve. Alvy Ray Smith covers this evolution through the early 1980's, with particular attention to the movie industry [Smith 82][Smith 97]. Because of the overpowering influence of the personal computer, as well as desktop publishing, most of these systems evolved into high-end photograph retouching systems.

Our focus in this chapter is user-assisted painting programs which simulate painting with natural media. John Lansdown and Simon Schofield [Lansdown, Schofield 95] review the beginnings of non-photorealistic rendering systems in their 1995 paper. Paul Haeberli [Haeberli 90] built an image-based system that re-samples photographic images to create impressionistic paintings. His system allows a user to control the shape, size, and orientation of individual brushstrokes. The user then chooses the placement of the strokes by moving a "brush" over a reference image. Brush-stroke colors are sampled from the reference image. Siu Chi Hsu and Irene H. H. Lee [Hsu et al. 94] present a drawing and animation system, "Skeletal Draw," based on skeletal strokes. They demonstrate their system with animation sequences, including a vector graphics motion-blurring technique.

The masters thesis of Eric Wong [Wong 99] presents a method of generating a charcoal sketch portrait from a photograph. Using Wong's system the user is coached in the artistic process to identify and separate regions of the photograph. These regions are then "drawn in" using simulated charcoal pencil by the system. Jorg Hamel and Thomas Strothotte introduced techniques and tools for re-using the effort invested in lighting, shading and texturing a model for the rendering of other models [Hamel, Strothotte, 99].

Pat Hanrahan and Paul Haeberli [Hanrahan, Haeberli 90] built a three-dimensional object space paint program. Their system allows a user to "paint" directly onto a three-dimensional computer model. Daniel Teece [Teece 98a][Teece 98b] extended this work by building an interactive, three dimensional painting system which can be used to produce animations with a hand-drawn look. Although Teece's work is proprietary, fortunately his images are not, and are shown in Figure 4.1.

Simon Schofield [Schofield 94][Schofield 96] designed an interactive NPR system for architectural rendering. Using this system, an artist is able to create non-photorealistic animations and stills interactively. In addition, the power of standard computer graphics hardware is leveraged to allow the creation of hybrid renderings. An example of Schofield's process is shown in Figure 4.2. Barbara Meier [Meier 96] uses a particle system based on three-dimensional geometry to create painted animations with a hand-crafted look and without temporal artifacts.

Figure 4.1.   Left: "Cezanne Fruit Bowl" Right: "Pen and Ink Fruit Bowl." See Color Plate VI. Copyright 1998 Teece [Teece 98a] and ACM. Used by permission.

Figure 4.2. Three stages in the painterly re-rendering of a model of London. Left: The original image from the viewing/modeling system. Middle: Urban textures brushed onto the model. Right: Re-rendered using a soft painterly brush that clips against geometric planes found in the scene. Model courtesy Miller-Hare Ltd, London. Copyright 1999 Schofield et al. [Green et al. 99] and ACM. Used by permission.

A number of researchers have attempted to simulate the copperplate engraving process. Yachin Pnueli and Alfred Bruckstein demonstrated "Digidurer," a digital engraving system [Pnueli, Bruckstein 94]. Victor Ostromoukhov [Ostromoukhov 99] introduced basic techniques for imitating copperplate engraving to produce digital facial engravings. Mestetskii [Mestetskii 00] describes a method for creating images which simulate engraving using a Bézier representation.

The following set of references about the artistic process are mentioned by the researchers whose work we cover in this chapter:

For painting and animation:

- *Techniques of the Impressionists* by A. Callen [Callen 82].
- *Creative Painting with Pastel* by C. Katchen [Katchen 90].
- *Problem Solving for Oil Painters* by G. Kreutz [Kreutz 86].
- *The Big Book of Painting Nature in Oil* by S.A. Schaeffer [Schaeffer 91].
- *The Artist's Handbook* by R. Smith [Smith 87].
- *Disney Animation—The Illusion of Life* by F. Thomas and O. Johnston [Thomas, Johnston 81].

For engraving:

- *A Handbook of Graphic Reproduction Processes* by F. Brunner [Brunner 84].
- *How Prints Look* by W. M. Ivins, Jr. [Ivins 88].

4.2   Artistic Rendering of Portrait Photographs

Eric Wong [Wong 99] presents a user-assisted software tool for rendering charcoal-style portraits using a reference image. Wong's system coaches the user in segmenting the source image into five feature categories. This approach gives Wong's system an excellent division of labor: the user performs the segmentation task which is very difficult to automate via computer, while the computer aids the user by performing the actual drawing tasks. Throughout the process, the user maintains complete artistic control. Owing to the complexity of the system and the large number of specialized algorithms, we describe Wong's system at a high level. Interested readers are encouraged to consult Wong's thesis for more detailed information.

Wong's system segments the source image, a portrait photograph, into five categories.

- The background area.

- The hair.

- Lines and edges in the image.

- Facial features.

- Facial tone.

Examples of a source image and the five categorical images that result from the separation process, as well as an image of the final results of Wong's system, are shown in Figure 4.3.

Wong's method for separating the background from the subject in the source image is straightforward. He requires that the photograph be taken in front of a blue screen, and uses flood-fill segmentation to isolate the background region. Wong stores the isolated background image to use as an image mask in future segmentation processes. An example of this process is shown in Figure 4.4.

The segmentation and rendering of hair regions is a much more lengthy process. First the user must segment the hair regions by hand. Hair regions include all facial hair except eyebrows. These regions are then added to the background image mask. Eyebrows are handled later, during the facial-feature recognition phase of the process. After the hair regions are segmented, the segmented hair image is converted to grayscale and blurred using a Gaussian blur. A line detection algorithm is applied to the grayscale hair image, and a Hough orientation filter [Hough 62] is applied to the line-detected image. The Hough transform is a standard computer vision method for finding a mathematical description of lines and shapes in an

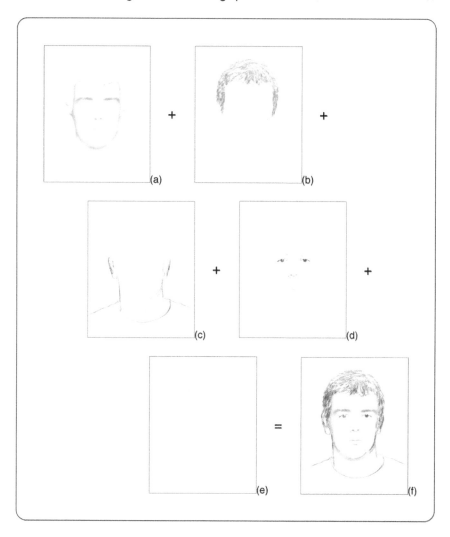

Figure 4.3. An overview of the artistic rendering process. The (a) facial tone, (b) hair, (c) edges, (d) facial features, and (e) background region are composited to form (f) the final artistic rendering. Copyright 1999 Wong [Wong 99]. Used by permission.

image. The orientation field resulting from the Hough transform is next smoothed using a relaxation technique, and used as the basis for the hair-rendering algorithm. An example of the hair segmentation and rendering process is shown in Figure 4.5.

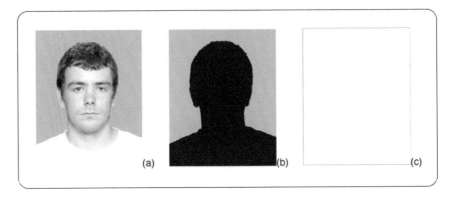

Figure 4.4.   A typical image stack for the rendering of the background region.
(a) The original image. (b) The background region after it has been selected. (c)
The final artistically rendered result. Copyright 1999 Wong [Wong 99]. Used by
permission.

The identification of edges to be drawn in the final image is the most
user-intensive portion of Wong's process. An edge-detection algorithm is
used to create an edge image. The image mask is used to remove all
of the lines in the background and hair regions of the image. Then a
despeckle filter is used to remove false edges created by noise. The user
manually removes any additional unwanted lines from the image. The
removal process is simple and straightforward and takes from three to five
minutes. Figure 4.6 shows an example of the steps in this process.

Wong's facial-feature finding algorithm rests on the assumption that
darker features in the facial region are significant indicators of facial features. This assumption holds because of the controlled lighting of the source
photographs, but may cause errors if the subject has a dark skin tone, or
has facial birth marks, tattoos, or wears glasses. Once again the user must
manually select the facial region, and the image mask is subtracted from
this region to remove any facial hair from the region. Next the lighting in
the facial image is normalized. This is done in a user-assisted fashion by
having the user select points on skin regions across the face. It is also as-
sumed that the face is roughly cylindrical and that the light in the portrait
comes from the direction of the camera. The normalized image is converted
to grayscale and its brightness and contrast are increased. These increases
aid the thresholding process by removing any remaining shadows. The facial features are found using a clustering algorithm, with expert knowledge
of how facial features occur. This clustered image is used as input to a rendering algorithm that draws the facial features. An example of the facial
segmentation and rendering process is shown in Figure 4.7.

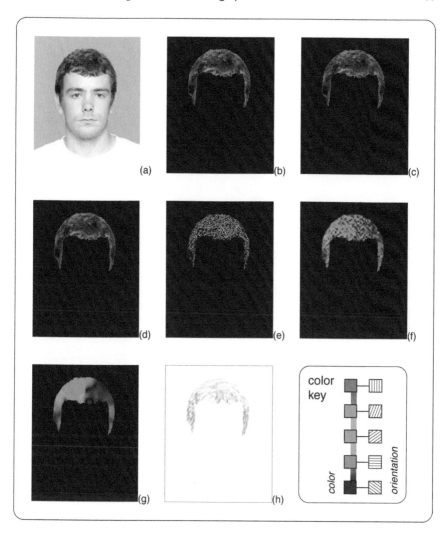

Figure 4.5. A typical image stack for the rendering of hair. (a) The original image. (b) The hair region after is has been selected. (c) The hair region converted to grayscale. (d) The hair region blurred. (e) The line-detected version of the hair region. (f) The result of applying the orientation filter. (g) The smoothed orientation field. (h) The final artistically rendered result. Copyright 1999 Wong [Wong 99]. Used by permission.

The final step in Wong's system is the generation of facial tone. After subtraction of the area mask from the source image, the resulting tone image is converted to grayscale and strongly blurred, and its brightness is greatly increased. The area-mask portion of the image is removed, and the

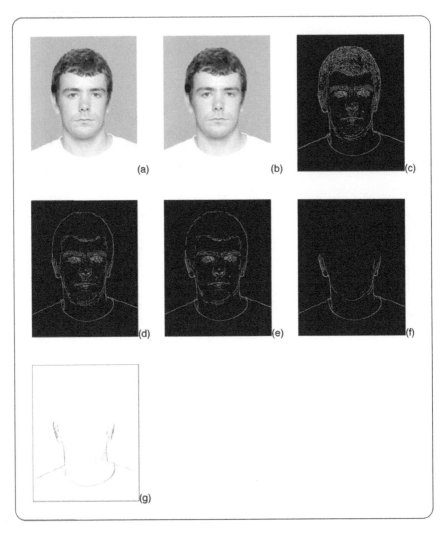

Figure 4.6.   A typical image stack for the rendering of edges. (a) The original image. (b) The image after blurring. (c) The edge-detected image. (d) The image after subtracting the image mask. (e) The image after despeckling. (f) The result after a user has removed unwanted edges. (g) The artistically rendered result. Copyright 1999 Wong [Wong 99]. Used by permission.

image is again blurred. The result is a smoothed and washed-out version of the source image. This image is then blended with a paper texture to yield the appearance of smudged charcoal. Figure 4.8 shows an example of this process.

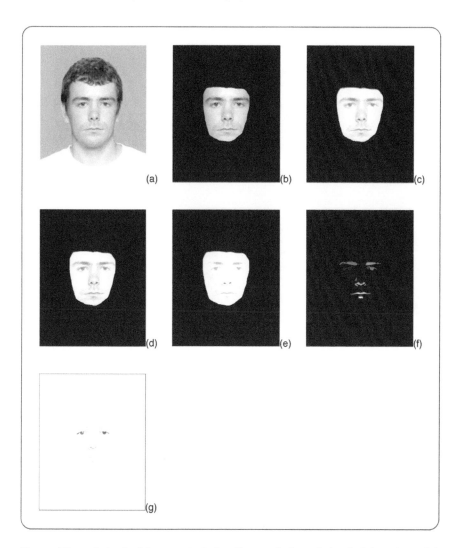

Figure 4.7.   A typical image stack for the rendering of the facial region. (a) The original image. (b) The facial region after being selected by the user and subtracting the image mask. (c) The result of the lighting normalization process. (d) The image after converting to grayscale. (e) The image after increasing the brightness and contrast. (f) The image after the facial-feature finding algorithm. (g) The final artistically rendered result. Copyright 1999 Wong [Wong 99]. Used by permission.

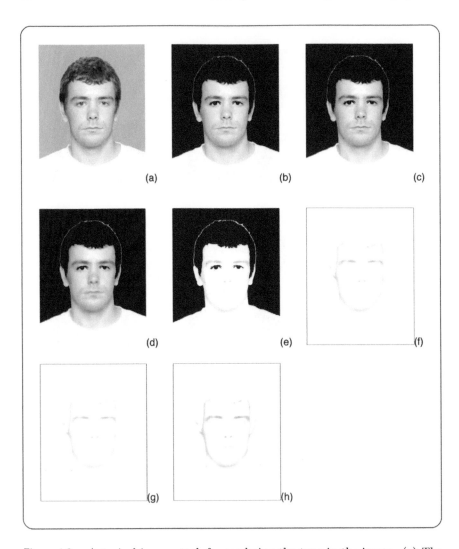

Figure 4.8. A typical image stack for rendering the tone in the image. (a) The original image. (b) The image after subtracting the image mask. (c) The image after converting to grayscale. (d) The result after blurring. (e) The image after increasing the image brightness. (f) The image after the removal of the masked area created by the subtraction process. (g) The image is again blurred. (h) The final tonal shading. Copyright 1999 Wong [Wong 99]. Used by permission.

4.3 Paint By Numbers: Abstract Image Representations

Paul Haeberli [Haeberli 90] presents an interactive program that allows a user to create an impressionistic image from a source photograph. Haeberli also shows how this system can be expanded to use computer-modeled scenes instead of an image, as well as techniques for automating his program. By creating impressionistic images, Haeberli is among the first researchers to explore the paradigm of images as a communication medium instead of as the result of a physical simulation.

Haeberli's program works by point-sampling the source image at a set number of locations, then rendering brushstrokes at these positions. The user interactively selects the brushstroke positions by moving a mouse across the "canvas" to be "painted." An example of this painting process is shown in Figure 4.9.

In Haeberli's program, each painting is composed of a list of brushstrokes. Each brushstroke contains the following attributes:

- Location—The position of the brushstroke.

- Color—The RGB color and Alpha value of the stroke.

- Size—The size of the stroke.

- Direction—The angle of the stroke relative to the canvas.

- Shape—The look of the brushstroke.

Brushstroke location and color are determined by moving a mouse and sampling the source image. Points along the path of the mouse are sampled,

Figure 4.9.   An example of creating a painting and the inset source image. Copyright 1990 Haeberli [Haeberli 90] and ACM. Used by permission.

Figure 4.10.   Three paintings derived from a single source image each using different type of brush. See Color Plate VII. Copyright 1990 Haeberli [Haeberli 90] and ACM. Used by permission.

and based on the currently selected brushstroke attributes, brushstrokes are painted onto the canvas. The brushstroke positions are perturbed using a stochastic process. Brushstroke size is set by the user in one of two ways: by pressing keyboard keys as the mouse is moved, or by varying the size of the stroke by the speed with which the mouse is moved. The latter method allows the user to add fine details to the painting slowly and carefully. The angle of brushstrokes can be controlled in a variety of ways. Examples include placing brushstrokes in the same direction as the mouse is being moved, placing all strokes on the canvas in a similar direction, allowing the user to set each brushstroke direction interactively, or placing brushstrokes according to image gradients in the source image. Brushstroke shape strongly influences the look of the final painted image. The user may select the brushstroke shape using a pop-up menu. Examples of a source image and three very different paintings that result from the use of different brush shapes are shown in Figure 4.10.

Haeberli also describes a number of tools that have been added to his original system. The first is a toolkit that allows a user to manipulate some or all of the brushstrokes that compose a painting. Another allows brushstroke orientations to be guided by a second source image. He also describes a method for using texture-mapped brushstrokes, and a number of methods for enhancing the color content of the resulting paintings. Haeberli's paint system is avalible for use at http://reality.sgi.com/grafica/impression/.

4.4   Painterly Rendering for Animation

Barbara Meier [Meier 96] presents a technique for rendering animation in a painterly style. Meier's method provides frame-to-frame coherence in animations by modeling surfaces as three-dimensional particle sets that are

Figure 4.11. Frames from a painterly rendered animation. The painterly renderer is particularly well suited to abstracting natural textures like the cloudy sky, hay, and plowed ground in this example. Note that the haystack texture does not exhibit the problems of traditional texture-mapping in which the gift-wrapped texture gets dense near silhouette edges. The overlapping brushstrokes on the plowed ground imply volume rather than flat, painted texture as the view animates, even though the surface is planar. Barbara Meier uses the largest brushstrokes to paint the sky, using brush texture and random hue variation to create clouds that do not exist in the color reference picture. The original haystack geometry is simply a cone resting on a cylinder. Meier represents the hay with a brushstroke shorthand that eliminates the need to model and color every piece of hay. See Color Plate VIII. Copyright 1996 Meier [Meier 96] and ACM. Used by permission.

rendered as two-dimensional strokes in screen space. Her method is similar to an artist painting brushstrokes on a canvas. Brushstroke appearance is controlled using the three-dimensional information contained in the modeled scene. She is able to create a variety of painting styles by varying the brushstroke and lighting parameters. Meier's goal in this work is to provide a tool that automates the rendering of brushstrokes while leaving the artistic decisions to the user. Example frames from an animation created using her system are shown in Figure 4.11.

Meier's system begins by creating a particle set that describes the geometry of a modeled scene. This set is built by tessellating the modeled three-dimensional scene into triangles, and distributing particles onto each triangle based on its area relative to the total area of the scene. The particles are then transformed into screen space and sorted by depth. Each particle has five attributes: image, color, orientation, size, and position. The brush image is a color image that may be solid or textured. Orientation, color, and size are assigned by the user or can be computed from a reference image assigned to an object. Position comes from the position of the particle in screen space. An example of Meier's rendering pipeline is shown in Figure 4.12. By varying these brushstroke parameters, animations with different painterly styles can be created. Examples of variations in the painted style of images created from the same geometric source are shown in Figure 4.13.

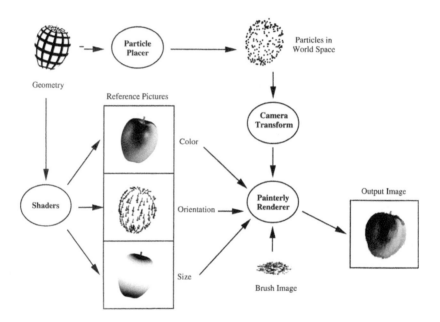

Figure 4.12.   An example of the painterly rendering pipeline. The particle placer populates a surface with particles. The surface geometry is rendered using various shaders to create brushstroke attribute reference pictures. Note that the arrows in the orientation image are representational in this diagram; the orientations are actually encoded in the color channels of the image. The particles, which are transformed into screen space, the reference pictures, and the brush image are input to the painterly renderer. The renderer looks up brushstroke attributes in the reference pictures at the screen space location given by each particle's position, and renders brushstrokes that are composited into the final rendered image. Copyright 1996 Meier [Meier 96] and ACM. Used by permission.

Figure 4.13. Four styles of painterly rendered fruit. By choosing different brush images and painting parameters, Meier has created four different looks from the same sets of reference pictures. The upper left image has the soft, blended quality of a pastel painting. The pointillistic version, in the upper right, remaps the original saturations and values from the color reference picture to a new range. A squiggle brush image and increased hue variation were used to create marker-style strokes in the lower left image. The brush used to create the lower right image contained some opaque black that helps to create a woodcut-print style. See Color Plate IX. Copyright 1996 Meier [Meier 96] and ACM. Used by permission.

4.5 Digital Facial Engraving

Victor Ostromoukhov [Ostromoukhov 99] introduces techniques for creating digital facial engravings that imitate traditional engraving practices. He establishes a set of rules to build an engraving in layers using a source image as a reference. Layers are then merged according to a set of merging rules. The merging rules use shift and scale operators on parametric surfaces specially introduced for this purpose. Ostromoukhov also illustrates techniques for engraving-specific image enhancements, mixing regular engraving lines with mezzotint and irregular perturbations of engraving lines.

Ostromoukhov's process begins by having the user segment a source image, from a photograph or a computer-generated image, using a commercially available software product. For each segment, the user then fits a Coons patch over the region that will define the orientation of the curves that make up the engraved lines. A Coons patch is a parametric spline

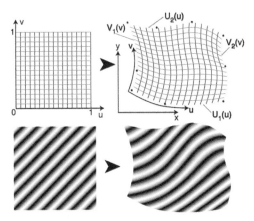

Figure 4.14.   A Coons patch is morphed to fit a two-dimensional region. This establishes a mapping for a basic engraving pattern. Copyright 1999 Ostromoukhov [Ostromoukhov 99] and ACM. Used by permission.

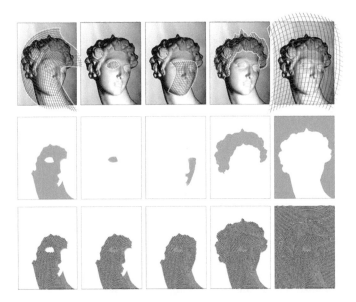

Figure 4.15.   The process of building the engraving. Upper row: A series of parametric grids manipulated to fit the segmented image. Middle row: The corresponding range shift masks. Lower row: The succession of resulting engraving layers during the superimposition process. Copyright 1999 Ostromoukhov [Ostromoukhov 99] and ACM. Used by permission.

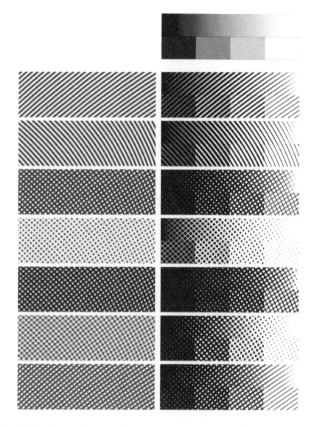

Figure 4.16. The first column show a series of basic engraving patterns. The second shows the effects of using a standard dithering algorithm to compute discrete or continuous blends between the layers of an engraving. Copyright 1999 Ostromoukhov [Ostromoukhov 99] and ACM. Used by permission.

representation of a surface patch that allows explicit control of the patch boundary and tangent plane continuity. The Coons patch shown in Figure 4.14 is fitted by moving only the border points to line up the features in the source image with the grid of the patch. Figure 4.15 shows an example of this process for a rendered image of Michelangelo's Giuliano de Medici.

The next step in Ostromoukhov's process is to use standard dithering algorithms to merge separate layers by adjusting the widths of the engraving marks to match the local intensity of the source image. An example of using dithering to adjust the intensity of a simulated engraved patch is shown in Figure 4.16. These methods are then applied to produce an engraved image such as in Figure 4.17.

Figure 4.17.   The engraving produced using the engraving shown in Figure 4.15. Copyright 1999 Ostromoukhov [Ostromoukhov 99] and ACM. Used by permission.

Ostromoukhov also describes methods for interactively enhancing the automatically generated portions of the digital engravings. He shows how additional layers can be added to the engraving to sharpen facial features. Additionally abrupt changes in orientation and frequency in the engraved lines can be used for contrast and to add detail as shown in the glasses and cheek in Figure 4.18. He also mentions that color engravings can be made using standard RGB color separation methods.

Figure 4.18. An engraving from a photograph, showing various enhancement techniques: an abrupt change in the orientation and frequency of the etching (in the glasses), and an additional layer for sharper appearance of the nasolabial fold. Copyright 1999 Ostromoukhov [Ostromoukhov 99] and ACM. Used by permission.

4.6 Summary

This chapter covered systems whose goal is to provide high-level tools to non-artists, in order to enable them to produce images with a professional look. A maxim of engineering is that simple tools require expert users, while simple users require expert tools. This maxim is reflected in the software tools demonstrated in this chapter. All of these systems required a large coding effort, and a great deal of thought about the user interface. However, the systems covered in this chapter are examples of the highest achievement in computer science. To paraphrase Fred Brooks, "A man and a machine can do more together than either alone." User-assisted systems for the creation of art are still an open problem in non-photorealistic rendering.

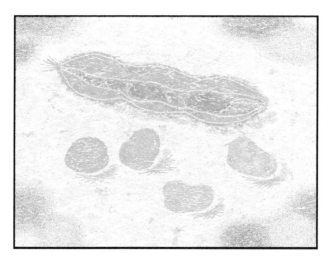

Plate I. Bean pod on washi paper using the method of Takagi et al. [Takagi et al. 99].

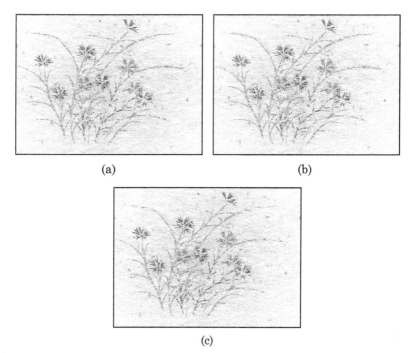

(a)

(b)

(c)

Plate II. Colored pencil drawings: (a) Volume CPD, (b) with wash effects, (c) with eraser effects [Takagi et al. 99]. See Figure 2.9.

Plate III. A source image and an example of an automatically generated wa
color image [Curtis et al. 1997]. See Figure 3.14.

Plate IV. An example of the effects possible with the method of Curtis et al. [Curtis et al. 97]. See Figure 3.15.

Plate V. An example of Curtis et al.'s watercolorization technique [Curtis et 1997]. See Figure 3.17.

Plate VI. Top: "Cezanne Fruit Bowl." Bottom: "Pen and Ink Fruit Bowl" [Teece 98]
[Teece 98b]. See Figure 4.1.

Plate VII. Three paintings derived from a single source using Paul Haeberli's painting system [Haeberli 90]. See Figure 4.10.

Plate VIII. Frames from a painterly rendered animation created using Barbara Meier's system [Meier 96]. See Figure 4.11.

Plate IX. Four styles of painting from the same reference picture using Barba Meier's system [Meier 96]. See Figure 4.13.

Plate X. Example worlds created using the Cohen et al.'s Harold system [Cohen et al. 00]. See Figure 5.11.

Plate XI. A lorax-like figure, generated with graftals using the method of Kowalski et al. [Kowalski et al. 99]. See Figure 5.12.

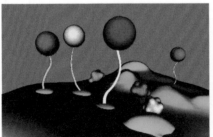 

Plate XII. Left: A simple geometric scene. Right: Graftals [Kowalski et al. 99] geometric complexity as well as a Dr. Suess-like look. See Figure 5.13.

Plate XIII. Simple models rendered with graftals by Markosian et al. [Markosian et al. 00]. See Figure 5.14.

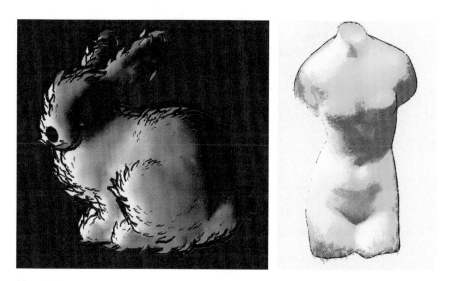

Plate XIV. Graftals can be used to capture a wide range of artistic effects [Kaplan et al. 00].

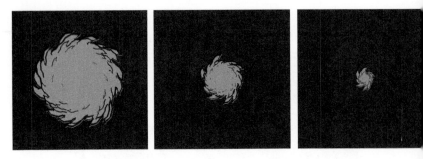

Plate XV. As objects move away from the viewer some of the geograftals shrink size while a randomly selected few grow in size [Kaplan et al. 00]. See Figure 5.1

Plate XVI. Example images using the system of Kaplan et al. [Kaplan et al. 0
See Figure 5.16.

Plate XVII. A frame from Cassidy Curtis' NPR animation "The New Chair." See
Figure 6.1.

Plate XVIII. Using three-dimensional geometric scenes to create a multiperspect panaroma [Wood et al. 97]. See Figure 6.5.

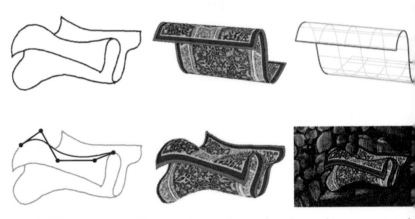

Plate XIX. Process of creating one frame of an animation, using computer-ai texture mapping [Corrêa et al. 98]. See Figure 6.6.

Plate XX. Automatically calculated shadow mattes complete a scene made of hand drawn art of a figure, trees, and background matte [Petrovic et al. 00]. See Figure 6.9.

Plate XXI. Hand drawn art, shadow matte, and the final frame produced usi
Petrovic et al.'s system [Petrovic et al. 00]. See Figure 6.10.

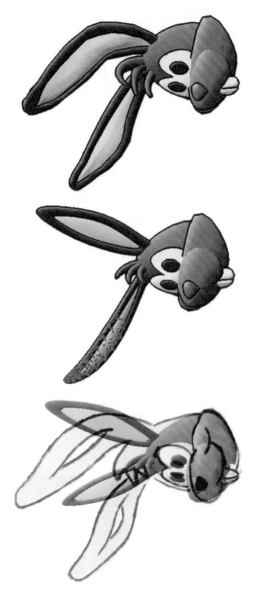

Plate XXII. Creating the view-dependent model using Paul Rademacher's system [Rademacher 99]. See Figure 6.12.

Plate XXIII. View-dependent geometric model deformations [Rademacher 9
See Figures 6.13, 6.14, and 6.16.

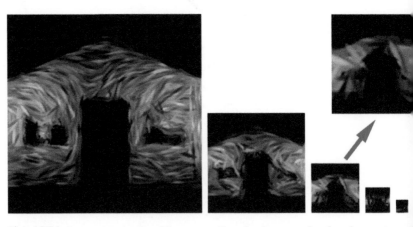

Plate XXIV. Art-maps work with conventional mip-mapping hardware to ma
tain constant stroke size at interactive frame rates [Klein et al. 00].
Figure 6.19.

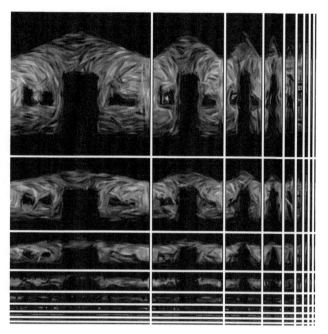

Plate XXV. Rip-maps help solve the problem of texturing obliquely viewed polygons [Klein et al. 00]. See Figure 6.20.

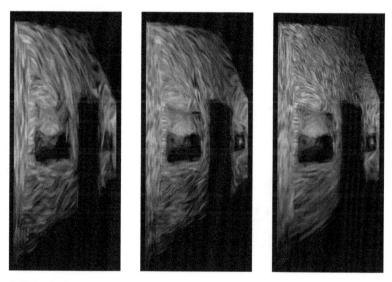

Plate XXVI. Left: Applying only art maps. Middle: Adding rip-maps. Right: Rip-maps can be used to place various sized strokes [Klein et al. 00]. See Figure 6.21.

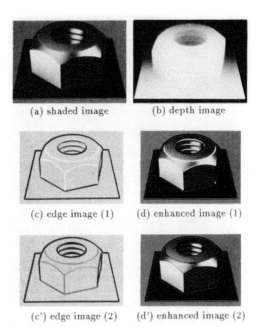

(a) shaded image   (b) depth image

(c) edge image (1)   (d) enhanced image (1)

(c') edge image (2)   (d') enhanced image (2)

Plate XXVII. Example of edges found through image processing [Saito, Takahas 90]. See Figure 7.6.

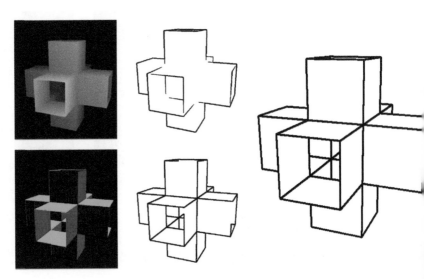

Plate XXVIII. Decaudin's image-based crease and surface boundary finding meth [Green et al. 99]. See Figure 7.7.

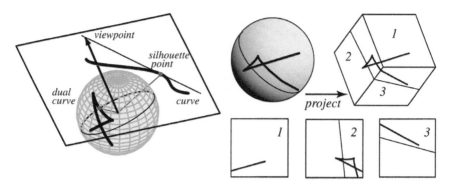

Plate XXIX. Top: Using a dual curve to find silhouette points. Bottom: Reducing the intersection problem [Green et al. 99]. See Figure 7.13.

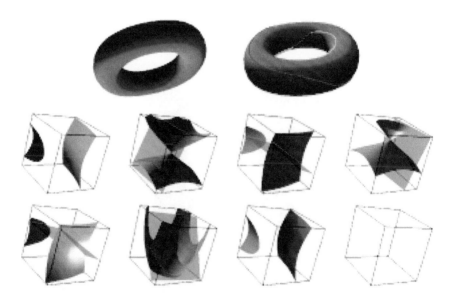

Plate XXX. Silhouettes under duality correspond to intersection curves of a plane with the dual surface [Hertzman, Zorin 00]. See Figure 7.14.

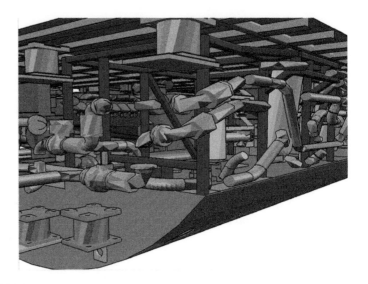

Plate XXXI. Real-time rendering of 250,000 triangle machine room with silh ette edges [Raskar, Cohen 99].

Plate XXXII. Non-photorealistic filters applied to texture maps on an archi tural model [Klein et al. 00]. See Figure 8.5.

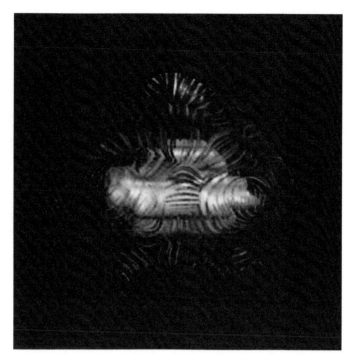

Plate XXXIII. Principal curvature lines on a volumetric data set [Interrante 97]. See Figure 8.6.

Plate XXXIV. Lake et al.'s cartoon shading. Reprinted by permission of Intel Corporation [Lake et al. 00]. See Figure 8.25.

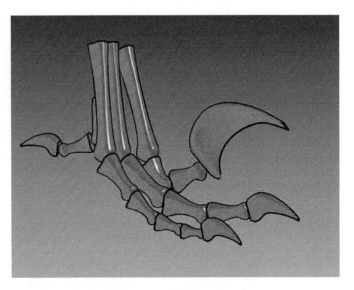

Plate XXXV. Approximately constant luminance tone rendering using the syte
of Gooch et al. [Gooch et al. 98]. See Figure 8.33.

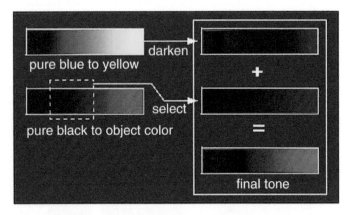

Plate XXXVI. Tone shading is created for a red object using the sytem of Gooch
al. [Gooch et al. 98]. See Figure 8.34.

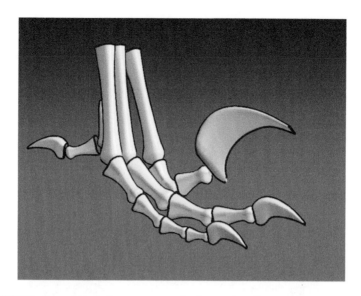

Plate XXXVII. Luminance/hue tone rendering using the sytem of Gooch et al. [Gooch et al. 98]. See Figure 8.35.

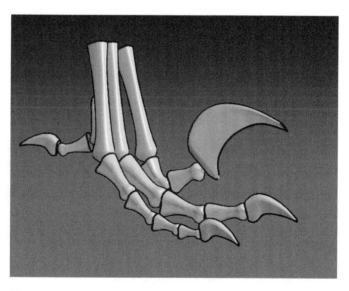

Plate XXXVIII. Another luminance/hue tone rendering using the sytem of Gooch et al. [Gooch et al. 98]. See Figure 8.36.

Plate XXXIX. Comparing Phong-shaded and tone-shaded spheres [Gooch et
98]. See Figure 8.37.

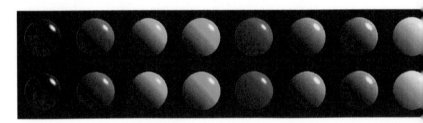

Plate XL. Varying the background of the spheres may seem to blend away
silhouettes, making the ball appear more like spheres and less like flat d
[Gooch et al. 98]. See Figure 8.38.

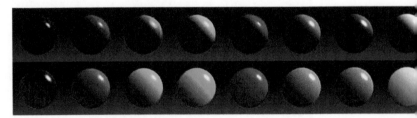

Plate XLI. Shaded spheres without edge lines created with the sytem of Gooc
al. [Gooch et al. 98]. See Figure 8.39.

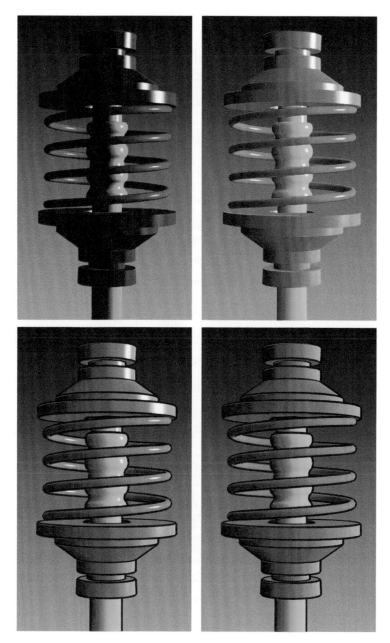

Plate XLII. Comparison of traditional computer graphics techniques and the technique of Gooch et al. [Gooch et al. 98]. See Figure 8.40.

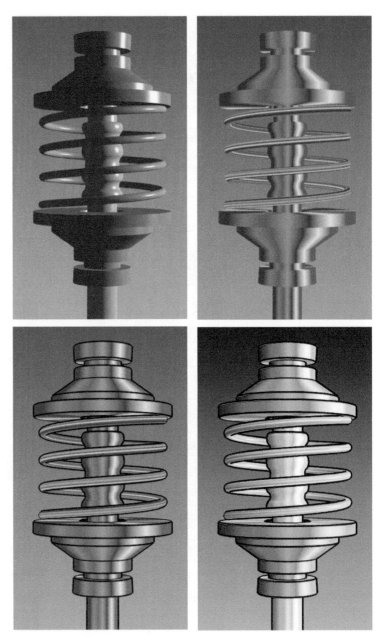

Plate XLIII. Representing metallic material properties using the technique
Gooch et al. [Gooch et al. 98]. See Figure 8.42.

Plate XLIV. Kaplan's "Tea-sselation" image [Kaplan, Salesin 00]. See Figure 9.2

Plate XLV. Additional examples of the "Impressionist" system [Litwinowicz 97].

Plate XLVI. Another example of automatic painterly rendering [Litwinowicz 97

Plate XLVII. An example of Hertzmann's system in it's "impressionist" m
[Hertzmann 98]. See Figure 9.9.

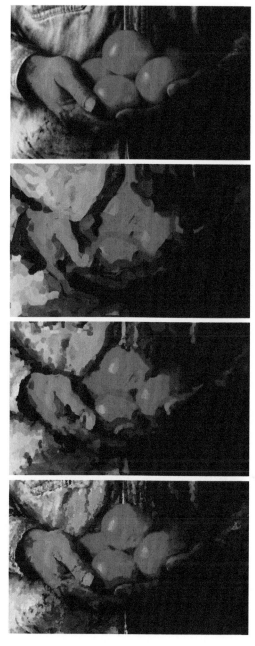

Plate XLVIII. Automatic painting given a source image, developed in layers [Hertzmann 98]. See Figures 9.10–9.13.

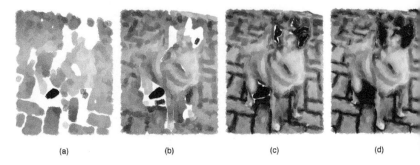

(a) (b) (c) (d)

Plate XLIX. An example of a canvas image being built up using the system Shiraishi and Yamaguchi [Shiraishi, Yamaguchi 00]. See Figure 9.17.

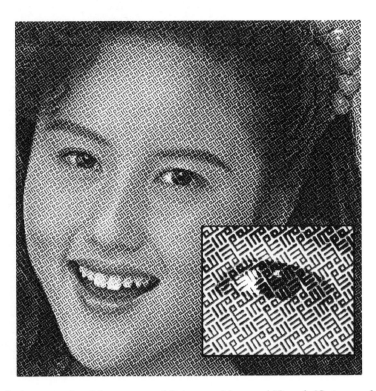

Plate L. An example of the process of Ostromoukhov and Hersch [Ostromoukh Hersch 95]. See Figure 9.23.

Chapter 5

Assisting a User: Modeling and Graftals

Non-photorealistic rendering isn't only about the images. NPR has also had an effect on geometric modeling. In this chapter we review several systems that use a two-dimensional sketching paradigm to create three-dimensional geometric models. Robert C. Zeleznik, Kenneth P. Herndon, and John F. Hughes [Zeleznik et al. 96] introduce the SKETCH system, which combines NPR with gesture recognition to create three-dimensional geometric models. Takeo Igarashi, Satoshi Matsuoka, and Hidehiko Tanaka's Teddy system allows a user to draw the silhouette of an object, which the system uses to create a three-dimensional polygon mesh [Igarashi et al. 99]. Taking motivation from the children's book "Harold and the Purple Crayon," [Johnson 77] Jonathan M. Cohen, John F. Hughes, and Robert C. Zeleznik have built an immersive system that allows users to draw their own world and move around in it [Cohen et al. 00]. Lee Markosian, Jonathan M. Cohen, Thomas Crulli, and John F. Hughes [Markosian, et al. 99] present a particle-based system for modeling smooth polygonal surfaces. A user of their "Skin" system interactively guides a particles system to grow over a given collection of polyhedral elements yielding smooth surfaces. Sidney W. Wang and Arie E. Kaufman [Wang, Kaufman 95] present a volume-modeling technique based on a sculpting metaphor. Sculpting is accomplished with their system using three-dimensional tools in a volumetric voxel-based model.

Another NPR-based approach to modeling covered in this chapter renders the appearance of complex geometry with a specialized rendering process called graftals. Graftals can be described as procedural geometric surface-generation structures.

The following artistic references are mentioned by the researchers whose work we cover in this chapter:

For drawing and sketching:

- *Using Technical Art: An Industry Guide* by G. Magnan [Magnan 70].

- *Harold and the Purple Crayon* by C. Johnson [Johnson 77].

- *Technical Illustration: Materials, Methods, and Techniques* by J. Martin [Martin 89b].

For modeling and graftals:

- *Cognition and the Visual Arts* by R. L. Solso [Solso 99].

- *The Lorax* by Dr. Seuss [Geisel 71].

- *The Foot Book* by Dr. Seuss [Geisel 88].

5.1   Sketching to Create Models

5.1.1   SKETCH: An Interface for Sketching Three-Dimensional Scenes

Consider trying to create a three-dimensional model of a chair. The easiest way to begin the chair design process may be with a simple sketch on paper. However, on paper you can't explore the chair idea in three-dimensions, and it may be difficult even to roughly specify the width, height, and depth of the chair without producing multiple sketches. The SKETCH system created by Robert C. Zeleznik, Kenneth P. Herndon, and John F. Hughes [Zeleznik et al. 96] provides a solution to this problem by combining non-photorealistic rendering and gesture recognition in a system for building three-dimensional geometric models and scenes. Their system allows users to conceptualize and edit geometric models quickly using a 3-button mouse augmented with occasional key strokes.

Zeleznik et al. begin by defining a few simple gesture strokes generated by using the first mouse button. The five stroke classes are:

- Click and release—creates a dot.

- Click and drag—produces an axis-aligned line.

- Click and drag then gesture—creates a non-axis-aligned line; the click and drag is followed by a "tearing" motion to "rip" the line from the axis.

- Click, pause, and draw—allows the user to draw a freehand curve.

- Shift-click and draw—allows the user to draw freehand curves on objects in the scene.

For ease of implementation and use, strokes are axis-aligned unless they are freehand strokes. Geometric models are created using a series of gesture strokes, as shown in Figure 5.1.

The middle mouse button is used for "interactors" that select, move, or delete objects. In order to keep interactions simple, every object has an interaction handler that contains constraint information, including the plane or axis that an object is constrained to translate or rotate about. For example, to move a block in the x-axis, the user needs to click and drag along the x-axis with the first mouse button. Then a click-and-drag gesture with the middle mouse button will transform or rotate the block.

Zeleznik et al. also use gestures with the third mouse button to manipulate the camera and rendering style:

- Click and drag—pans the camera. A point on the film plane beneath the mouse will remain beneath the mouse.

- Click, pause, drag—zooms the camera. Dragging horizontally zooms in/out towards clicked-on point, dragging vertically pans up/down.

- Click near the window boundary and drag—rotates the camera. This performs continuous xy rotation around the center of the screen.

- Clicking on an object brings it into "focus"—The object is centered in the window.

- Shift-click—cycles through available rendering styles.

Shadows can be an important cue for contact between objects or for determining depth and absolute position of objects. The SKETCH system allows users to sketch shadows, which in turn edit the object's position. The system also allows copying and hierarchical grouping of objects to make scene creation rapid and simple.

SKETCH renders orthographic views of three-dimensional scenes using a conventional z-buffer. Objects are originally created with a random color which can be changed by the user. The system renders objects with a sketchy style, which draws the users' attention away from imperfections in the approximate scenes they are creating.

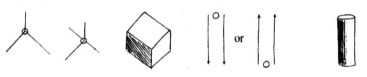

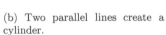

(a) Three perpendicular lines create a cube.

(b) Two parallel lines create a
cylinder.

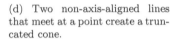

(c) Two non-axis-aligned lines
that meet at a point create a cone.

(d) Two non-axis-aligned lines
that meet at a point create a trun-
cated cone.

(e) A closed curve followed by a
dot creates a sphere.

(f) Two perpendicular axis-
aligned lines and a dot create a
pyramid.

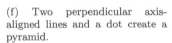

(g) Two pairs of perpendicular
axis-aligned lines create a trun-
cated pyramid.

(h) Two perpendicular axis-
aligned lines and two parallel
lines create a tri-prism.

Figure 5.1. Just a few of the basic gestures for creating and manipulating shapes.
Continued on the following page. Copyright 1996 Zeleznik et al. [Zeleznik et al.
96] and ACM. Used by permission.

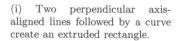

(i) Two perpendicular axis-aligned lines followed by a curve create an extruded rectangle.

(j) An unclosed curve creates an object of revolution.

(k) A non-axis-aligned line, a series of dots forming a closed polyline, then an axis of extrusion create an extruded polyline.

(l) A closed curve, an axis-aligned line, and a curve create a duct. The line is the normal of the plane in which the curve lies.

Figure 5.1 continued.

Figure 5.2. SKETCH allows the user to create objects and scenes quickly with a few simple gestures. Copyright 1996 Zeleznik et al. [Zeleznik et al. 96] and ACM. Used by permission.

A reduced set of the SKETCH interface is available as a Java applet by Adam Doppelt, using a modified three-dimensional visualization package by Chris Genly © 1997, Brown University and the NSF Graphics and Visualization Center: http://www.cs.brown.edu/research/graphics/research/sketch/java-sketch/

The SKETCH system simplifies three-dimensional model creation, and is especially desirable as a communication tool. A novice user only needs a simple tutorial and possibly a "cheat-sheet" to create a scene like the one shown in Figure 5.2. By leveraging non-photorealistic rendering methods, SKETCH's models convey information about the draft-stage of a scene, a feature that is lacking in most modeling systems.

5.1.2   Teddy: A Sketching Interface for Three-Dimensional Free-Form Design

Another critically acclaimed sketching interface uses two-dimensional sketches to create three-dimensional free-form models. The Teddy system by Takeo Igarashi, Satoshi Matsuoka, and Hidehiko Tanaka allows users to specify the silhouette (in two dimensions), which the system then "pops" into a three-dimensional polygon mesh [Igarashi et al. 99]. Their method restricts model generation to models with a spherical topology, i.e., the user cannot create a torus. The Teddy system has four basic stages of model building: creation, extrusion, smoothing, and painting. An example of the extrusion stage is shown in Figure 5.3.

Figure 5.3.   Teddy enables users to create simple three-dimensional models by simply sketching silhouettes. Copyright 1999 Igarashi et al. [Igarashi et al. 99] and ACM. Used by permission.

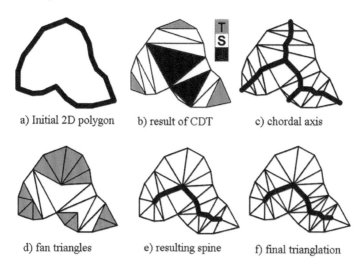

a) Initial 2D polygon   b) result of CDT   c) chordal axis

d) fan triangles   e) resulting spine   f) final trianglation

Figure 5.4. Finding the spine. Part (b) illustrates the three different types of triangles: T = terminal triangle; S = sleeve triangle; J = junction triangle. Copyright 1999 Igarashi et al. [Igarashi et al. 99] and ACM. Used by permission.

Modeling

Figure 5.4 shows an overview of the algorithm. To model an object, the user first draws a non-self-intersecting silhouette of the object. A closed planar polygon is generated by connecting the first and last points of the user's stroke. Constrained Delaunay Triangulation (CDT) is applied to the planar polygon. The triangles that compose the polygon are then divided into three categories: triangles with two external edges (*terminal triangle*), triangles with one external edge (*sleeve triangle*), and triangles without external edges (*junction triangle*).

To prepare the two-dimensional region to become a three-dimensional polygonal mesh, the terminal triangles are modified using the following algorithm, shown in Figure 5.5.) Let T be a terminal triangle which has two exterior edges and one interior edge. Erect a semicircle whose diameter is the internal edge. If all three vertices of T lie on or within the semicircle, then the internal edge is removed and T is merged with the triangle on the other side of the interior edge. This algorithm continues with T and its one interior edge until some vertex lies outside the semicircle, or until the newly-merged triangle is a junction triangle (Figure 5.5, parts e and f). If one of the vertices is outside the semicircle, then T is triangulated with a triangle fan, pivoting around the midpoint of the internal edge. If the algorithm is terminated due to a junction triangle, then a fan of triangles

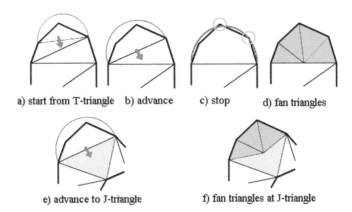

a) start from T-triangle   b) advance   c) stop   d) fan triangles

e) advance to J-triangle   f) fan triangles at J-triangle

Figure 5.5.   Pruning. Copyright 1999 Igarashi et al. [Igarashi et al. 99] and ACM. Used by permission.

is created from the midpoint of the junction triangle. A pruned spine of the planar polygon is created by connecting the midpoints of the remaining sleeve and junction triangle's internal edges. The mesh with the spine is then fully triangulated as shown in Figure 5.4(f).

Figure 5.6 shows that each vertex along the spine is raised by an amount proportional to the average distance between that vertex and the external vertices that are directly connected to the vertex. Each internal edge of each fan triangle, excluding spine edges, is converted to a quarter oval, and the final polygonal mesh is generated by sewing together the neighboring elevated edges. The final closed mesh is created by copying the elevated mesh to the other side. Igarashi et al.'s system then refines the mesh, removing short edges and small triangles.

Extrusion

Users can specify an extrusion with two strokes: a closed stroke on the surface (called the base ring), and a stroke depicting the silhouette of the

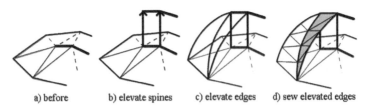

a) before   b) elevate spines   c) elevate edges   d) sew elevated edges

Figure 5.6.   Polygonal mesh construction.   Copyright 1999 Igarashi et al. [Igarashi et al. 99] and ACM. Used by permission.

extruded surface. Their system first calculates the normal of the ring using the following algorithm:

- Project the points of the ring to the original xy-plane.

- Compute the enclosed "signed area":

$$A_{xy} = 0.5 * \sum_{i=0}^{i=n-1} x[i] * y[i+1] - x[i+1] * y[i],$$

  where the indices are wrapped such that $x[n] = x[0]$.

- Calculate A_{yx} and A_{zx} similarly.

- The normal of the ring is the vector $v = (A_{xy}, A_{zx}, A_{xy})$.

The Teddy system then computes the projection plane of the extruding stroke. This plane passes through the base ring's center of gravity, is parallel to the normal of the base ring, and faces the camera as much as possible. The two-dimensional polygonalized extruding stroke is next projected onto the plane. Copies of the base ring are created along the extruding stroke so that they are perpendicular to the direction of the extrusion and are resized to fit the stroke. This process is accomplished by tracking both sides of the extrusion stroke with two vectors (left and right), each representing an edge along the stroke. The system chooses either to advance the left vector, advance the right vector, or advance both, as illustrated in Figure 5.7a. The vectors advance if the angle between a line connecting the tip of the vector and the direction of the stroke at each vector is close to 90 degrees. The extrusion is complete when the two vectors meet. The polygonal mesh is then created by sewing the rings together. The same algorithm can also be used to create pockets in the surface.

Cutting and Smoothing

Surfaces can also be cut or smoothed with the Teddy system. A cut is specified by a line that starts and ends outside of an object's silhouette. The line is projected onto the front- and back-facing polygons. The polygons to

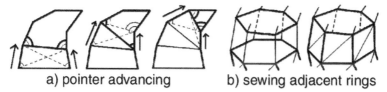

a) pointer advancing   b) sewing adjacent rings

Figure 5.7. Copyright 1999 Igarashi et al. [Igarashi et al. 99] and ACM. Used by permission.

the left of the line are deleted, and the edges along the cutting stroke are connected with a planar polygon. A user can also smooth a region by selecting a ring and then "scribbling" in the region. The polygons in the ring are removed and replaced by a surface which smoothly interpolates along the edge of the ring. Smoothing is accomplished by translating the object into a coordinate system where the z-axis is parallel to the normal of the ring. The ring is then projected onto the xy-plane in the new coordinate system, and a triangulated surface is created. (Note, this part of the algorithm will fail, unless special care is taken, if the ring contains creases or folds when projected onto the xy-plane.) The new z-values of each vertex on the newly created surface patch are calculated so that they lie on the two-dimensional Bézier curve that smoothly interpolates the ring.

Painting on the Surface

Teddy also allows users to paint strokes on object surfaces by projecting line segments onto the object's surface. Object painting is accomplished by calculating a plane consisting of all rays shot from the camera through the segment on the screen. All intersections between this plane and each polygon of the object are computed, and the resulting three-dimensional line segments are connected. The painting will fail if the three-dimensional line segments cannot be fully connected.

The Teddy system is implemented in Java and is freely available at http://www.mtl.t.u-tokyo.ac.jp/~takeo/Welcome.html/. It is interactive, with some short pauses when the model becomes complicated. Teddy models reflect their method of creation: They lack both hard edges and the geometric severity that is common with most modelers. The Teddy system's strongest recommendation is that it is intuitive, allowing fast creation of simple objects.

5.1.3   A World Made of Drawings

Motivated by the children's book "Harold and the Purple Crayon," [Johnson 77] Jonathan M. Cohen, John F. Hughes, and Robert C. Zeleznik have built an immersive system that allows users to draw their own world and move around in it [Cohen et al. 00]. Like SKETCH and Teddy, a user can create a three-dimensional model of an environment. However, in this case, the world is populated by drawings.

The world is initially modeled as a large ground plane (the earth) inside a sphere (the sky). Users are provided with a toolbar that allows them to change the drawing color, stroke style, stroke width, and drawing mode. Drawing modes include drawing on the sky, drawing terrain, drawing on the ground, creating billboards, and bridging billboards. Drawings made

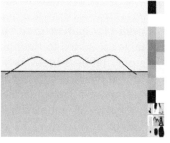 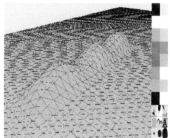

(a) Drawing of a stroke starting and ending on the ground,
indicating the silhouette of a
hill.

(b) The hill is created by
warping the ground to try to
match the stroke.

Figure 5.8. Drawing terrain. Copyright 2000 Cohen et al. [Cohen et al. 00] and
ACM. Used by permission.

on the sky, stick to the sky. In terrain-drawing mode, strokes that start and
end on the ground can be used to create a bump in the terrain, making it
easy to create hills or raised ground in the distance, as shown in Figure 5.8.
Drawing on the ground forces the strokes to follow the terrain, making it
easy to create sidewalks or railroad tracks. If the user's stroke crosses the
silhouette of the terrain, the stroke will be projected onto that terrain,
filling in to make a continuous stroke, as shown in Figure 5.9.

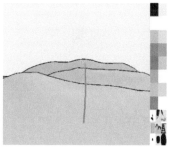 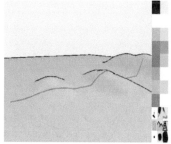

(a) A ground stroke crossing
the silhouette of a hill.

(b) The same stroke seen from
a different view, demonstrating how their system has filled
in the "gap" with a segment.

Figure 5.9. Drawing on the ground. Copyright 2000 Cohen et al. [Cohen et al. 00]
and ACM. Used by permission.

The primary primitive of the Harold system is the billboard, which represents a collection of planar strokes. After a stroke is drawn, a bounding rectangle is computed and displayed as a semi-transparent gray polygon. All strokes that start in this bounding rectangle are added to the billboard. However, as Cohen et al. explain, providing only billboards severely limits the type of scenes that can be drawn in three dimensions. They use the example of creating a fence to enclose a herd of animals: if the user moves to a position perpendicular to the drawn fence, the animals will now be beside instead of behind the fence. To solve this problem, Cohen et al. provide bridging billboards that are created by starting a stroke in one billboard and ending the stroke in some other billboard. Bridging billboards allow users easily to create telephone poles strung with wires or to represent an object like a hammock, as shown in Figure 5.10.

The Harold system also allows the changing of colors, erasing of lines, and camera controls. The camera controls are specified by drawing a stroke on the ground and then clicking to specify the look-at point. The camera will move along the drawn path at a constant speed, at two meters above ground. The user can also swivel and tilt the camera. Cohen et al. note that they provide the option to fly through the world, but provide it hesitantly because flying via the keyboard seems to break the drawing metaphor.

Strokes may be rendered in styles simulating marker, ink, or watercolor, using the method of Northrup and Markosian [Northrup, Markosian 00], which is discussed in Chapter 8.

Although this method of creating three-dimensional worlds restricts the camera position, it allows users to create interactive drawings that they can walk into and through, drawing all the time, just as Harold did. Some

Figure 5.10. The hammock is a bridge billboard, so that as the view changes, the hammock stays tied to the trees. Copyright 2000 Cohen et al. [Cohen et al. 00] and ACM. Used by permission.

Figure 5.11. Example worlds created using the Harold system, demonstrating how Harold can be used to capture the liveliness of children's drawings. See Color Plate X. Copyright 2000 Cohen et al. [Cohen et al. 00] and ACM. Used by permission.

examples of the expressive and visually rich interactive three-dimensional worlds created with the Harold system are shown in Figure 5.11.

5.2 Graftals

One of the most exciting results of non-photorealistic rendering is the ability to make simple, even crude, models expressive and artistically detailed. It is fast and easy for human artists to draw a teddy bear or a grassy field rapidly with a few well-placed strokes. However, in computer graphics, modeling and rendering fur and grass are complex and time-consuming processes.

Researchers in NPR have built on the idea of graftals, introduced by Alvy Ray Smith [Smith 84], as recursively defined L-systems. Graftals have also been described more generally as structures that "create surfaces via an implicit model that produces data upon request" [Badler, Glassner 97]. In this chapter we will define more precisely how NPR researchers have used graftals to mimic a number of different artistic techniques. Michael A. Kowalski, Lee Markosian, J. D. Northrup, Lubomir Bourdev, Ronen Barzel, Loring S. Holden, and John Hughes first explored the idea of non-photorealistic graftals for the rendering of fur, grass, and trees [Kowalski et al. 99]. These ideas were further refined by Lee Markosian, Barbara J. Meier, Michael A. Kowalski, Loring S. Holden, J. D. Northrup, and John F. Hughes [Markosian, et al. 00]. Kowalski et al. and Markosian et al. create imagery similar to the Dr. Seuss illustrations by using graftals, as shown in Figure 5.12 of "The Lorax." Matthew Kaplan, Bruce Gooch, and Elaine Cohen [Kaplan et al. 00] extended this idea to incorporate strokes that simulate those produced with pastels or paints by an artist.

Figure 5.12.   A Lorax-like figure, generated with graftals. See Color Plate XI.
Copyright 1999 Brown Computer Graphics Group [Kowalski et al. 99] and ACM.
Used by permission.

The most important contribution of graftals to NPR is that the burden
of modeling complex scenes can be transfered to the rendering pipeline, as
shown in Figure 5.13. The range of styles is generally limited only by the
creativity of the user.

5.2.1   Geograftals

Graftals in NPR have been generalized still further to include procedural geometric entities, termed geograftals [Kaplan et al. 00]. Using geograftals,

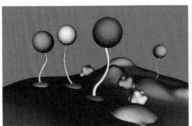

Figure 5.13.   Left: A simple geometric scene. Right: Graftals add geometric
complexity as well as a Dr. Seuss-like look. See Color Plate XII. Copyright
1999 Brown Computer Graphics Group [Kowalski et al. 99] and ACM. Used by
permission.

information such as normal, position, and color can be precomputed while waiting until runtime to calculate view- or lighting-dependent characteristics of the geograftals such as size, orientation, or highlight placement.

Geograftals contain:

- width

- height

- type: shape of the geograftal and stroke effects (pen, pencil, paint brush, etc.)

- color

- scaling functions (control geograftal's size and shape).

Using the system of Kaplan et al., geograftals can either be placed on an object interactively by a user, or automatically placed at random by the system. Random placement is achieved by parameterizing the surface and computing random u and v values, based on a user-specified density. Kaplan et al.'s system allows user refinement of desired areas, as well as multiple layers and types of geograftals. Once placed, geograftals can be individually edited, or the user can change the features of all an object's geograftals globally.

Individual geograftals are stored with an associated surface polygon, based on an idea presented by Meier [Meier 96], see Chapter 4, Section 4. Each geograftal procedurally determines how it is drawn at run time, and because geograftals are statically placed on an object's surface, they maintain viewpoint invariance under animation.

5.2.2 Drawing Geograftals

Graftals can be geometry-based procedural objects [Kaplan et al. 00] [Markosian, et al. 00] or textures [Kowalski et al. 99]. Using textures restricts the resolution of the graftals and the type of scaling functions available, therefore we only discuss geometry-based graftals.

Geograftals are displayed as a triangle strip, and each geograftal silhouette as a line strip. Points that define the strips are described as a linear combination of two basis vectors: the geograftal normal, $\vec{n_g}$, and the cross product of the geograftal normal with the view vector, $\vec{n_g} \times \vec{v}$. Other bases can be used to create different types of graftals. For example, to create graftals for a pine tree, as shown in Figure 5.14, Markosian et al. use the surface normal and $\vec{n_g} \times (\vec{n_g} \times \vec{y})$, where $\vec{y}$ is a constant vector, pointing straight up. The length of the basis vectors is specified by user-defined

Figure 5.14. Night scene. All objects are simple models, but are rendered with graftals to create clouds, bumpy ground, and foliage. See Color Plate XIII. Copyright 2000 Brown Computer Graphics Group [Markosian, et al. 00] and ACM. Used by permission.

width and height values. This basis will maintain a constant orientation via the view vector, while realistically foreshortening the geograftals.

Frame-to-frame coherence is maintained by drawing all of the geograftals every frame. Unlike regular geometry, where it isn't necessary to render back-facing surfaces, all of the geograftals must be drawn, since they may protrude from behind an object. A popping artifact will occur if geograftals are back-face culled. The same popping artifact will occur if geograftals are no longer drawn in the interior of the object. In order to create geograftals that gradually fade in and out, scaling functions are used for each geograftal. The scaling function affects the size of the geograftal based on its position and orientation in relation to the view vector.

A general scaling function described by both Kaplan et al. and Markosian et al. is:

$$f_g = 1 - |\vec{n_g} \cdot \vec{v}|$$

where f_g is the scaling factor (between 0 and 1), $\vec{n_g}$ is the geograftal normal, and $\vec{v}$ is the view vector. The basis vectors that define each geograftal are multiplied by f_g. Thus the geograftal's size and shape will change continuously over the surface of the object, insuring frame-to-frame coherence. In order for the edge lines of the graftals to have the same frame-to-frame coherence, Kaplan et al. use two additional scaling factors. The first scaling factor changes the width of the geograftal's edge, making graftal edges that are close to the silhouette of the model more prominent and those drawn in the interior less visible. The second scaling function changes the color of the geograftal edges to match the color of the object as the geograftals move toward the interior of an object. Other methods for modifying the width of a silhouette with respect to lighting are discussed in Chapter 8, Section 1.

As the distance from the viewer to the object increases, many traditional artists will draw a smaller number of disproportionately large strokes. In order to avoid adding and removing geograftals with respect to distance, another scaling factor can be used:

$$f_d = d_g/d_m$$

where d_g is the distance from the geograftal to the viewer, and d_m is the maximum distance from the viewer to the far clipping plane. To minimize the geograftal's appearance with distance, features such as width and height are multiplied by f_d. To make the geograftal features larger with distance, the features are multiplied by $1 + (1 - f_d)$.

Kaplan et al. mention that although distance scaling of geograftal geometry works well as shown in Figure 5.15, leaving the size and number of geograftals constant while correcting the geograftal edge width with distance (f_d) has a more pleasing effect. This results in line-weight depth cuing, establishing the distance from the viewer to the object based on the boldness of the silhouette. Depth cuing is also discussed in Chapter 8, Section 1. Kaplan et al. and Markosian et al. both note that although more complex functions can be used to scale geograftals, linear methods seem to be the most visually pleasing.

5.2.3 Additional Effects

Because geograftals can have any associated drawing routine, they can be used to mimic different artistic stroke styles. Kaplan et al. represent these strokes with single lines that overlap the edge of the surface they are assigned to, producing a loose and hand-drawn effect. The goal is to represent a tone—the relative amount of light a surface receives as seen by the viewer—with a number of strokes.

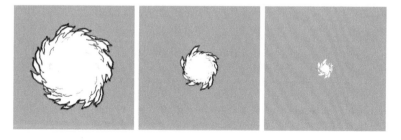

Figure 5.15.   As objects move away from the viewer, some of the geograftals shrink in size, while a random few grow in size. See Color Plate XV. Copyright 2000 Kaplan et al. [Kaplan et al. 00] and ACM. Used by permission.

Since stroke shading can require a large number of geograftals for each surface, an array of N stroke geograftals is initialized for each polygon/surface. Kaplan et al. also precompute the lighting for each surface using the algorithm described in Chapter 8.2.6. Given RGB_{total} as the sum of the RGB color values at each of the vertices of the surface, and RGB_{max} as the maximum RGB color value for those vertices that make up the surface, then the number of strokes T to produce a tone is given by:

$$ T = \left(1 - \frac{RGB_{total}}{RGB_{max}} \right) N. $$

T is used as an index in the array of strokes. Only those strokes with an index less than T are drawn. An example of this is shown in Figure 5.16.

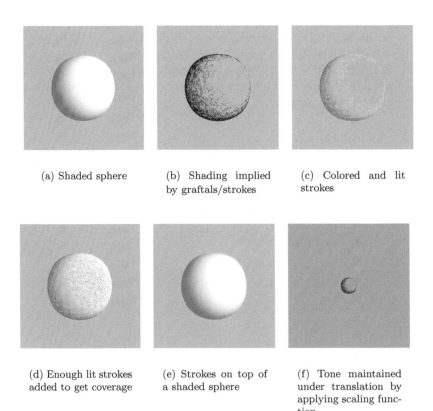

(a) Shaded sphere

(b) Shading implied by graftals/strokes

(c) Colored and lit strokes

(d) Enough lit strokes added to get coverage

(e) Strokes on top of a shaded sphere

(f) Tone maintained under translation by applying scaling function

Figure 5.16. See Color Plate XVI. Copyright 2000 Kaplan et al. [Kaplan et al. 00] and ACM. Used by permission.

For a given lighting condition, this algorithm maintains frame coherence because the same strokes are always drawn, even if the viewpoint changes. In order to maintain scale invariance, Kaplan et al. use a scaling function that increases the stroke index as the distance from the user increases. However, this function has to be tweaked per object, since it depends upon the surface area of the polygon as well as the size of the view frustum relative to the stroke widths. A variety of effects can be produced by coloring and lighting these strokes, as well as by changing the size and orientation of the geograftals.

A geograftal system could also be used to capture three-dimensional strokes painted by the user directly onto the surface of an object. The system would simply need to seed a geograftal object based on the user's placement of strokes. Geograftals remove problems such as the surface distortion and parametric overlapping common to three-dimensional painting systems, since only the position of the geograftal is tied to the object. Another desirable characteristic of these painted geograftals is that they are completely editable after being attached to the surface.

Geograftals have added a new process for rendering complex-looking three-dimensional objects in a large range of artistic styles. This approach is based on previous particle system research that allows these effects to be viewed with inter-frame coherence.

Chapter 6

Assisting a User: Animation and Three-Dimensional Environments

Researchers have created tools and systems that assist both artists and non-artists in the process of creating animations. As discussed by Cassidy Curtis in his course notes from the 1999 SIGGRAPH Course on Non-Photorealistic Rendering, having the tools is simply not enough; it is how the tools are used that matters most. In making a non-photorealistic animation or three-dimensional environment, it is rarely sufficient to just add an NPR-look at the end of the process. If a project calls for an artistic look, it is essential that the look of the finished piece be considered at every step in the process.

In creating an NPR animation, a vision of the final look and feel of the animation is necessary from the start. Cassidy Curtis [Green et al. 99] lists the following static items that define the "style" of the project:

- *Texture of the substrate:* Is the image painted on canvas, carved into wood or stone, or simply drawn on paper? Each kind of substrate has its own texture.

- *The Medium:* Is it oil paint, pencil, pen-and-ink, watercolor?

- *Geometry of the screen-space marks:* Are the marks (strokes) long or short? Fat or thin? Curved or straight?

- *Character of the marks:* Loose, flowing, rigid? Rough or smooth? Calm or energetic?

- *Texture of marks:* Transparent or opaque? Matte or glossy? Smooth or globby?

- *Visual function of the marks:* Do they represent outlines, highlights, or shadows? Do they convey properties about the surface, such as texture? Are entire objects represented by individual marks?

- *Semantic function of marks:* Do the marks express qualities, such as emotional state?

In animation, there also exist dynamic qualities that are less well-defined and usually more dependent upon imagination and intuition. It is hard to say how Van Gogh would have approached making "The Starry Night" into an animated film instead of a single image. In animation, one must consider motion. One of the hardest things to ensure with non-photorealistic rendering techniques is frame-to-frame coherence of marks. If these marks are to move, what kind of coherence is desired? Do we want coherence with the canvas or with an object's surface, or perhaps none at all? Does the motion of the marks represent the motion of the object, a change in the way in which the artist placed the marks, or some other non-literal quality? We also have to consider how objects or characters move or change as the viewpoint changes.

In the remainder of this chapter, we review the major issues in NPR animation and three-dimensional environments by looking at both two- and three-dimensional systems.

6.1   A Study of an Example NPR Animation

In Cassidy Curtis' animation "The New Chair," he found that using NPR may make some stages of the animation process more difficult, while others become simpler or even disappear entirely. A frame from his animation is shown in Figure 6.1.

In this animation, the artistic focus is on the appearance of the silhouettes. Modeling was easy, since the animator had no need to worry about intersecting surfaces, surface smoothness, or textures. Lighting was also easy, because Curtis used only two fill lights and a single shadow-casting light to create ground shadows. If the animation had used a more standard computer-graphics look, more attention and time would have gone into adding "kicker" lights to separate the foreground from the background.

All of the objects were rendered to separate layers to allow different scene elements to be rendered in different styles. Due to the layered approach, object-space intersections are of little concern to the animator. However, the addition of the layers made it difficult to composite all of the

Figure 6.1. A frame from Cassidy Curtis' NPR animation "The New Chair." See Color Plate XVII. Copyright 1999 Curtis. Used by permission.

parts into a final frame. Curtis had to worry about effects such as animation of line styles, combining different line styles, hidden-line removal, ordering of layers, and the ability to combine color backgrounds with lines.

Using NPR in this animation gave Curtis the ability to convey emotion and personality easily in the character through the rendering style, an effect which may have been tedious to achieve with traditional computer-rendering techniques.

6.2 Two-Dimensional Systems

For the last 75 years, millions of people across the world have been enjoying two-dimensional animated movies. These animated movies are by their very nature non-photorealistic. Computers in two-dimensional animation studios are generally there to support the process rather than play a central role. Walt Disney Feature Animation is the exception, having integrated computers into its animation process in 1987. This latency in computer-aided two-dimensional animation is at the root of why we should pay close attention to the path that NPR takes. It is not enough to solve the technical problems associated with animation, we must be sure to preserve the artistic process and the artist.

Several researchers have examined the two-dimensional animation process and created tools and algorithms that aid the artist in some tedious processes, such as choreographing motion, tweening, and the filling of cells. Genesys, a system developed in 1969, enabled an animator to create hand-drawn pictures, arrange and transform them, and then specify how to play back the frames [Baecker 69]. Another early system [Burtnyk, Wein 71] morphed drawings by breaking up or combining lines as necessary. The Tween commercial system developed at the New York Institute of Technology allowed the creation of animations with colored antialiased lines and regions [Catmull 83].

The Inkwell system by Peter Litwinowicz [Litwinowicz 91] provides a user with an interface for creating two-and-a-half-dimensional animations based on polygons, ellipses, and splines. A two-and-a-half-dimensional animation system is defined to be a system that maintains a drawing order for two-dimensional objects, causing objects to be layered on top of each other. Inkwell uses a patch primitive that allows users to animate and deform texture regions. The primitives of this system can be outlined and filled with a variety of patterns or textures to create simple characters and cartoons. The system is keyframe based, allowing users to edit shape and timing. Litwinowicz stresses that character animation is often the most difficult challenge presented in computer animations. Therefore, Inkwell was created with two goals in mind. The first is to allow a user to create character animation easily, with believable feelings, personalities, and expressions, through motion. The second is to provide an animation system that makes drawing and painting as natural and intuitive as possible.

6.2.1   TicTacToon: A Paperless System for Professional Two-Dimensional Animations

Most of the published research on computer-related two-dimensional animation focuses on building or automating a part of the animation process. Jean-Daniel Fekete, Érick Bizouarn, Éric Cournarie, Thierry Galas, and Frédéric Taillefer [Fekete et al. 95] created TicTacToon, a paperless system for professional two-dimensional animation. In order to understand which tasks a paperless animation system needs to solve, it is necessary to understand the traditional animation process, illustrated in Figure 6.2. Most stages of the traditional animation process involve an exposure sheet, which lists all of the frames in a scene. Each frame includes information about the mouth shape (phoneme) of each character in the frame, as well as the order and position in which the camera will capture the figures and the background. In addition each scene requires a set of stages:

- *Story board:* splits the script into scenes with dialogue and music.

- *Sound track:* records dialogue and music.

- *Sound detection:* fills in the dialogue column of an exposure sheet.

- *Layout:* manages drawing of backgrounds and main character positions; specifies camera movement and other animation characteristics.

- *Background painting:* paints background, based on layout stage.

- *Key frame animation:* draws extreme positions of characters specified by layout stage; provides instructions for in-betweeners.

- *Cleaning:* cleans the drawings to achieve final quality of the strokes.

- *Paint:* puts clean drawings onto acetate celluloid (cels) and fills areas with watercolor paints.

- *Check:* verifies animation and background according to layout specification, and certifies that the animation is camera-ready.

- *Record:* captures frame-by-frame onto film or video.

Robertson's 1994 survey of commercial computer-graphics systems divided animation systems into two categories: ink-and-paint, and automated in-betweening [Robertson 94a]. Ink-and-paint systems start with scanned images of an animated character that are cleaned up (to remove noise and close gaps between strokes). The images are then painted using a seed-fill algorithm, and composed with backgrounds, applying zoom, rotation, and pans. Automated in-betweening systems begin with a scanned key frame, which is then cleaned. Next the lines in the image are vectorized, sometimes using semi-automatic methods. Pairs of drawings are then matched,

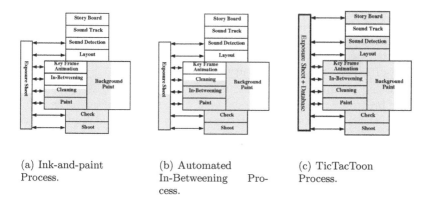

(a) Ink-and-paint Process.

(b) Automated In-Betweening Process.

(c) TicTacToon Process.

Figure 6.2. Diagram shows the work flow of the different stages in the creation of a two-dimensional animation. Computers are used for the darkened portions. Copyright 1995 Fekete et al. [Fekete et al. 95] and ACM. Used by permission.

painted if necessary, and the in-betweens are interpolated according to an exposure sheet. Each frame is rendered, composed with the characters and backgrounds, and then recorded onto film or video.

Unlike these ink-and-paint and automatic in-betweening systems, Tic-TacToon computerizes the traditional animation pipeline as a whole (with the exception of the soundtrack process). The system avoids changing media from paper to computer to cels. It is resolution-independent, which enables the reuse of drawings at any zoom level. The researchers replicate the tools used by animators on paper, and provide an environment proven acceptable to traditional animators.

One of the most important parts of creating a paperless animation system, in addition to making the system natural and intuitive to use, is making it as similar as possible to the traditional methods. Traditional animators work on a table with a sheet of translucent plastic that can be back-lit. Papers are punched and inserted onto pegs attached to the table. The workspace can be rotated in the plane of the table. TicTacToon enhances this paradigm by allowing artists to stack drawings, turn the light on or off for any number of drawings in the stack, change the position of the drawings without actually modifying the drawings themselves, flip quickly between successive sketches, and zoom, pan, or rotate the viewpoint.

Sketching with TicTacToon is done on a pressure-sensitive tablet, which vectorizes each stroke using Pudet's brushstroke model, discussed in Chapter 5. The authors tried several different setups, including a cordless digitizer on an LCD screen, but discovered that most animators preferred to draw on a flat surface, looking at the drawing on the screen. One animator commented that after working with TicTacToon for three months and then switching back to paper, he was annoyed that his hand was always hiding a portion of the drawing. The authors of TicTacToon also noticed that although they provided unlimited undo/redo and curve-editing abilities, the artists make very few mistakes, and prefer to erase and redraw the stroke instead of editing the resulting curves.

A layout module supports the entire animation process. The layout module provides a three-dimensional view of the current drawing as well as a view of the exposure sheet. In traditional two-dimensional animation, the final shot of each frame is captured using a rostrum, shown in Figure 6.3. A rostrum includes a camera, a set of movable transparent trays holding the cels, and a background. The camera is always perpendicular to the layers of cels, but can be panned, moved forward or back, and zoomed in or out. The cels may also be moved or rotated on the trays. The rostrum makes managing perspective difficult, and animators must keep this in mind when creating the drawings. In contrast, TicTacToon manages all of the elements of each frame. TicTacToon also optimizes an animator's time by

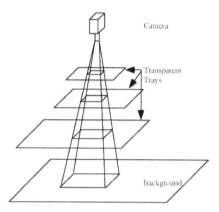

Figure 6.3. A rostrum used in filming traditional two-dimensional animations. Copyright 1995 Fekete et al. [Fekete et al. 95] and ACM. Used by permission.

saving reusable walk and movement cycles. TicTacToon makes it easy to tune object placement and trajectory precisely.

Overall, TicTacToon is a good study on how to automate an artistic process like two-dimensional animation. At every stage, the artist's traditional methods were evaluated and mimicked as closely as possible, with the intent not of replacing the artist, but of allowing the computer to complete tedious tasks, assisting the artists and the animators. With TicTacToon, all stages of the work are performed on a computer, avoiding the cost of transferring from paper to computer. Their vector-based strokes provide resolution independence and allow transparency through the alpha channel. Each stage has access to the entire animation pipeline, which enables animators to test scenes at any time without having to risk moving paper from location to location. TicTacToon was tested by over one hundred professional animators; over 90% were able to immediately switch from paper to TicTacToon with no nasty side effects. Some traditional layout animators were more familiar with the rostrum model, having learned how to "cheat" with perspective, and reported problems using the three-dimensional paradigm.

6.2.2 Multiperspective Panoramas for Cel Animation

Walt Disney's 1940 animation Pinocchio opens with a long continuous flyover of a small village, gradually descending into the cobbled streets, ending in front of Geppetto's cottage. This fly-through was accomplished with the creative filming of a single two-dimensional multiperspective panorama,

Figure 6.4. A multiperspective panorama from Disney's *Pinocchio*. © Disney Enterprises, Inc. Used by permission.

shown in Figure 6.4. Daniel N. Wood, Adam Finkelstein, John F. Hughes, Susan E. Thayer, and David H. Salesin [Wood et al. 97] explored generating similar multiperspective panoramas based on three-dimensional scenes and a planned camera path. As shown in Figure 6.5, their process starts with a three-dimensional model and a camera path. The output of their program is one or more panoramas, each with a specification for a two-dimensional window per frame of the animation. The panorama appears to be strangely warped when viewed as a whole, because it is created to be locally correct for a specific camera path. The result of Wood et al.'s calculations can then be painted or sketched by an artist to simulate any artistic effect. Similarly, the two-dimensional panoramic image could also be fed to any of the non-photorealistic filters mentioned in this book, to generate automatic non-photorealistic multiperspective panoramas. This effect may be useful for any application in which predefined camera moves are applied to three-dimensional scenes such as computer-games or virtual reality walk/fly throughs.

The creation of multiperspective panoramas combines the strengths of the computer and the artist. Using a computer allows the generation of more complex camera paths, facilitating experimentation and editing. The artist is free to give life to the panorama and is not limited to computer rendering techniques. Using a computer to generate these "warped perspective" images also allows the easy addition of two- or three-dimensional elements into the final playback, since there is a known three-dimensional representation of the camera path and the backdrop.

6.3   Three-Dimensional Systems

Recent years have seen an explosion of animations, even full length movies, that use three-dimensional computer-generated elements. These movies include everything from computer-generated crowds for Disney's *Hunch-*

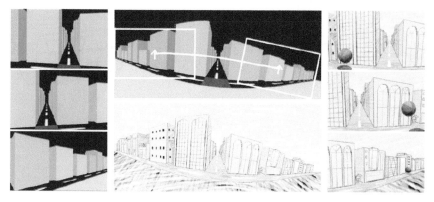

Figure 6.5. Left column: views from a three-dimensional camera path. Middle top: computer-generated layout. Middle bottom: illustrated panorama. Right column: frames from the illustrated panorama with computer-animated bounding ball. See Color Plate XVIII. Copyright 1997 Wood et al. [Wood et al. 97] and ACM. Used by permission.

back of Notre Dame or grass blowing in the wind in Disney's *Mulan*, to combining two-dimensional character onto three-dimensional backgrounds and objects in *Titan A.E.* In Disney's *Tarzan*, jungle backgrounds were painted in three dimensions using Disney's proprietary tool "Deep Canvas," in order to provide extra depth to a scene and allow complex camera flythroughs. The giant in the movie *The Iron Giant* was entirely modeled and animated in three dimensions, and then rendered with a cartoon shader. Three-dimensional computer graphics provide complex lighting and shading effects, make camera motion easier, allow automatic in-betweening and the reuse of scene elements, and more. In this section we review techniques that demonstrate how three-dimensional computer graphics techniques help artists and animators.

6.3.1 Texture Mapping for Cel Animation

In traditional cel animation, background scenery is painted in subtle, yet exquisite, detail because it can often be reused from frame to frame. Moving characters are usually kept simple due to efficiency and time constraints. If complex textures are applied to moving characters, temporal inconsistencies may make the textures seem to "boil" or "swim" on the animated element. Research by Wagner Toledo Corrêa, Robert J. Jensen, Susan E. Thayer, and Adam Finkelstein [Corrêa et al. 98] allows animators to combine complex artistic textures with hand-drawn artwork, retaining the expressiveness of traditional cel animation while leveraging the strengths

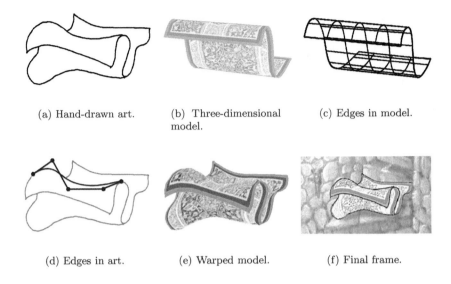

(a) Hand-drawn art.   (b) Three-dimensional   (c) Edges in model.
                              model.

(d) Edges in art.   (e) Warped model.   (f) Final frame.

Figure 6.6.   Process of creating one frame of an animation, using computer-aided texture mapping. See Color Plate XIX. Copyright 1998 Corrêa et al. [Correa et al. 98] and ACM. Used by permission.

of three-dimensional computer graphics. For each frame of the animation, they do the following, shown in Figure 6.6:

(a) The user scans in the cleaned-up hand-drawn artwork.

(b) The user creates a simple three-dimensional model that roughly approximates the shape of the hand-drawn character, including major features found in the drawing.

(c) A computer algorithm is used to find the visible border and silhouette edges in the three-dimensional model.

(d) The user traces over the edges in the line art that correspond to border and silhouette features of the three-dimensional model.

(e) The computer warps the three-dimensional model to match the shape of the line art, and then renders the model with the complex texture. (Details of implementation of the warping algorithm can be found in Corrêa et al.'s paper [Corrêa et al. 98].)

(f) The computer composites the rendered model with the background scenery.

Corrêa et al.'s process allows the use of complex textures on artwork that can be represented by a simple model. The task of matching silhouette and boundary features in the artwork and in the computer-generated model is labor-intensive and may be solvable as a computer-vision problem. However this is a good example of how computers can be leveraged to complete tedious tasks that may not be economical otherwise.

6.3.2 Shadows for Cel Animation

Shadows give contact cues for elements in a scene that anchor figures to the ground. Without shadows, characters or objects seem to float arbitrarily or may appear to be stuck to the background. In traditional cel animation, shadow mattes have to be drawn by hand, for every frame. Research by Lena Petrovic, Brian Fujito, Adam Finkelstein, and Lance Williams [Petrovic et al. 00] provides a semi-automatic method for creating shadow mattes. Their process begins with hand-drawn line art of a figure created by a traditional animator, and of the background scenery that the figure is to be placed on.

The first stage of Petrovic et al.'s process is to create a three-dimensional mockup of the scene based on the background. They use gesture strokes, inspired by the SKETCH system of Zeleznik et al. [Zeleznik et al. 96], discussed in Chapter 5, to construct the three-dimensional scene. Petrovic et al. assume a fixed field-of-view and aspect ratio. They also set the camera roll and ground plane tilt to be upright. In order to establish the pitch of the camera relative to the ground plane, a user sketches over the background art with a pair of parallel lines in the ground plane. The pitch θ is determined by $\theta = arctan(h/d_c)$, where h is the height of the horizon relative to the center of the image, and d_c is the distance from the camera to the image plane, which is set to 1. Then the user creates a three-dimensional model of the background by sketching in the background geometry.

Petrovic et al. then create a model based on the hand-drawn line art of the figure. The line art is divided into character mattes, which separate out parts of the figure, e.g., arms from legs and torso. Each of these layers is then inflated to create a collection of three-dimensional models. They use the inflation algorithm described by Igarshi et al. [Igarashi et al. 99] covered in Chapter 5. The inflation algorithm provides a model as viewed with an orthographic camera. To correct for perspective projections, Petrovic et al. adjust the shape of the inflated surface by sending every point p in the model through the following transform: $p' = p_0 + d\vec{v}$ where every point p on the lofted surface is a signed distance d from its corresponding point p_0 and $\vec{v}$ is the normalized vector from the camera to p_0, as shown in Figure 6.7.

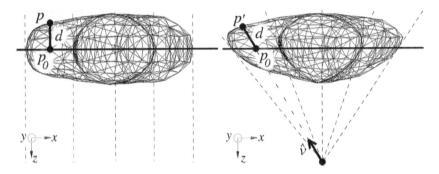

Figure 6.7. Inflating a three-dimensional figure from two-dimensional line art. Left: orthographic extrusion. Right: perspective extrusion. Copyright 2000 Petrovic et al. [Petrovic et al. 00] and ACM. Used by permission.

In order to place the inflated character into the three-dimensional background, the character must be placed at a certain depth while preserving the model's image plane projection. Petrovic et al. allow the user to control the depth of the character by adjusting two parameters: depth-translation and depth-shear, as shown in Figure 6.8.

By manipulating depth-translation, a user can move the figure out of the image plane while the image plane projection is maintained using a uniform scale around the camera center. Depth-shear allows a user fine control over how the shadows will be cast by the character. The user specifies an axis and an angle θ. For every point p on the unsheared object, Petrovic et al. calculate a value p_s, the result of sending p through a conventional shear

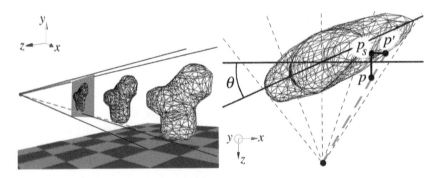

Figure 6.8. Adjusting the depth of a figure. Left: depth translation. Object grows as it moves back. Right: depth-shear preserves the perspective outline. Copyright 2000 Petrovic et al. [Petrovic et al. 00] and ACM. Used by permission.

Figure 6.9. Character with a flower produces a shadow on the ground. The trees are also producing shadows on the character. See Color Plate XX. Copyright 2000 Petrovic et al. [Petrovic et al. 00] and ACM. Used by permission.

by θ. The final point p' is the point on the ray from the camera through p that has the same depth value as p_s.

Based on the lights, the inflated character, and the three-dimensional scene, the computer generates three types of complex shadow mattes. *Contact shadow mattes* emphasize contact between the character and the ground. *Cast shadow mattes* specify shadows cast by the character onto the scenery. *Tone mattes* indicate self-shadowing and shadows cast by other objects onto the character, such as the shadows cast by the trees onto the arm of the man carrying the flower in Figure 6.9.

Shadow mattes allow the animator to edit and experiment with the shadows easily, a process that would be quite tedious to draw by hand. Figure 6.10 shows a character with two different backgrounds. It took two hours to build mattes for a 16-frame cycle with four layers. To create nine other cycles, the character mattes were simply offset with no additional user effort.

6.3.3 View-Dependent Geometry

Non-photorealistic rendering allows researchers to look at modeling and animation from an artistic perspective. Another result of NPR research is the acknowledgment that artists, especially cartoonists, often encode view-dependent characteristics into their "flat" drawings. For example, an artist who draws a bunny like the one shown in Figure 6.11 may position the ears differently depending on whether we are looking at the side or the front of the bunny. Animators who work with three-dimensional geometry often encode these subtle artistic changes, but the process of doing so can

Figure 6.10.   Three examples of hand-drawn art, shadow mattes, and the final frame produced with two different backgrounds for a stomping character. See Color Plate XXI. Copyright 2000 Petrovic et al. [Petrovic et al. 00] and ACM. Used by permission.

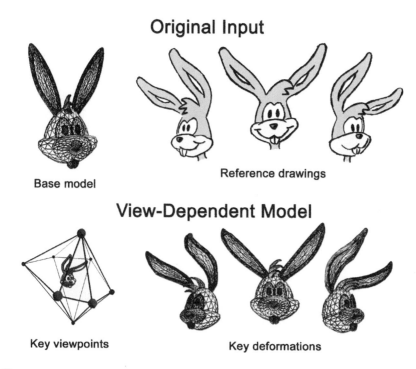

Original Input

Base model

Reference drawings

View-Dependent Model

Key viewpoints   **Key deformations**

Figure 6.11.   Components from an example of a view-dependent model. Copyright 1999 Rademacher [Rademacher 99] and ACM. Used by permission.

be tedious and requires the animator to know the camera path. Paul Rademacher [Rademacher 99] proposes encoding the view dependencies in the model during the modeling phase.

A view-dependent model consists of a base model and a complete description of the model's shape from key viewpoints. Rademacher's process starts with reference drawings for various viewpoints and a base three-dimensional model. For each of the viewpoints, the software user rotates and translates the camera, manually aligning the model with the corresponding drawing. The user then moves model vertices to deform the three-dimensional model to match the drawing, as shown in Figure 6.12. Since the model's shape is valid for a specific viewpoint, the majority of the transformations on the vertices can be done in two dimensions. The deformation process begins with the user selecting a control vertex. All vertices within distance r are automatically selected to move as well. As the user moves the control vertex in the image plane, the automatically selected

Figure 6.12.   Creating the view-dependent model. Left: establish the key view-point and align the base model to the line art reference drawing of a character. Middle: deform the model to match the drawing by selecting vertices of the model. Right: final key deformation for the given viewpoint. See Color Plate XXII. Copyright 1999 Rademacher [Rademacher 99] and ACM. Used by permission.

vertices are moved in the same direction with a scaling factor of $\left(1 - \frac{d}{r}\right)^2$, where d is the distance between the control vertex and the current vertex. This scaling factor provides smooth deformations of the automatically selected vertices. Although this method will preserve the topology of the model, the user must make sure the mesh doesn't become self-intersecting.

After mesh deformations are defined from various viewpoints, it is possible to render the model from an arbitrary camera direction. Rademacher makes two simplifying assumptions: only the view direction is considered for calculating the deformations of the model; the view direction points towards the centroid of the model. These assumptions allow key viewpoints to be mapped to a viewing sphere.

In order to render the model from an arbitrary camera direction, Rademacher finds the three nearest key viewpoints surrounding the current viewpoint. These three viewpoints form a spherical triangle that can be projected to a planar triangle. This process is equivalent to finding the convex hull of all of the viewpoints, and can be computed as a preprocess. Then the positions of the surrounding viewpoints are computed at runtime using ray intersection tests.

Given the three nearest key viewpoints, blending weights for the associated deformations must be computed. Blending coefficients can be computed directly from the barycentric coordinates of the point at which the ray intersection test intersected the triangle made of the surrounding viewpoints. These coefficients, w_1, w_2, w_3, are scaled exponentially such that: $w_i' = \frac{w_i^{\alpha}}{w_1^{\alpha} + w_2^{\alpha} + w_3^{\alpha}}$ where α controls how sharply the blended model moves towards the nearest key deformation, i.e., a smaller α will make the blend more gradual.

The key deformations are interpolated using a simple linear interpolation scheme. For each vertex v, let v^1, v^2, v^3 be the deformed vertices for each of the three key viewpoints. Then the new vertex for the arbitrary camera is: $v = v^1 w_1' + v^2 w_2' + v^3 w_3'$

In cases where there are no more than four deformations specified, or if the viewpoints all fall on one side of the viewpoint sphere, Rademacher suggests filling in the sphere with "dummy deformations," which are simply copies of the base model, in order to fully enclose it.

Another solution is to gradually revert to the base model by blending the deformation with the base model. Given the case illustrated in Figure 6.13, only one deformation was specified. As the camera moves to the back of the building, the building resumes its base shape. This was accomplished by:

$$\text{newModel} = \max(0, (\vec{V_{key}} \cdot \vec{V_{eye}})) * \text{deformedModel} +$$
$$\max(0, 1 - (\vec{V_{key}} \cdot \vec{V_{eye}})) * \text{baseModel}$$

where $\vec{V_{key}}$ is the view vector for the single key deformation and $\vec{V_{eye}}$ is the view vector for the current eye point.

Rademacher also demonstrates methods for creating animations by deforming models over time. Deformations over time are given sparsely, and don't necessarily correspond to the underlying animation in key frames, so they can not be interpolated directly. Instead, Rademacher propagates the

Figure 6.13.   The base model in this figure is a simple rectangular building. For the viewpoint directly facing the building, a single deformation is applied. The final model gradually reverts to the base model as the view changes from facing the front of the building to facing the side of the building. See Color Plate XXIII. Copyright 1999 Rademacher [Rademacher 99] and ACM. Used by permission.

Figure 6.14.   An animation cycle for a base (undeformed) model, viewed by a rotating camera.   See Color Plate XXIII. Copyright 1999 Rademacher [Rademacher 99] and ACM. Used by permission.

deformations throughout the animation by factoring out the deformation offsets at each frame, interpolating between the offsets, and then adding them to the animated model. This technique allows changes caused by deformation to propagate over time while preserving the underlying motion.

For example, Figure 6.14 shows an animation walk cycle, given the deformations specified in Figure 6.15. The deformations are applied in the 2nd and 7th frames of Figure 6.16, and all other frames use offset-interpolated deformations.

Work by Martin, Garcia, and Torres [Martin et al. 00] generalizes the idea of view-dependent deformations using Hierachical Extended Non-Linear Transformations (HENLT), which use a control function to relate position and transformations. They use HENLT for orientation-dependent

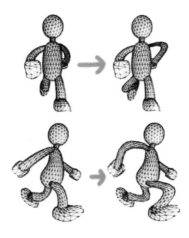

Figure 6.15.   Two different deformation are applied to an animated model. The left shows the base model, and the right shows the deformed version. Copyright 1999 Rademacher [Rademacher 99] and ACM. Used by permission.

Figure 6.16.   The animation cycle of Figure 6.14 has been changed by adding the distortions of Figure 6.15 in the 2nd and 7th frames; all other frames use offset-interpolated deformations. See Color Plate XXIII. Copyright 1999 Rademacher [Rademacher 99] and ACM. Used by permission.

functions such as those seen in Figure 6.17, and distance-dependent functions such as those shown in Figure 6.18. Their paper only provides an overview of their system, without implementation details.

6.3.4   Texturing with NPR-Filtered Textures

Consider an ancient palace of which we want to construct a three-dimensional representation. We cannot and probably do not want to do this with photographs or real textures, because they might misconvey the information. Non-photorealistic rendering may enable us to render such a three-dimensional environment much the way an architect creates a concept drawing. In order to make such an environment interactive, it might be

Figure 6.17.   The first row illustrates traditional view of a model as it rotates. The second row illustrates view-dependent deformations of a model, especially the eyes, mouth, and ears. Copyright 2000 Martin et al. [Martin et al. 00] and ACM. Used by permission.

Figure 6.18.   Examples of distance-dependent deformations.   Copyright 2000
Martin et al. [Martin et al. 00] and ACM. Used by permission.

advantageous to use non-photorealistic textures, which can contain the necessary level of abstraction. However, in order to texture a three-dimensional
world with NPR-filtered textures, special care must be taken to avoid noticeable artifacts. Work by Allison Klein, Wilmot Li, Misha Kazhadan,
Wagner Toledo Corrêa, Adam Finkelstein, and Thomas Funkhouser showed
that if NPR filters are applied to photographs, and the resulting NPR images are mapped onto the surfaces of a three-dimensional model, very noticeable artifacts tend to occur [Klein et al. 00]. If each texture undergoes a
different projective warp onto the image plane, seams along boundaries will
not be continuous. In order to avoid this, Klein et al. suggest constructing
a single texture image for each connected set of polygons, and applying the
NPR filter to the whole texture at one time. This method helps to alleviate
artifacts that occur at the seams of polygons and textures.

Another problem with NPR-filtered textures is the need for frame-to-
frame coherence in animations, while keeping the stroke size constant in
image space. Klein et al. address this problem through a type of mip-
map they call "art-maps." An example art map is shown in Figure 6.19.
Mip-mapping [Williams 83] is the technique of precomputing antialiased
textures, where each texture is one-quarter the size of the previous one.
Then the appropriate texture can be chosen based on the distance from
the viewer to the texture. Art-maps are created by applying the NPR
filter to each level of the mip-map. In an interactive environment or in
an animation, the strokes will slowly blend or blur into one another. This
method of blending strokes preserves frame-to-frame coherence, and keeps
strokes from popping in and out when they change. Without these art-
maps, the strokes will vary as the distance between the surface and the
camera varies.

Figure 6.19. Art-maps work with conventional mip-mapping hardware to maintain constant stroke size at interactive frame rates. See Color Plate XXIV. Copyright 2000 Klein et al. [Klein et al. 00] and ACM. Used by permission.

When a polygon is viewed obliquely and textured with art-maps, strokes in the texture appear stretched. Klein et al. explored a method called "rip-maps" [Packard 00] for solving the problem that all mip-maps face when viewed obliquely. Shown in Figure 6.20, rip-maps contain pre-filtered, off-axis images of the texture. Klein et al. render the scene by recursively

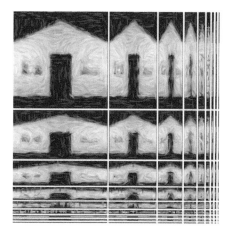

Figure 6.20. Rip-maps help solve the problem of texturing obliquely viewed polygons. In the case of art-maps, this helps to remove the stretching of strokes. See Color Plate XXV. Copyright 2000 Klein et al. [Klein et al. 00] and ACM. Used by permission.

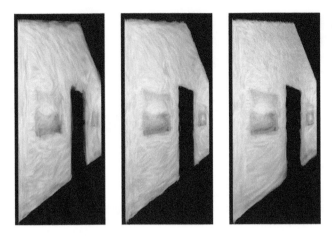

Figure 6.21.   Left: applying only art maps. Middle: adding rip-maps. Right: Klein et al. use their implementation of rip-maps to place small strokes at the top of the wall, gradually fading to larger strokes on the bottom of the wall. See Color Plate XXVI. Copyright 2000 Klein et al. [Klein et al. 00] and ACM. Used by permission.

subdividing polygons and selecting a rip-map texture to apply to a region, as shown in Figure 6.21. However, their implementation of rip-mapping is too slow for real-time rendering of complex scenes because of the necessary geometric complexity.

Part III

Automatic Systems

Chapter 7

Feature Edges: Silhouettes, Boundaries, and Creases

The ability to calculate and draw the feature edges of three-dimensional models is gathering momentum from both the NPR community and from scholars researching standard computer graphics. The calculation of feature edges is used in a variety of applications, including computer-generated technical or architectural illustration [Coutts, Greenberg 97][Coutts 98] [Dooley, Cohen 90][Schlechtweg 97][Masuch et al. 98][Markosian, et al. 97] [Gooch et al. 98][Raskar, Cohen 99][Interrante et al. 96] and coarse geometric renderings that preserve the exact silhouette of the original model [Sander et al. 00].

In this book we define feature edges to include silhouettes, surface boundaries, and creases, as shown in Figure 7.1 for a NURBS model.

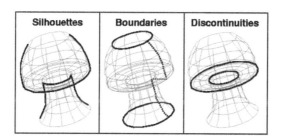

Figure 7.1. Feature edges include silhouettes, boundaries, and discontinuities (creases).

117

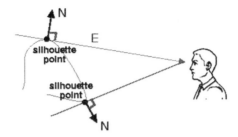

Figure 7.2.   Definition of a silhouette: At a point on a surface $\sigma(u, v)$, and given $V(u, v)$ as the eye vector and $n(u, v)$, as the surface normal, a silhouette point is defined as the point on the surface where $V(u, v) \cdot n(u, v) = 0$ or the angle between $V(u, v)$ and $n(u, v)$ is 90 degrees.

Definition of a Silhouette

At a point on a surface $\sigma(u, v)$, given $V(u, v)$ as the eye vector and $n(u, v)$ as the surface normal, a silhouette point is defined as the point on the surface where $V(u, v) \cdot n(u, v) = 0$ or the angle between $V(u, v)$ and $n(u, v)$ is 90 degrees, as shown in Figure 7.2. To generalize this definition for polygons, an edge between two polygons is a silhouette edge if the edge is shared by a front-facing and a back-facing polygon, as illustrated in Figure 7.3.

For uniformity throughout this book, we assume a standard definition of a polygon normal, such that polygon normals point outward from surfaces. This assumption yields the following:

if $N \cdot V < 0$ then the polygon is front-facing;

if $N \cdot V > 0$ then the polygon is back-facing;

if $N \cdot V = 0$ then the polygon is perpendicular to the view direction.

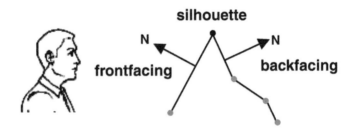

Figure 7.3.   For polygons, an edge between two polygons is a silhouette edge if the edge is shared by a front-facing and a back-facing polygon.

Definition of a Surface Boundary

A surface boundary can only occur on a non-closed model. For a polygonal model this means that at least one polygon has at least one edge that is not shared with any other polygon.

Definition of a Crease

For a non-polygonal mesh, such as a NURBS surface, a crease can be defined as any region where the surface normal changes abruptly, i.e., C^1 discontinuities. For a polygonal model, a crease is defined as an edge between two front-facing polygons whose dihedral angle, θ, is above some threshold, illustrated in Figure 7.4.

Other Facts about Feature Edges

- Silhouette lines are view-dependent.

- Surface boundaries and creases are model dependent and can be pre-computed.

- Model geometry can occlude feature edges.

Another term associated with feature edges is "cusp;" Markosian et al. [Markosian, et al. 97] give the following definition: A vertex is defined to be a *cusp vertex* or *cusp* if one of the following is true:

1. The vertex is adjacent to exactly two silhouette edges which are part of one front-facing polygon and one back-facing polygon.

2. The vertex is adjacent to more than two silhouette edges.

3. The vertex is adjacent to a boundary edge.

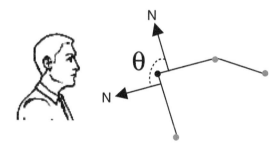

Figure 7.4. For a polygonal model, a crease is defined as an edge between two front-facing polygons whose dihedral angle, θ, is above some threshold.

In this chapter we review and provide algorithms for calculating feature edges. The calculation of feature edges can be done either in image space or in object (three-dimensional model) space.

7.1   Image Space Algorithms

7.1.1   Using First- and Second-Order Differentials in Image Space

Takafumi Saito and Tokiichiro Takahashi [Saito, Takahashi 90] provide the data structure and algorithms necessary for drawing discontinuities, edges, contour lines, and curved hatching from the image buffer. Saito and Takahashi further classify edges into two subcategories: external silhouette edges, i.e., a halo around the outside border of an object, and internal silhouette edges, i.e., silhouette lines that, from the current viewpoint, fall inside the border.

Saito and Takahashi start with a depth image that is calculated using the relationship,

$$z_s = \frac{d^2}{wz_v}, \tag{7.1}$$

where d is the distance between the viewpoint and the screen, z_v is the depth of the object, and w is one pixel length on the screen. The depth image is a grayscale image that maps $[d_{min}, d_{max}]$ to $[0, 255]$. Every pixel in the depth image corresponds to the depth of the closest point of an object at that pixel. The geometric layout of this equation is shown in Figure 7.5. The depth image equalizes the gradient value of the depth image with the slope of the surface. In OpenGL, the depth map image can be extracted by calling glReadPixels with GL_DEPTH_COMPONENT.

Profile edges are defined by Saito and Takahashi as C^0 (0th order) discontinuities in the depth image. Profile edges can be computed by taking a first-order differential of the depth image. Internal edges are C^1 discontinuities in the depth image, and can be obtained by taking a second-order differential of the depth image. Saito and Takahashi recommend using Sobel's filter such that for a pixel X and its neighbors (A - H) as shown below,

$$
\begin{array}{ccc}
A & B & C \\
D & X & E \\
F & G & H
\end{array}
$$

the C^0 discontinuities can be written as a new image, g, where

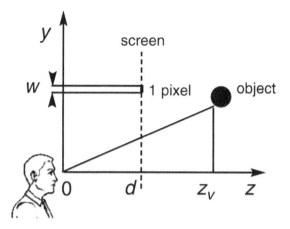

Figure 7.5.   Perspective depth. Copyright 1990 Saito and Takahashi [Saito, Takahashi 90], NTT, and ACM. Used by permission.

$$g(X) = (|A + 2B + C - F - 2G - H| +$$
$$|C + 2E + H - A - 2D - R|)/8. \tag{7.2}$$

Note that Equation 7.2 is normalized so that it corresponds to the gradient per pixel.

C^1 discontinuities in the depth image can be extracted with a second-order differential operator; Saito and Takahashi recommend

$$l = (8X - A - B - C - D - E - F - G - H)/3. \tag{7.3}$$

Problems may still occur in the computation of silhouettes. Using the first-order differential operator, it is hard to distinguish discontinuities from large continuous changes. In addition, the second-order differential operator may have a double-line artifact, as shown in Figure 7.6(c).

Saito and Takahashi normalize both images, g and l, as follows:

$$p = \begin{cases} \frac{g_{min} - g}{g_{max} - g_{min}} & \text{if } (g_{max} - g_{min} > k_g) \\ \frac{g_{min} - g}{k_g} & \text{if } (g_{max} - g_{min} <= k_g); \end{cases} \tag{7.4}$$

$$e = \begin{cases} l & \text{if } (g_{max} - g_{min} <= k_l) \\ \frac{l}{\frac{g_{max}^2}{k_l}} & \text{if } (g_{max} > k_l), \end{cases} \tag{7.5}$$

where g_{max} and g_{min} are the maximum and minimum gradient values in the 3×3 matrix of neighboring pixels. The constant k_g distinguishes discontinuities from continuous changes, and the value of k_g depends only upon the original image. The constant k_l is the limit of the gradient for the elimination of 0th order discontinuities. In Figure 7.6, $k_g = 10$ and $k_l = 2$.

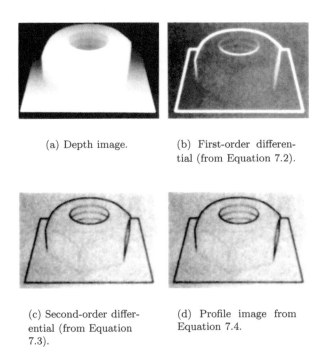

(a) Depth image.

(b) First-order differential (from Equation 7.2).

(c) Second-order differential (from Equation 7.3).

(d) Profile image from Equation 7.4.

(e) Internal edge image from Equation 7.5.

Figure 7.6.   Example of edges found through image processing. Copyright 1990 Saito and Takahashi [Saito, Takahashi 90], NTT, and ACM. See Color Plate XXVII. Used by permission.

The benefits of Saito and Takahashi's method include algorithmic stability and independence from the surface representation of the model. However, the feature edges computed are not exact, as with any image space algorithm.

7.1.2 Using Normal Maps to Find Creases and Boundaries

Philippe Decaudin presents a method for finding creases, C^0 discontinuities, and object boundaries that may not be detected by image space algorithms that use a depth map. Decaudin's method augments the depth map with surface normals or a normal map. The normal map represents the surface normal at each point on an object. Each pixel is represented by an (R, G, B) value that corresponds to the (x, y, z) surface normal for the corresponding point on the object.

The normal map is obtained using the following algorithm. First, the object's color is set to white and its material property to diffuse reflection. Then a red light is placed on the x-axis, a green light on the y-axis, and a blue light on the z-axis, each light facing the object. Next negative lights (lights with negative intensity) are placed on the opposite side of the object from each of the three colored lights. The normal map is produced by rendering the scene with these six lights, shown in Figure 7.7.

Both C^0 and C^1 discontinuities (silhouettes and creases) can now be found in image space by augmenting standard image space algorithms with Decaudin's normal map.

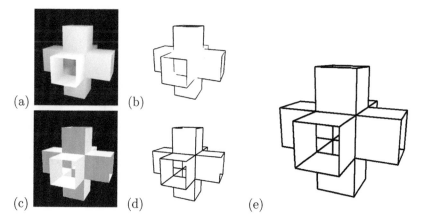

Figure 7.7.   Image-based silhouette finding: a) depth map. b) edges of the depth map. c) normal map. d) edges of the normal map. e) combined edges from the depth map and the normal map. See Color Plate XXVIII. Copyright 1999 Hertzmann [Green et al. 99] and ACM. Used by permission.

7.1.3   Image Processing with a Particle System

Cassidy Curtis' [Curtis 98] "loose and sketchy" filter automatically draws
the visible silhouette edges of three-dimensional models. His method uses
image processing and a stochastic, physically-based particle system. The
method starts with a depth-map image. The depth map is then converted
into two additional images, a template image and a force-field image, shown
in Figure 7.8.

The template image is obtained by calculating the magnitude of the
gradient of the depth map, thresholding it to a binary value (0 or 1), and
blurring the result. Each pixel in the template image represents the amount
of ink needed in its immediate neighborhood.

The force-field image is obtained by calculating unit vectors perpendicular to the depth map's gradient. This vector field is used to push particles
along silhouette edges.

Curtis' algorithm proceeds by generating a fixed number of particles,
one at a time. Each particle's position is chosen at random from within the
template image, placing particles only in areas where the template image
has a value of 1. At each time step, the particle moves based on the force
field and additional user-manipulated coefficients such as randomness and
drag. The particle erases the inked pixels from the template image as it
travels, and the particle's movement is rendered with an anti-aliased line. If
a particle wanders into an area that needs no ink, the current particle dies

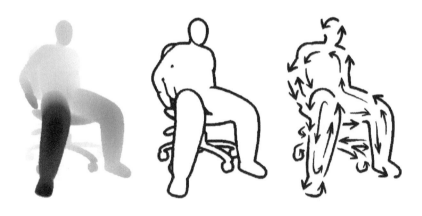

(a) A depth map.   (b) A template image.   (c) The force field.

Figure 7.8. Curtis' loose and sketchy filter starts with a depth map, which is then
converted into two images, a template image and the force-field image. Copyright
1999 Curtis [Green et al. 99] and ACM. Used by permission.

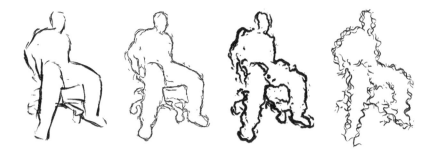

Figure 7.9. Just a few of the styles that can be achieved with Curtis' loose and sketchy filter. Each image took around 10-60 seconds to render. Copyright 1999 Curtis [Green et al. 99] and ACM. Used by permission.

and the algorithm generates a new particle in a random place. Particles may also die after a user-determined number of steps, depending on the length of strokes desired.

Curtis' method allows a software user to create a variety of line styles ranging from precise to gestural sketch. Curtis demonstrates in Figure 7.9 that his method can give life to line drawings, even in static images, conveying both motion and emotion with a few simple lines. However, the method may not capture all silhouettes and creases, because the computation is carried out based on the contents of the image buffer.

7.1.4 Using Hardware

Hardware methods for drawing silhouettes assume no prior knowledge or preprocessing of the model, and heavily leverage commodity graphics hardware. These methods are useful because of the ease of implementation. Most rely on multi-pass rendering to extract silhouettes.

Ramesh Raskar and Michael Cohen [Raskar, Cohen 99] give a simple algorithmic overview of how to render the silhouettes of polygonal models:

Generate two sets of polygons:

- P1: the layer of all visible polygons nearest the viewpoint.

  For a collection of polygonal models of closed objects, P1 consists of front-facing polygons that are completely visible, and the visible sub-parts of front-facing polygons that are partially visible.

- P2: second layer of polygons from the same viewpoint.

The second layer is computed by removing all polygons in P1, and performing the same visibility algorithm used for P1 with the remaining polygons.

Silhouettes are the intersection of P1 and P2 (assuming the user is not inside a closed object and that the interiors of polygons don't intersect). Using the z-buffer in image space, the locations where the depth values of P1 and P2 are equal correspond to silhouette points.

In the remainder of this section we present several methods which use graphics hardware to accelerate the calculation of the silhouettes of polygonal models.

Algorithm 1

This method which renders silhouette edges in black on a white background was presented in the 1999 SIGGRAPH OpenGL Course [Blythe et al. 99] and also by Raskar and Cohen [Raskar, Cohen 99]. Algorithm 1 may miss pixels close to the silhouette because of pixel sampling and z-buffer quantization. It also only generates silhouette edges at most one pixel wide.

- Fill background in white.

- Enable back-face culling, set depth function to "Less Than."

- Render front-facing polygons in white.

- Enable front-face culling, set depth function to "Equal To."

- Draw back-facing polygons in black.

- Repeat for a new viewpoint.

Algorithm 2

A modified algorithm designed to render edges of back-facing polygons instead of filling back-facing polygons. It was originally presented by Rossignac [Rossignac, van Emmerik 92]. Algorithm 2 creates visible silhouette edges with constant thickness at the same depth value as the corresponding polygon edge. Algorithm 2 is easy to implement and works well when the dihedral angle between the adjacent front- and back-facing polygons is not large. However, as the line width increase, gaps may occur between silhouette edges.

- Fill background with white.

- Enable back-face culling, set depth function to "Less Than."

- Render front-facing polygons in white.

- Enable front-face culling, set depth function to "Less Than or Equal To."

- In black, draw back-facing polygons in wireframe mode.

- Repeat for a new viewpoint.

Algorithm 3

Algorithm 3, presented by Raskar and Cohen, increases the area of intersection at silhouettes. Front-facing polygons are rendered, then back-facing polygons are pulled slightly towards the camera with depth function set to "Less Than or Equal To" and rendered filled. Algorithm 3 overcomes the precision problems of the depth buffer and allows a larger portion of the back-facing polygons to be rendered.

The OpenGL API provides the function glPolygonOffset() that can be used to offset the polygon. It allows z-dependent scaling, and takes into account the orientation of the polygon with respect to the camera. Alternatively, all polygons can be moved a fixed distance toward the camera. However, translating back-facing polygons will not create uniform width silhouettes as illustrated in Figure 7.10.

- Fill background with white.

- Enable back-face culling, set depth function to "Less Than."

- Render front-facing polygons in white.

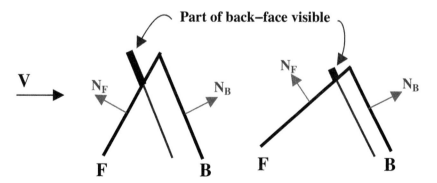

Figure 7.10. The projection width of the visible part of the back-facing polygon depends on the normals of the adjacent front-facing and back-facing polygons. Copyright 2000 Raskar and Cohen [Raskar, Cohen 99] and ACM. Used by permission.

- Enable front-face culling, set depth function to "Less Than or Equal To."

- Offset back-facing polygons towards camera.

- Draw back-facing polygons in fill mode black.

- Repeat for a new viewpoint.

Algorithm 4

Raskar and Cohen propose a method for drawing constant-width silhouette edges using "fat" back-facing polygons:

$$
\begin{aligned}
\text{Given} \quad z &= \text{distance to midpoint of the edge from the camera,} \\
N_B &= \text{normal for a back-facing polygon,} \\
V &= \text{viewpoint vector,} \\
E &= \text{the edge vector so that } \cos(\alpha) = V \cdot E,
\end{aligned}
$$

then, the required fattening for the edge E is proportional to

$$z * \sin(\alpha)/(V \cdot N_B).$$

This process fattens each edge individually, allowing individual lines to be thickened by differing amounts. Raskar and Cohen note that in general, z and V can be approximated and calculated only once for the centroid of each polygon.

After fattening, an n-sided polygon has $2n$ vertices connected with n original edges that may contain small gaps between vertices. Any potential gaps are closed by connecting the shifted vertices and triangulating. The most efficient method of triangulating is to create a triangle fan from the centroid of the original triangle. Raskar and Cohen's method involves only the drawing of polygons, instead of using polygons and wireframe as in Algorithm 3.

Algorithm 5

A slightly different algorithm for creating uniform line-width silhouettes using a stencil buffer and polygon offset was presented by Gooch et al. [Gooch et al. 99] and Blythe et al. [Blythe et al. 99].

- Clear the depth and color buffers and set the stencil buffer to zero.

- Disable color buffer writes.

- Draw the depth-buffered geometry using glPolygonOffset() to offset the image towards the far clipping plane.

- Disable writing to the depth buffer and glPolygonOffset().

- Set the stencil function to always pass and set the stencil operation to invert.

- Enable back-face culling.

- Draw the geometry as lines using glPolygonMode().

- Enable writes to the color buffer, disable back-face culling.

- Set the stencil function to pass if the stencil value is 1.

- Render a rectangle that fills the entire window (this will produce the silhouette image).

- Draw the true edges of the geometry.

- Enable writes to the depth buffer.

7.2 Object Space Algorithms

7.2.1 Brute Force for Polygons

A straightforward technique for drawing silhouettes is to test every edge explicitly in the polygonal model. A silhouette edge can only occur on a shared edge between a front-facing and a back-facing polygon. This computation can be done in parallel while the model is being rendered, especially in the cases where the z-buffer is primed for hidden surface elimination, or if the model is to be shaded.

While brute-force computation is simple, it can become a bottleneck for large models. Creases and model boundaries are view-independent, and therefore can be precomputed and stored. However, silhouettes are view-dependent, so more efficient software algorithms may be necessary for detecting silhouette edges at interactive frame rates.

7.2.2 Probabilistic Testing

Lee Markosian, Michael A. Kowalski, Samuel J. Trychin, Lubomir D. Bourdev, Daniel Goldstein, and John F. Hughes [Markosian, et al. 97] demonstrate a method for real-time non-photorealistic rendering that trades accuracy for speed. Their method improves upon and simplifies Appel's hidden-line algorithm by performing rapid probabilistic identification of silhouette edges [Appel 67]. The interframe coherence of silhouette edges and fast visibility determination are leveraged to further increase the speed of silhouette computation.

Markosian et al.'s algorithm can be summarized as follows:

- Determine the silhouette edges of the model.

- Determine the visibility of the feature edges using the modified Appel's algorithm.

- Render the feature edges.

Finding Silhouettes

In order to maintain real-time frame rates on large polygonal models, Markosian et al. developed a randomized algorithm for rapidly detecting silhouettes. Their method tests a percentage of the edges of a model at each time step to determine if any of the tested edges are silhouettes. Once a silhouette edge is found, the algorithm traces out a silhouette curve by recursively testing neighboring edges. Using this method, Markosian et al. are most likely to detect the long, more visually important, silhouettes of a model for a given viewpoint. However, their method does not guarantee that all silhouette edges will be found.

Markosian et al. increase their chances of finding silhouettes by ordering edges according to dihedral angles, starting with the largest. Thus the probability that an edge is a silhouette is proportional to $(\pi - \theta)$, where θ is the dihedral angle of the edge. The frame-to-frame coherence of silhouette edges is leveraged by checking silhouette edges from the previous frame.

Visibility Testing in Image Space and Silhouette Linking

In Markosian's dissertation and in a paper by Northrup and Markosian [Northrup, Markosian 00], a new method is described for determining silhouette visibility. Each polygon face and silhouette edge is tagged with a unique ID reference color. An ID reference image is generated by rendering the scene without lighting. Using the ID reference image, a list of edges that contribute at least one pixel to the image, L, is constructed. Each edge in L is scan-converted and compared to the ID reference image to determine which portions of each edge are visible. Each visible portion is recorded as a segment, which consists of two image-space endpoints and a pointer to the associated edge.

Prior to linking the image space segments, Markosian and Northrup carry out two correction steps to promote longer and smoother silhouette curves. First, segments that overlap and are nearly parallel are simplified by deleting the shorter segment. Two edges are nearly parallel if the angle between them is less than 1 degree. Next, segments which are adjacent and nearly parallel to each other are merged as shown in Figure 7.11.

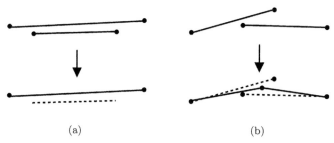

(a)   (b)

Figure 7.11. In order to connect segments into strokes, two correction steps are taken. a) The first method deletes the shortest segment of the two segments that overlap and are nearly parallel. b) The second method merges the strokes by refining their overlapped endpoints to be the midpoint between them. Note that in this figure, the angle between the segments is exaggerated for clarity and the deleted strokes are shown as dotted segments. After an image by Northrup et al. [Northrup, Markosian 00]

To link segments together into paths, Northrup and Markosian search near each segment's endpoints for potential neighbors. The search is an $m \times m$ local pixel search in the ID reference image, with $m = 3$. The following algorithm determines if segments s and n are suitable for linking:

Given two segments, s and n:

$$
\begin{aligned}
\theta &= \text{angle between } s \text{ and } n; \\
\theta_{max} &= \text{max angle allowed to link (they use } \theta_{max} = 45^\circ); \\
D &= \text{distance between endpoints of } s \text{ and } n; \\
D_{max} &= \text{max distance allowed to link (they set} \\
&\quad D_{max} = 2 \text{ pixels});
\end{aligned}
$$

if s is already linked to n

    reject n;

if $\theta \geq \theta_{max}$

    reject n;

if endpoints of s and n don't overlap

    and $D \leq D_{max}$

    and $\theta \leq$ angle of s's current neighbor (if any)

    and $\theta \leq$ angle of n's current neighbor (if any)

        link s and n.

7.2.3   Using Software Data Structures

Edge Buffer Data Structure

John W. Buchanan and Mario C. Sousa [Buchanan, Sousa 00] present the
edge buffer data structure to speed the computation of silhouette edge
detection when all of the polygons are going to be processed. The edge
buffer data structure stores a minimum of two bits per edge, with the bits
corresponding to a front-facing (F) or a back-facing (B) flag. Every vertex
is given a unique vertex index. The flags are stored in a hash table that is
indexed using the lowest valued vertex index of the edge. The second vertex
index is stored as a field in the edge buffer entry. In their implementation,
the edge buffer is a static array of size $v - 1 \times v$ where v is the number of
vertices.

The edge buffer array is updated on a per-polygon basis. As the polygons are sent to the rendering engine, each polygon is tested to determine
whether it is front- or back-facing. If a polygon is front-facing then the F
field in the edge buffer array corresponding to each of the polygons edges
is XOR'd with 1; if the polygon is back-facing then the B field is XOR'd
with 1.

Further explanation of Buchanan and Sousa's algorithm based on the
closed polyhedral object defined by five vertices and six polygons is shown
in Figure 7.12.

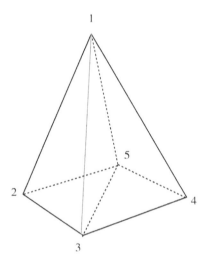

Figure 7.12.   A closed polyhedral object defined by five vertices and six polygons.
Copyright 2000 Buchanan and Sousa [Buchanan, Sousa 00] and ACM. Used by
permission.

The array is initialized for each frame as shown below:

Vertex	VFB	VFB	VFB	VFB
1	200	300	400	500
2	300	500	x00	x00
3	400	500	x00	x00
4	500	x00	x00	x00
5	x00	x00	x00	x00

First test polygon defined by the vertices 1, 2, and 3 (P[1, 2, 3]). Since P[1, 2, 3] is a front-facing polygon, the edge buffer has the following values:

Vertex	VFB	VFB	VFB	VFB
1	*210*	*310*	400	500
2	*310*	500	x00	x00
3	400	500	x00	x00
4	500	x00	x00	x00
5	x00	x00	x00	x00

After processing polygon P[1, 3, 4]:

Vertex	VFB	VFB	VFB	VFB
1	210	*300*	*410*	500
2	310	500	x00	x00
3	*410*	500	x00	x00
4	500	x00	x00	x00
5	x00	x00	x00	x00

Note that the entry of edge (1, 3) now has the value 00 since it has been visited twice.

After processing polygon P[3, 4, 5]:

Vertex	VFB	VFB	VFB	VFB
1	210	300	410	500
2	310	500	x00	x00
3	*411*	*501*	x00	x00
4	*501*	x00	x00	x00
5	x00	x00	x00	x00

After the remaining polygon edges are processed the edge buffer table becomes:

Vertex	VFB	VFB	VFB	VFB
1	211	300	411	500
2	311	500	x00	x00
3	411	500	x00	x00
4	500	x00	x00	x00
5	x00	x00	x00	x00

Edges whose entries have FB = 11 are silhouette edges. In the example the silhouette edges are: (1, 2), (2, 3), (3, 4), (1, 4). Edges with FB != 00 are boundary.

Although this algorithm does not detect creases, an additional bit could be added to allow edges to be marked as "always draw." A problem occurs, however, when the "always draw" edges are back-facing, In this case the back-facing "always draw" edges have array values FB=00, making the rendering choice indeterminate. Buchanan and Sousa fix this problem by adding F^α and B^α. They also allow another bit they call the artist flag, A, which the user can set for edges they always want to draw. When a front-facing edge is being updated, the current value of F^α is OR'd with 1, similarly for B^α. Thus the flags for a front-facing "always draw" edge will be $AFBF^\alpha\ B^\alpha$ = 10010 and the back-facing "always draw" edge will be $AFBF^\alpha\ B^\alpha$ = 10001.

Buchanan and Sousa's method is advantageous for closed polyhedral objects because the back-facing polygons do not need to be submitted to the edge test. In addition, the compact data structure allows processing of silhouette edges, boundary edges, and edges marked by an artist or another process. The algorithm has very little overhead in applications where all of the polygons are accessed during the rendering process.

Duality

Aaron Hertzmann and Dennis Zorin [Hertzmann, Zorin 00] use the concept of a dual surface for fast detection of silhouette curves defined as zero sets for smooth surfaces or silhouette edges of polygonal meshes.

Barequet et al. [Barequet et al. 99] presented the idea for using dual surfaces to calculate silhouette in three dimensions. They define the dual space to be a space of the same dimension such that each m-dimensional object in the primal space is represented by a $(2 - m)$-dimensional object in the dual space. Then let f be a face in the plane $Ax + By + Cz + D = 0$. The dual of f is a point f' in the dual space: $(\frac{A}{D}, \frac{A}{D}, \frac{A}{D})$.

Hertzmann and Zorin expand upon this method in four dimensions, making the method numerically stable. Given a surface M and its dual M', the points of M' are the images of the tangent's planes where each plane $Ax + By + Cz + D = 0$ is mapped to the homogeneous point $[A, B, C, D]$.

Thus, given point p on the surface M and its unit normal, $n = [n_1, n_2, n_3, 0]$, the dual surface, M', can be obtained by mapping each point of a surface, M, to a homogeneous point $N = [n_1, n_2, n_3, -p \cdot n]$.

In order to find a silhouette, Hertzmann and Zorin use the inverse: each plane in the dual space corresponds to a point in the original three-dimensional space. Let $C = [c_1, c_2, c_3, c_4]$ be the viewpoint in homogeneous form. The silhouette of the surface consists of all points p for which C is in the tangent plane at that point. Under perspective projection, this means that $(C \cdot N) = (c-p) \cdot n = 0$. For orthographic projections, the homogeneous form is the same, so $(C \cdot N) = (c \cdot n) = 0$, where c is the viewpoint direction.

Hertzmann and Zorin have reduced the problem of finding silhouettes to the problem of intersecting a plane with a surface. A complication is introduced by the fact that some points of the dual surface may be at infinity. Hertzmann and Zorin deal with this problem by identifying the entire three-dimensional project space with the boundary of a hypercube in four-dimensional space. A demonstration of the algorithm for a two-dimensional example is shown in Figure 7.13.

The algorithm takes as input a polygonal mesh. In order to compute silhouettes using zero-crossings, normals must be specified at vertices. Hertzmann and Zorin divide their algorithm into two parts: 1) initializing the

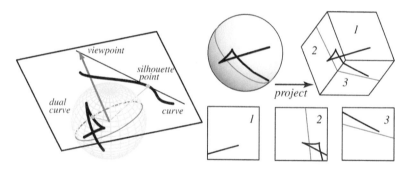

Figure 7.13. Left: Using a dual curve to find silhouette points. The figure shows a curve in the $z = 1$ plane and its dual on a sphere. The arrow is the vector c from the origin in 3D to the viewpoint in the plane. The circle around the sphere is the intersection of the plane passing through the origin perpendicular to c. The silhouette point can be found by intersecting the circle with the dual curve and retrieving the corresponding point on the original curve. Right: Reducing the intersection problem to planar subproblems. The upper hemisphere containing the dual curve is projected on the surface of the cube and at most five (in this case three) planar curve-line intersections are solved on the faces of the cube. See Color Plate XXIX. Copyright 2000 Hertzmann and Zorin [Hertzmann, Zorin 00] and ACM. Used by permission.

spatial partition; 2) intersection of the dual surface with the plane corresponding to the viewpoint.

Algorithm for Initializing the Spatial Partition

- For each vertex p with normal n, compute the dual position $N = [n_1, n_2, n_3, -(p \cdot n)]$.

- Normalize each dual position N using an l_∞-norm, i.e., divide by $\max(|N_1|, |N_2|, |N_3|, |N_4|)$. After this step, at least one of the components N_i, $i = 1..4$, will become 1 or -1. The resulting four-dimensional point is on the surface of the unit hypercube. The three-dimensional face of the cube on which the vertex is located is determined by the index and sign of the maximal component.

- Next, create an octtree for each three-dimensional face of the cube. Place each triangle from the dual mesh into the octtree if any of the triangle's vertices are on that face of the cube.

Part one of Hertzmann and Zorin's algorithm breaks the hypercube into eight three-dimensional cubes. Part two uses the octtree to find silhouette edges by intersecting the dual plane with the dual surface given the camera position. An example is shown in Figure 7.14.

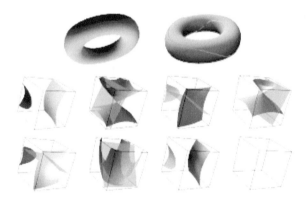

Figure 7.14. Silhouette lines under the duality map correspond to the intersection curve of a plane with the dual surface. Top: Torus shown from the camera viewpoint and from the side viewpoint. Bottom: The eight 3D faces of the hypercube, seven of which contain portions of the dual surface. The viewpoint dual is shown as a light blue plane. Silhouettes occur at the intersection of the dual plane with the dual surface. See Color Plate XXX. Copyright 2000 Hertzmann and Zorin [Hertzmann, Zorin 00] and ACM. Used by permission.

Anchored Cones

Pedro V. Sander, Xianfeng Gu, Steven J. Gortler, Hugues Hoppe, John Snyder [Sander et al. 00] provide a software method for fast silhouette extraction. They calculate silhouettes at every viewpoint for a detailed mesh, and use them to clip the rendering of a coarse mesh in order to eliminate artifacts of the coarse mesh.

Sander et al. calculate silhouettes by entering polygonal edges into a hierarchical search tree, or as they put it, a forest. Each node, n, in the forest contains a list of edges, where the node is the set of polygons attached to edges contained in that node and in all of its descendants. This data structure allows them to easily determine, for any viewpoint, whether all of the polygons in a node are front-facing or back-facing. If all the polygons in a node are front-facing or back-facing, then those edges cannot be silhouettes, and only the remainder of the nodes need to be searched. Their paper contains the pseudocode and a more detailed explanation of their forest-of-edges algorithm. The most important contribution of this paper is, however, the idea of anchored cones.

Sander et al. optimize the front-facing or back-facing test using two anchored cones, one front-facing anchored cone, a_f, and one back-facing anchored cone, a_b. The anchored cones represent a cone of normals for the node. Each anchored cone, a, is specified by an anchor origin, a.o, the central axis (normal) of the cone a.$\vec{n}$, and a cone angle θ, as illustrated in Figure 7.15.

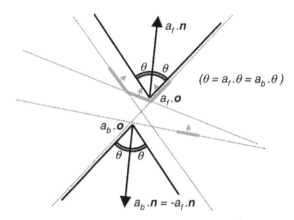

Figure 7.15.   Anchored cones provide conservative bounds on the front-facing and back-facing regions of a set of faces, illustrated here in 2D for four oriented line segments. Copyright 2000 Sander et al. [Sander et al. 00] and ACM. Used by permission.

Anchored cones are constructed by creating the cone with the largest angle θ inside the front-facing region. The value of θ is computed as the complement of the maximum angle from $\vec{n}$ to the set of face normals. For any given node, Sander et al. assign $a_f.\vec{n} = -a_b.\vec{n} = \vec{n}$ $a_f.\theta = a_b.\theta = \theta$. They find the best cone origins, $a_f.o$ and $a_b.o$, by solving the linear programs: $a_f.o = \min \vec{n} \cdot o$, where o is equal to each vertex of each front-facing face and $a_b.o = \min -\vec{n} \cdot o$, where o is equal to each vertex of each back-facing face.

To remove the polygons that are entirely front-facing or entirely back-facing from testing, the following test is made: A vector p is in an anchored cone if $cos^{-1}\left(\frac{p-a.o}{\|p-a.o\|} \cdot a.\vec{n}\right) \leq a.\theta$.

To reduce computation, they store the scaled normal $a.\vec{n_s} = a.\vec{n}/\cos(a.\theta)$.

With careful precomputation, a node can be tested using only two dot-product operations and no square roots or trigonometric operations.

A vector p is in an anchored cone if

$$(p - a.o) \cdot a.\vec{n_s} \geq 0 \text{ and}$$

$$((p - a.o) \cdot a.\vec{n_s}))^2 \geq \|p - a.o\|^2.$$

Using anchored cones allows the fast rejection of entirely front-facing and entirely back-facing polygons. The code and a demo program are available at http://www.deas.harvard.edu/~xgu/, with a mirror version available at http://www.cs.utah.edu/npr/repository.html.

Gauss Map

Bruce Gooch, Peter-Pike Sloan, Amy Gooch, Peter Shirley, and Richard Riesenfeld [Gooch et al. 99] use a more complex preprocess and search algorithm when classifying edges becomes a bottleneck. Their algorithm is similar in spirit to Zhang et al. [Zhang, 97], but requires looking at arcs on the Gauss map instead of points. The Gauss map of an edge on a polyhedral model is a great arc on the sphere of orientations (Figure 7.16). Under orthographic projection, a plane through the origin in this sphere defines the view. All of the faces on one side of the plane are front-facing, and on the other side they are back-facing. If the "arc" corresponding to an edge is intersected by this plane, it is a silhouette edge. To search for such edge/plane intersections, they store the arcs in a hierarchy on the sphere to quickly cull edges that cannot be silhouettes. Gooch et al. implemented a decomposition of the sphere starting with a platonic solid (octahedron or icosahedron), and all successive levels are four-to-one subdivisions consisting of spherical triangles. An arc is stored at the lowest possible level of the hierarchy. This makes silhouette extraction logarithmic in the number of edges for smooth models where the arcs tend to be short. One problem

Figure 7.16. The arc in a Gauss map seen in two dimensions. The two bold line segments are faces that share a vertex. The orientations of their normals can be represented as points on the circle. The arc between those two points represents all orientations swept out between the two normals. In three dimensions the same reasoning applies, and the arc is an arbitrary segment on a great circle.

with this hierarchy is that the edges of the spherical triangles on the sphere interfere with the arcs and limit how far they can be pushed down the hierarchy. The probability of being stored in a leaf node that can contain an arc of a given length decreases as the size of the triangles shrink, because the boundaries of these spherical triangles become denser with recursion. An ad hoc solution to this problem is to use multiple hierarchies, whose spherical triangles are different, and store an arc in the hierarchy with the spherical triangle with the smallest area that contains it. A more attractive alternative would be to use "bins" on the sphere that overlap and/or to make data-dependent hierarchies.

Under perspective viewing, the region to check grows, based on planes containing the object and intersecting the eye vector. Building a spatial hierarchy over the model as in [Zhang, 97] would minimize this effect.

7.2.4   Calculating Silhouettes for Implicit Surfaces

David Bremer and John Hughes [Bremer, Hughes 98] explore an approach similar to that of Markosian et al. [Markosian, et al. 97] for finding silhouettes for implicit surfaces. Their algorithm finds approximate silhouettes by first locating a point on the surface through ray–surface intersection. They then trace along the surface to a point on the silhouette, and then trace out the silhouette, shown in Figure 7.17.

Bremer and Hughes' algorithm assumes that the surface model S is the zero-set of a twice continuously differentiable function f on R^3. Their algorithm treats the implicit function as a "black box" from which they can

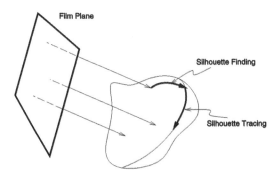

Figure 7.17.   Rays from the image plane are intersected with the surface. Upon
a surface intersection, the surface is traced in the direction of the view plane
projection of the gradient, attempting to find a silhouette point. Once a silhouette
point is found, a silhouette curve is traced out. Copyright 2000 Bremer and
Hughes [Bremer, Hughes 98] and ACM. Used by permission.

compute the value of the function, the gradient, and the Hessian (matrix
of second derivatives) at any point. They also use an orthographic camera
with view direction v, and assume that the surface fits within the camera's
image plane. Given p with coordinates p_1, p_2, p_3, they further assume the
existence of a constant $K > 0$ such that at every point p, the gradient of f
is given by

$$\nabla f(p) = \left(\frac{\delta f}{\delta p_1}(p), \frac{\delta f}{\delta p_2}(p), \frac{\delta f}{\delta p_3}(p), \right),$$

and is bounded in magnitude by K.

The Hessian of f is denoted by

$$H f(p) = \begin{bmatrix} \frac{\delta^2 f}{\delta p_1 \delta p_1}(p) & \frac{\delta^2 f}{\delta p_1 \delta p_2}(p) & \frac{\delta^2 f}{\delta p_1 \delta p_3}(p) \\ \frac{\delta^2 f}{\delta p_2 \delta p_1}(p) & \frac{\delta^2 f}{\delta p_2 \delta p_2}(p) & \frac{\delta^2 f}{\delta p_2 \delta p_3}(p) \\ \frac{\delta^2 f}{\delta p_3 \delta p_1}(p) & \frac{\delta^2 f}{\delta p_3 \delta p_2}(p) & \frac{\delta^2 f}{\delta p_3 \delta p_3}(p) \end{bmatrix}.$$

Given a point on the image plane o, the algorithm begins by searching
for a surface intersection along the ray $o + tv$. They check the ray at
discrete steps, guarantying that no intersections will be missed by taking
a step the size of $f(p)/K$. For example at p, the next location along the
ray is $p' = p + (f(p)/K)v$. The search proceeds along this ray from the eye
point until the function value is nearly zero.

After finding a ray-surface intersection q, the algorithm computes the
function gradient at q and uses it to find a tangent vector in the plane
spanned by v and ∇f by the following:

$$F(q) = \frac{\nabla f(q) \times (v \times \nabla f(q))}{||\nabla f(q)||^2}.$$

This vector field F is traced along until $v \cdot \nabla f$ changes sign, indicating a silhouette point.

Starting with a silhouette point acquired using the first portion of the algorithm, a three-dimensional polygonal silhouette line is traced out, with each point being approximately ϵ apart. If a point is found within ϵ of any other silhouette point, it is discarded and the silhouette-finding process starts over with a new ray intersection. The silhouette-tracing procedure is based on the following observation:

A curve h lies on the silhouette of the surface S along v if $h(t)\epsilon S$ for every t, and the tangent plane to the surface at $h(t)$ contains v for every t.

Bremer and Hughes rephrase this as

$$\nabla f(h(t)) = 0,$$
$$v^t \nabla f(h(t)) = 0.$$

Allowing $w = h'(t)$, where w is the tangent vector to $h(t)$ at t and using the chain rule to differentiate the above equations, then

$$\nabla f(h(t))w = 0,$$
$$v^t H \nabla f(h(t))w = 0.$$

The silhouette is traced by computing

$$w = \nabla f(q) \times v^t H \nabla f(q).$$

The tangent vector to the silhouette curve is orthogonal to both the gradient and the product of the Hessian with the view direction. Silhouette curve tracing will stop if $w = 0$ (occurring at cusps), or if it reaches the starting point.

Bremer and Hughes also perform occlusion testing by examining every 4th vertex for occlusion, then testing and removing the intervening vertices when necessary.

Instead of rendering only the polyline, Bremer and Hughes have modified their rendering pipeline to take into account the curvature information given in the Hessian matrix, noting that the curvature at a silhouette point p is

$$\kappa(p) = \frac{v^t H f(p)v}{||\nabla f(p)||^2}.$$

They draw several copies of the silhouette curves with spacing proportional to $1/\kappa(p)$, which creates tightly-curved sections with closely-spaced curves and wide-spaced curves for areas of little curvature, as shown in Figure 7.18.

Figure 7.18. Approximate silhouette of an implicit surface of a Mickey-Mouselike figure, with closely-spaced curves in areas of high curvature (the nose) and wide-spaced curves in areas of low curvature (backside of the head). Copyright 2000 Bremer and Hughes [Bremer, Hughes 98] and ACM. Used by permission.

7.2.5   Calculating Silhouettes for NURBS Surfaces

Amy Gooch [Gooch 98], presented methods for calculating silhouettes from nonuniform rational B-spline (NURBS) surfaces. Her work follows Elber and Cohen's [Elber, Cohen 90] "Hidden Curve Removal for Free Form Surfaces." Elber and Cohen's methods rely on splitting surfaces into regions bound by silhouette curves and surface boundaries. He uses ray casting and arbitrary surface refinement to extract silhouettes. Elber and Cohen's methods were aimed at generating images of NURBS models that included visible silhouettes, isoparametric lines, C^1 discontinuities, and surface boundaries. Unlike Gooch, Elber and Cohen's methods are not optimized for interactive scenes.

Let:

$$\sigma \equiv \text{the surface;}$$
$$\sigma(u,v) \equiv \text{a point on the surface at parametric values } u, v;$$
$$E(u,v) \equiv \text{vector from the eye point to } \sigma(u,v);$$
$$n(u,v) \equiv \text{the normal at } \sigma(u,v);$$
$$\theta \equiv \text{the angle between the vectors } E(u,v) \text{ and } n(u,v);$$
$$m_{i,j} \equiv \text{control point of the mesh indexed by } i, j.$$

Given $E(u,v)$ and $n(u,v)$, a silhouette point is defined as the point on the surface where $E(u,v) \cdot n(u,v) = 0$ or the angle between $E(u,v)$ and $n(u,v)$ is 90 degrees, as shown in Figure 7.2.

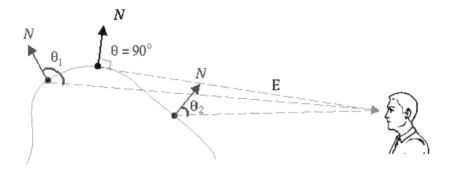

Figure 7.19. Interpolating silhouettes: After two neighboring surface points with different δ's are found, the point where $E(u,v) \cdot n(u,v) = \delta = 0$ can be found by linearly interpolating in u or v with the two angles as calculated in Equation 7.7. Note: $\theta_1 = E_1 \cdot n_1 > 0$ and $\theta_2 = E_2 \cdot n_2 < 0$.

Linear interpolation, as explained in Figure 7.19, is done only in one parametric dimension, u or v, keeping the other constant. Given two surface points at parametric values t_1 and t_2, such that $t_1 = (t_1, v_o)$ and $t_2 = (t_2, v_o)$, θ_i can be defined by $n(t_i)$, the normal at t_i, and $E(t_i)$, the eye vector, as seen in Equation 7.6:

$$\theta_i = \arccos\left(\frac{E(t_i) \cdot n(t_i)}{\|E(t_i) \cdot n(t_i)\|}\right). \tag{7.6}$$

Given θ_1 and θ_2 and the corresponding parametric values, t_1 and t_2, linear interpolation will give an approximate t_* where the angle is 90 degrees or $\frac{\pi}{2}$:

$$t_* = t_2 - (t_2 - t_1)\frac{(\theta_2 - \frac{\pi}{2})}{(\theta_2 - \theta_1)}. \tag{7.7}$$

One way to find silhouettes on NURBS surfaces is to use the control mesh of a surface, σ, to supply information on where a silhouette can occur. Due to the variation diminishing properties of the control mesh, regions of the surface that cannot contain silhouettes may be culled from further searches.

A two-dimensional marching-cube data structure is necessary for holding the silhouette points and assembling them into silhouette curves. The marching-cube data structure contains four control points and their (u,v) values, as well as a list of possible silhouette points (four silhouette points are possible between the mesh points, and four additional points possible at the mesh points).

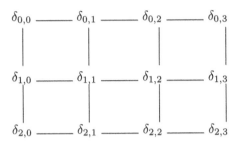

Figure 7.20.   Visualization of Gooch's method as a table of signs $(\delta_{i,j})$, where $\delta i, j$ can be +, -, or 0.

Gooch uses the intrinsic property of NURBS surfaces, called nodes, to identify places to look for silhouettes. Nodes correspond to parameter values that are the average of consecutive sets of $(order-1)$ knots from the knot vector, ignoring the first and last. There are exactly the same number of nodes as there are control points on a NURBS surface. A normal is calculated for every node point on a surface, as a preprocess.

$E(u, v) \cdot n(u, v)$ is calculated for every view and every node point, where $n(u, v)$ is the surface normal at the node point and $E(u, v)$ is the vector from the eye point to the point on the surface. The resulting signs of the dot products, $\delta_{i,j}$, are stored in a table, one per node point, as shown in Figure 7.20 and 7.22. If $\delta_{i,j}$ is zero, there is a silhouette at that node point on the surface. By searching the table in the u direction and then in the v direction, a silhouette can be found by comparing $\delta_{i,j}$ to $\delta_{i+1,j}$ and $\delta_{i,j}$ to $\delta_{i,j+1}$, respectively. If a sign changes from + to - or from - to +, then there is a silhouette between those two points on the surface, as shown in Figure 7.22.

When a region containing a silhouette point is found between two node points, a silhouette point can be linearly interpolated from the node values, as shown in Figure 7.19. The interpolation is based on two surface points and the respective angles formed by the normal and the eye vector, calculated as in Equation 7.6 and 7.7.

In order for Gooch's algorithm to be successful, the surface needs to be sufficiently refined, or the algorithm may miss silhouettes, as discussed in Figure 7.21. Surface refinement can be done as a preprocess over the whole surface. However, the refinement increases the number of control points and thus the number of checks necessary to locate silhouette points. It may be better to refine the surface in areas where a silhouette is known to be based on testing the control mesh.

The two-dimensional marching-cube data structure makes it easy to connect the silhouette points to form linear silhouette curves. Figure 7.22

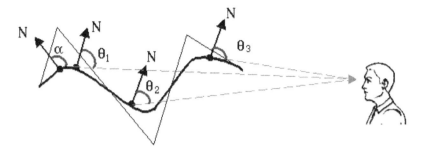

Figure 7.21. Gooch's Method can result in missed silhouettes, depending upon the node points. If, for example, the node points were those that correspond to θ_1, θ_2, and θ_3, there would be three missed silhouette points, because θ_1, θ_2, and θ_3, are all less than 90 degrees and there would be no sign change. However, if the nodes points were α, θ_2, and θ_3, then α is greater than 90 degrees and θ_2 is less than 90 degrees, so the silhouette between the two corresponding node points would not be missed and could be interpolated. The problem of missing these silhouettes can be remedied by refining the control mesh.

provides a visualization of the $\delta_{i,j}$ and the approximate silhouette lines. The marching-cube method results in edge lines as displayed in Figure 7.23.

7.3 Summary

There are many methods for finding feature edges, either with image-space or object-space algorithms. Image-space methods work without knowledge of the surface representation, as long as a depth buffer is available. However, these methods are limited by the resolution of the depth image.

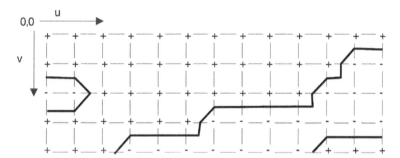

Figure 7.22. This image shows the control mesh (in uv-space) for a surface, with approximations to the silhouettes. The sign of the dot-product $E(u, v) \cdot n(u, v)$ are denoted by +, -, or 0.

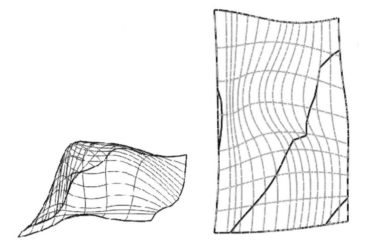

Figure 7.23. A NURBS-surface with silhouettes and boundary lines generated with Gooch's method, as well as a view from above the surface. Compare this image with the two dimensional projection and approximation of silhouettes shown in Figure 7.22.

Hardware methods make the implementation simple, leveraging the speed of APIs such as OpenGL, but these methods give less control over line width and style. Software object-space methods allow more control over how the feature edges are drawn, and can be faster for large, complex models.

While it is not certain that one of these methods for finding feature edges is definitely better than another for a broad range of applications, the one thing we do know is that real-time visibility culling of feature edges is very hard and unsolved. Most of the examples here use the z-buffer to resolve the visibility of feature edges by drawing these edges first, and then rendering the polygons either in the background color or by using some other shading method.

Chapter 8

Automatic Systems: Illustration

Examining technical manuals, illustrated textbooks, and encyclopedias reveals shading and line-illustration conventions that are quite different from traditional computer graphics conventions. Line and shading techniques used by illustrators can convey a more accurate representation of shape and material properties than traditional computer graphics methods. These illustration techniques can improve or replace traditional representation of models, such as wireframe or Phong-shaded.

Several researchers have used illustrators' techniques to improve the communication of ideas ranging from mechanical assemblies [Driskill 96] and user-interfaces, to physical objects, [Seligmann, Feiner 91] to creating artistic images such as those sought after in cel animation [Lebaredian 96]. In this chapter, we present techniques for line rendering, NPR shading techniques, hatching, and cartoon shading.

8.1 Artistic Line Drawing

8.1.1 Which Lines to Draw

Several studies in the field of perception [Biederman, Ju 88][Braje et al. 95] [Christou et al. 96][Tjan et al. 95] conclude that subjects can recognize three-dimensional objects at least as well, if not better, when the edge lines (feature edges) are drawn. Christou et al. [Christou et al. 96] concluded in a perceptual study that "a few simple lines defining the outline

The following artistic references are mentioned by the researchers whose work we cover in this chapter.

For drawing:

- *Technical Drawing* by F. Giesecke, A. Mitchell, and H. Spencer [Giesecke et al. 36].

- *Rendering in Pen and Ink* by A. L. Guptill [Guptill 76].

- *Line: an Art Study* by E. J. Sullivan [Sullivan 22].

- *The Drawing Handbook* by F. Lohan [Lohan 78a].

For illustration:

- *Technical Illustration, 2nd Edition* by T. A. Thomas [Thomas 68].

- *High Tech Illustration* by J. Martin [Martin 89a].

- *Using Technical Art: An Industry Guide* by G. Magnan [Magnan 70].

- *The Guide Handbook of Scientific Illustration*, by Elaine Hodges, ed. [Hodges 89].

- *Seeing Between the Pixels: Pictures in Interactive Systems* by C. Strothotte and T. Strothotte [Strothotte, Strothotte 97].

- *The New Complete Illustration Guide: The Ultimate Trace File for Architects, Designers, Artists, and Students* by L. Evans [Evans 96].

of an object suffice to determine its 3-D structure." (p. 712) As seen in children's coloring books, humans are good at inferring shape from line drawings. Lines help distinguish different parts and features of an object and draw attention to details that may be lost in shading.

Chapter 7 described how to calculate and draw feature edges such as silhouettes, creases, and boundaries. Silhouettes are view-dependent and have to be recalculated for every new view of the object, whereas lines such as creases and surface boundaries can be precalculated and are view-independent.

Several researchers have also looked at alternatives to feature edges. Gershon Elber [Elber, Cohen 90][Elber 95][Elber 98] has studied isoparametric curves extensively. Given a surface parameterized in u, v as shown in Figure 8.1, isolines need to be drawn sparingly to give the effect of placing a grid on an object, and may emphasize subtleties of shape that can be missed by only drawing feature edges.

Research concerning the display of lines related to principal directions of curvature by Victoria Interrante [Interrante 97] and Ahna Girshick, Victoria Interrante, Steven Haker, and Todd Lemoine [Girshick et al. 00] aim at

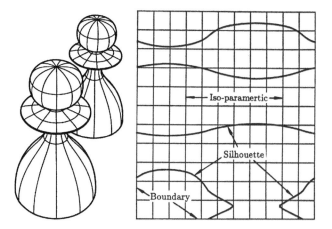

Figure 8.1. From left to right, Pawn model: with 1930 polygons; with 4215 polygons; 2 NURBS surfaces (56 rational patches). Far right: A parametric view of the NURBS pawn with extracted curves. Copyright 1990 Elber [Elber, Cohen 90] and ACM. Used by permission.

communicating surface shape, as shown in Figure 8.2, when feature edges and shading fall short. Adding curvature lines has been shown to be important in displaying three-dimensional volume data that has overlapping surfaces. Principal directions are advantageous because they are geomet-

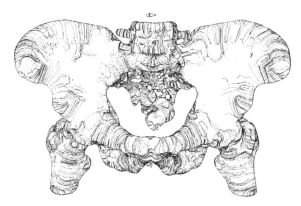

Figure 8.2. Principal-direction line drawing, including silhouette edges and hidden-line removal of a volume dataset. The line drawing exposes subtle shape information throughout the dataset, information which may be unavailable in traditional computer graphics renderings. Copyright 2000 Girshick et al. [Girshick et al. 00] and ACM. Used by permission.

rically invariant. Geometrically invariant cues are based on the surface geometry, and are thus viewpoint and light-source independent.

Victoria Interrante [Interrante 97] defines both principal directions and curvature, and explains how to calculate them. Given a point on a smoothly curving surface, there is one single direction in which the curvature of the surface is the greatest. This direction is called the *first principal direction*, and the curvature of the surface in this direction is called the *first principal curvature*, κ_1. The second principal direction is mutually orthogonal to both the first principal direction and to the surface normal, and represents the direction in which the curvature, κ_2, of the surface is at a minimum. Figure 8.3 illustrates κ_1 and κ_2 at various points over a vase-shaped model.

Principal directions and curvature can be found, given an orthonormal frame $(\vec{e_1}, \vec{e_2}, \vec{e_3})$ at a point $P_{x,y,z}$, where $\vec{e_1}$ and $\vec{e_2}$ are arbitrary orthogonal vectors lying in the tangent plane to the surface and $\vec{e_3}$ points in the direction of the surface normal.

Principal directions are determined by diagonalizing the *Second Fundamental Form*, a matrix of partial derivatives:

$$
A = \left[\begin{array}{cc} \omega_1^{13} & \omega_1^{23} \\ \omega_2^{13} & \omega_2^{23} \end{array} \right]
$$

in which the elements ω_j^{13} can be computed as the dot product of $\vec{e_i}$ and the first derivative of the gradient in the $\vec{e_j}$ direction. Diagonalizing A means computing the matrices:

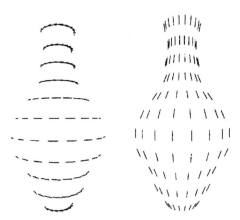

Figure 8.3. Left: continuous vector field of the greatest overall curvature. Right: continuous vector field of the least overall curvature. Copyright 2000 Girshick et al. [Girshick et al. 00] and ACM. Used by permission.

$$D = \begin{bmatrix} \kappa_1 & 0 \\ 0 & \kappa_2 \end{bmatrix}$$

and

$$P = \begin{bmatrix} \nu_{1u} & \nu_{2u} \\ \nu_{1v} & \nu_{2v} \end{bmatrix},$$

where $A = PDP^{-1}$ and $|\kappa_1| > |\kappa_2|$. The principal curvatures are the eigenvalues $|\kappa_1|$ and $|\kappa_2|$, and the principal directions are the corresponding eigenvectors, expressed in three-dimensional object space coordinates as $\vec{e_i} = \nu_{iu}\vec{e_1} + \nu_{iv}\vec{e_2}$.

Interrante further explains that it is useful to use full floating-point precision to represent the gradients, and use a Gaussian weighted-derivative operator over a $3 \times 3 \times 3$ neighborhood rather than central differences when computing the values of ω_j^{i3}.

8.1.2 Line Color

In almost all illustrations, edge lines are drawn in black. Occasionally, if the illustration incorporates shading, another convention is used, in which some of the interior lines are drawn in white like a highlight. Lines drawn in black and white suggest a light source, and denote the model's orientation, as shown in Figure 8.4.

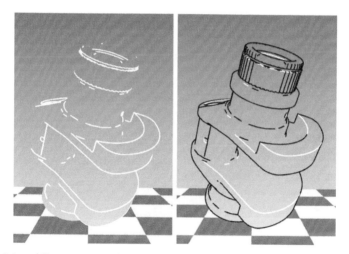

Figure 8.4.   All creases are drawn in white (left), and then all of the silhouette lines are drawn in black (right), overlapping the creases. Copyright 1999 Gooch et al. [Gooch et al. 99] and ACM. Used by permission.

For some applications, colored lines can provide the same separation as black lines without being distracting, as shown in Figure 8.5. Colored lines of the same hue but with a darker intensity can be used to separate individual objects, as show in the leaves or the puffs on the clouds in Figure 5.14 on page 88. Kaplan et al. [Kaplan et al. 00] blend their silhouettes from black to object color as the silhouettes move from external to internal lines. This was especially important for the fading in and out of graftals, as discussed in Chapter 5.2.

Adding color variation to lines provides an easy method for viewers to determine relationships between objects. Interrante [Interrante et al. 96] mentions that one of the most effective uses of color (hue) in line drawing applications is as a label. In the case of three-dimensional volume data, it may be useful to use color to separate out an inner from an outer surface and to indicate the distance between the outer and inner surface as in Figure 8.6.

8.1.3 Line Weight

There are many line weight conventions that traditional illustrators choose among, based on the intent of the image. Martin [Martin 89b] discusses three common conventions, shown in Figure 8.7: a single line weight used throughout the image, two line weights with the heavier describing the

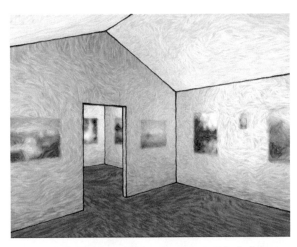

Figure 8.5. A non-photorealistic environment uses black feature edges to mask objectionable artifacts at seams and unnaturally hard edges at polygon boundaries. However, with a full-color image, the black lines may prove distracting. See Color Plate XXXII. Copyright 2000 Klein et al. [Klein et al. 00] and ACM. Used by permission.

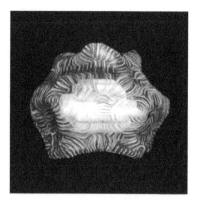

Figure 8.6. Principal curvature lines on this volumetric data set are given a color that is used to convey the relative magnitude of the depth distance between the two surfaces. The lines are whitest where the surfaces are further apart, and become redder as the distance between the two surfaces narrows. See Color Plate XXXIII. Copyright 1997 Interrante [Interrante 97] and ACM. Used by permission.

outer edges, and varying the line weight along a single line, emphasizing the perspective of the drawing with heavy lines in the foreground. One way of achieving the latter effect in raster graphics is to vary the line weight depending on the direction of the light source, giving a shadowed effect to the line. Most illustrators use bold external lines, with thinner interior lines to aid in the perception of spaces [Edwards 89].

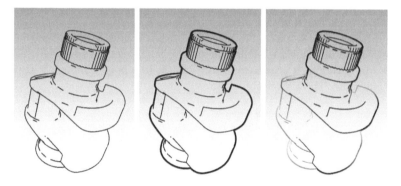

Figure 8.7. Three line conventions suggested by Martin [Martin 89b]. Left: single weight used throughout the image. Middle: heavy line weight used for outer edges; other lines are thinner. Right: varying line weight to emphasize perspective. Copyright 1999 Gooch et al. [Gooch et al. 99] and ACM. Used by permission.

Work by J. D. Northrup and Lee Markosian [Northrup, Markosian 00] further divides line-weight depth cuing into two different styles. Line weight can be based on "distance cues," in which there is an overall scale factor for the object. As the object gets closer to the viewer, the silhouettes widen, and when the object is moved away from the viewer, the silhouettes gradually thin. For an initial viewpoint, Northrup and Markosian compute the value D_i, which is the initial ratio of object space length to screen-space length of the object. For each successive frame, the current scaling factor D_c is computed. They then multiply the width of each stroke in the mesh by a non-linear scale factor of

$$f_D = \sqrt{\frac{D_c}{D_i}}.$$

Although the scaling factor doesn't present physically correct information, it gives a cue to the object's distance from the viewer.

A second line-weight style, "depth cue" foreshortens parts of the object by varying the line width of the strokes as the depth *within* an object varies. Northrup and Markosian compute the frame-buffer z-value bounds of each object, z_{min} and z_{max}. They then scale the width of each stroke vertex v based on its depth, z_v, so that the foremost vertices are scaled by a factor $1 + S$, and the rear-most vertices by $1 - S$, where S is a user-define scalar. The depth cue scaling factor f_v for vertex v is multiplied by the width of each vertex, where $f_v = max(0, 1 + S\frac{z_{max}+z_{min}-2z_v}{z_{max}-z_{min}})$.

Similar in spirit to the work of Northrup and Markosian, line weight based on distance was also explored by Kaplan et al. [Kaplan et al. 00] and Markosian et al. [Markosian, et al. 00] for the silhouettes of graftals. Graftals are discussed in Chapter 5, Section 2. Kaplan et al. also propose a method for changing silhouette line width with a scaling function associated with the tone of a surface along the surface's silhouette edges. Given the color and lighting effects at each of the vertices in a polygonal mesh Kaplan et al. calculates the silhouette width, s_w, as:

$$s_w = \left(1 - \frac{RGB_{total}}{RGB_{max}}\right) * w_{max}$$

where RGB_{total} is the sum of the RGB color values at the vertex, RGB_{max} is the maximum RGB color values for those points, and w_{max} is the maximum silhouette width. This process results in silhouette lines which change smoothly with the lighting on an object.

8.1.4   Line Style

While line width can be used to provide depth cues, line style can be used to convey the intent of an image, such as in the drawing of the shoe in Figure 8.8.

Figure 8.8.   An example of an ink-wash style rendering using variable stroke widths. Copyright 2000 Northrup and Markosian [Northrup, Markosian 00] and ACM. Used by permission.

Most graphics APIs restrict line drawing to a single width and style along the line. In order to vary the width and style of a line segment, Northrup and Markosian [Northrup, Markosian 00] use long triangle strips inspired by the work of Hsu et al. [Hsu et al. 94]. For every vertex v_i there is a corresponding width w_i of the stroke at v_i. The triangle strips are generated by creating a vector "rib" $\vec{r}_i$ along the angle bisector, shown in Figure 8.9. In order to maintain the desired path of the stroke, Northrup and Markosian used a scale factor for each of the ribs. The scale factor for each rib is computed as $f = |\frac{|\vec{r}_i|}{\vec{r}_i \cdot \vec{n}_i}|$ where n_i is the normalized vector perpendicular to the path direction between v_i and v_{i+1}, and $|\vec{r}_i| = \frac{w_i}{2}$. This corrects for the problem in Figure 8.10. Northrup and Markosian limit the scaling factor to 2 to keep the miter for a very sharp corner from becoming too large.

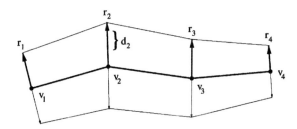

Figure 8.9.   Constructing rib vector $\vec{r}_i$ to add width to a four-vertex stroke. Copyright 2000 Northrup and Markosian [Northrup, Markosian 00] and ACM. Used by permission.

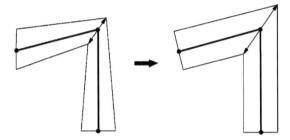

Figure 8.10. Effect of scaling rib vector to maintain constant path width. Copyright 2000 Northrup and Markosian [Northrup, Markosian 00] and ACM. Used by permission.

Once a triangle fan based on the ribs and vertices has been created, lines with artistic effects can be created. Northrup and Markosian sample stroke vertices, which can then be perturbed in location and width to achieve an uneven, hand-drawn look. Adding alpha fade, which linearly increases the transparency along the length of a stroke, produces a simple watercolor or ink-wash look. Another operation flares the overall width of the stroke from end-to-end to create a brush stroke shape. They use the flare function:

$$f = \sqrt{1 - t^2} \ \ \text{where} \ \ t = \frac{\text{current vertex index}}{\text{max vertex index}}.$$

Without using fine sampling along the stroke, texture maps could also be used to modify the style of the stroke.

Figure 8.11.   The cumulative effects of adding stroke operations. From left to right: raw stroke, antialiased, taper, flare, wiggle, alpha fade, and texture mapping. Copyright 2000 Northrup and Markosian [Northrup, Markosian 00] and ACM. Used by permission.

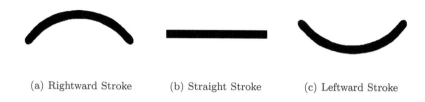

(a) Rightward Stroke   (b) Straight Stroke   (c) Leftward Stroke

Figure 8.12. Strokes used for stylized silhouette edges. Reprinted by permission of Intel Corporation, Copyright 2000 Intel Corporation [Lake et al. 00] and ACM.

Another interesting method for smoothing strokes without refinement is the use of curvature-driven textures by Lake et al. In order to draw smoother strokes, Lake et al. introduce the idea of three textures: rightward stroke, straight stroke, leftward stroke (shown in Figure 8.12 and used in Figure 8.13). Given an edge e_i, its successor edge e_{i+1}, and a user-determined threshold θ, the stroke to apply to e_i is determined by the following equation:

$$e_i \cdot e_{i+1} = \begin{cases} \leq -cos(\theta) & \text{apply leftward stroke texture} \\ -cos(\theta) < 0 < cos(\theta) & \text{apply straight stroke texture} \\ \geq cos(\theta) & \text{apply right texture} \end{cases}$$

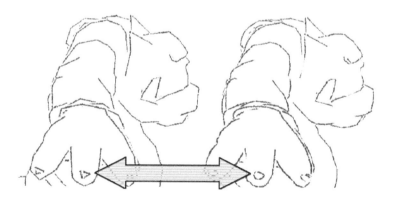

Figure 8.13. Left: A straight texture map applied to the silhouettes of Olaf. Right: Curvature-driven texture maps shown in Figure 8.12, applied to Olaf. Note the curvature of the fingernails. Reprinted by permission of Intel Corporation, Copyright 2000 Intel Corporation [Lake et al. 00] and ACM.

8.1.5   More Examples: Using Lines to Generate NPR Images

Line drawings are useful for generating images that vary in level of abstraction. The pen-and-ink trees by Oliver Deussen and Thomas Strothotte [Deussen, Strothotte 00a] are an excellent demonstration of this idea. Deussen and Strothotte start with highly detailed three-dimensional models of trees, and separately process the tree skeleton (the trunk and branches of the tree) and the foliage. Silhouettes of the tree skeleton are drawn, and its interior is shaded with hatches similar to the work of Salisbury et al. [Salisbury et al. 97], discussed in Chapter 2, Section 3.

Foliage is divided into three areas, all of which are rarely found in a single illustration. The leaves in the light are represented solely by their outline. The leaves in half-shadow are drawn with either a detailed outline or with silhouettes and cross-hatching. The regions in deep shadow are generally filled in with solid color.

Deussen and Strothotte observe that artists do not draw leaves "correctly," but instead represent the visual appearance of leaves using abstract primitives. The simplest of these abstract primitives used by the authors is a view-facing disk shown in Figure 8.14. Additional simple drawing primitives, such as those shown in Figure 8.15, can be used to create a more detailed illustration.

In order to illustrate foliage, Deussen and Strothotte draw each of the leaves, using the chosen primitive, as a solid. They then use the depth buffer to determine the outline of the primitives, in a manner similar to Saito and Takahashi [Saito, Takahashi 90]. Deussen and Strothotte start by accessing the value d from the depth buffer, where $d \epsilon [0..1]$. Then the depth, z, in the camera space is:

Figure 8.14.   A tree rendered from three different distances. The first three trees are rendered with primitive sizes and thresholds constant for all distances. Visual abstraction is automatically achieved. For the last two trees, the primitive sizes are enlarged (up to a factor of two for the smallest tree). Copyright 2000 Deussen and Strothotte [Deussen, Strothotte 00a] and ACM. Used by permission.

Figure 8.15.   Two sketches of a tree. The first image is a set of leaves rendered using interpolated polygons. The middle tree has a shadow drawn in black with the threshold variable set to 100. The threshold variable is set to 6,000 for the other tree, and shadows are represented by detail. Copyright 2000 Deussen and Strothotte [Deussen, Strothotte 00a] and ACM. Used by permission.

$$z = \frac{\frac{z_1 z_0 (d_1 - d_0)}{z_1 - z_0}}{d - \frac{(z_1 + z_0)(d_1 - d_0)}{2(z_1 - z_0)} - \frac{d_1 + d_0}{2}},$$

Example values used in these figures are: $d_0 = 0$, $d_1 = 65535$ (the far plane), $z_0 = 1$, and $z_1 = 11$.

For each pixel, the "depth difference" is computed by taking the maximal positive difference of the depth value at the current pixel with all of its neighboring pixels. Pixels whose maximal depth-difference value lies above a threshold are stored in a separate buffer, and are used to create a bitmap of the outlines. At higher resolution, these pixels can be used to create stroke paths.

In order to render trees at varying distances and varying levels of abstraction, Deussen and Strothotte make two modifications to their system. By increasing the ratio of z_1 to z_0, there will be less depth resolution in the background and thus a smaller number of strokes.

Another modification is to scale the primitives as the trees proceed into the background. Deussen and Strothotte simplify the scale factor used by Kowalski et al. [Kowalski et al. 99] (presented in Chapter 5, Section 2), using a scale factor, r, where $r = w(d/s)$, given the desired screen space, d, the current screen space of the object, s, and the weight, w. This method generates primitives of the same visual size throughout the scene. For the examples in Figure 8.14, the drawing primitive size was doubled for the distant trees.

8.2   Artistic Shading

A fundamental method for conveying the three-dimensional structure of an object in a two-dimensional image is shading. Most shading research in computer graphics is aimed at generating photorealistic images. In this section we present methods that use artistic shading techniques. These methods include hatching, cartoon shading, pencil-shading, and cool-to-warm shading.

8.2.1   Hatching

Hatching has been used by artists and illustrators for centuries as a substitute for surface coloring and shading. Hatched illustrations are easy to reproduce, consume less storage, and are capable of conveying information over various levels of detail. Methods for automatic hatching differ depending on the surface representation (parameterization), and the source of the input (two-dimensional images or three-dimensional data).

Georges Winkenbach and David H. Salesin [Winkenbach, Salesin 96] generate appealing pen-and-ink renderings of smooth surfaces by relying on the parametric lines of NURBS patches to determine the hatching direction. Winkenbach and Salesin focus on using hatch density in order to render complex texture and global illumination effects for pen-and-ink renderings. However, these parameterization-based methods are only suitable for well parameterized surfaces, and will not work for subdivision surfaces or implicit surfaces. Several researchers [Elber 95][Elber 98][Girshick et al. 00] [Interrante 97] have explored principal curvature that does not depend upon parameterization, captures important geometric features, and is common in most two-directional hatching patterns. Curvature methods also have disadvantages. Umbilical points (points with coinciding principal curvatures) produce singularities, which means that the principal direction is undefined at these points. Another problem is flat areas, which due to the small curvature in the area produce complicated and noisy direction fields.

In this section we review three hatching methods. The first uses image space algorithms, the second takes advantage of hardware to create the hatch lines using clipping planes. The final method combines principal curvature methods and an optimization technique to "fill in" the hatching field.

Hatching by Image Processing

Saito and Takahashi use two-dimensional image processing techniques to produce hatched illustrations with uniform density. Their algorithm thins the number of contour lines drawn in areas of the image where the gradient is large and the contour lines become dense. If the contours lines become sparse, new contours are added between existing lines. The functions below produce contour lines, approximately spaced at intervals of d_i on the screen.

Let:

$$
\begin{aligned}
s &= \text{pixel value of input image;} \\
g &= \text{gradient value at the pixel, determined in Equation 8.1;} \\
c &= \text{pixel value of the output contour image;} \\
c_c &= \text{density of contour lines;} \\
c_b &= \text{density of background;} \\
f_1(t) &= \text{function that defines the density change of the contours;} \\
p_d &= \text{standard interval in the scalar field.}
\end{aligned}
$$

Saito and Takahashi use the following differential operator instead of the Sobel Operator:

$$
g = (|A - X| + 2|B - X| + |C - X| + 2|D - X| + \tag{8.1}
$$
$$
2|E - X| + |F - X| + 2|G - X| + |H - X|),
$$

where A through H are X's neighboring pixel values, shown below.

$$
\begin{array}{ccc}
A & B & C \\
D & X & E \\
F & G & H
\end{array}
$$

Then the pixel value c of the output contour image, c, is

$$
c = c_b + f_d\left(\frac{s - kp_n}{g}\right) \cdot (c_c - c_b),
$$

where

$$
\begin{aligned}
f_d(t) &= f_1(t) + \left(\frac{p_n}{d_i g} - 1\right) \cdot f_1\left(\frac{p_n}{2g} - |t|\right), \\
p_n &= 2^n p_d, \\
n &= \lfloor log_2 \frac{d_i p}{p_d} + 1 \rfloor, \\
k &= \lfloor \frac{s}{p_n} + \frac{2}{1} \rfloor.
\end{aligned}
$$

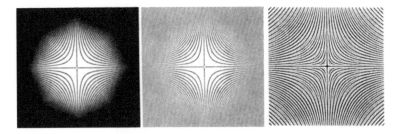

Figure 8.16. Left and middle: Contour lines produced by the function $s(x, y) = xy$. Right: Uniform-density curved hatching for an image produced by the function s(x,y)= xy. Copyright 1990 Saito and Takafumi [Saito, Takahashi 90], NTT, and ACM. Used by permission.

The function f_d has two terms: the first corresponds to the density of the normal contour line, and the second corresponds to thinned or added contour lines between normal lines. The simple box function $f_1(t)$ could be

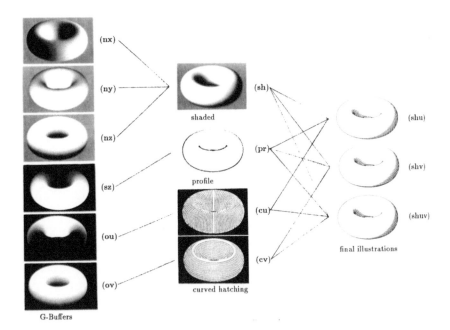

Figure 8.17. By combining a shaded image and a feature edge image with curved hatching, Saito and Takahashi produce a cross-hatched illustration. Copyright 1990 Saito and Takafumi [Saito, Takahashi 90], NTT, and ACM. Used by permission.

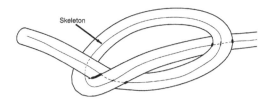

Figure 8.18. A geometric object and its skeleton. Copyright 2000 Deussen et al. [Deussen et al. 99]. Used by permission.

replaced with a higher-order function, which might be useful in reducing aliasing artifacts.

Given an image generated by the function s(x,y) = xy, Saito and Takahashi's algorithm produces a uniformly hatched surface, as shown in Figure 8.16. This hatching method can be combined with both a shaded and a feature edge image, as shown in Figure 8.17, to produce a cross hatched illustration.

Hatching Based on Hardware Intersection Planes and Skeletons

Deussen et al. provide a solution for creating hatched images based on geometric models. The hatched lines of their illustrations are derived from the models using intersection planes. First the model is segmented. Next the skeleton, shown in Figure 8.18, is calculated for each segmented part of the model based on an Raab's [Rabb 98] algorithm. Deussen et al. assume the object is represented as a triangular mesh and use Hoppe et al.'s edge collapse operation [Hoppe 96] to reduce the initial mesh is until no regular triangles exist. The remaining degenerate triangles are treated as line segments which are used to generate the skeleton. An outline of the algorithm follows:

```
sort all edges of the model according to length
while faces remain in the model
  take shortest edge $e(v_1,v_2)$
  collapse edge
  for all adjacent edges $e_v$ of $v_1$ and $v_2$
      if $e_v$ has no regular faces
              add $e_v$ to the skeleton
              delete $e_v$ from the model
      else
              resort edges with $e_v$
```

After performing the skeleton operation, the resulting line segments are converted into a spline curve. This curve is used to define an intersection plane perpendicular to the skeleton spline curve. Intersection curves are created by computing the intersection of the intersection planes with model parts. These curves can either be computed analytically or on a per pixel basis. Pixel methods are easiest but their accuracy depends on the screen resolution. Using graphics hardware (such as the OpenGL API) makes accuracy less of a problem and runs in reasonable time on most complex models. The algorithm for creating intersection curves is:

- Display model, take a snapshot;

- Extract pixels on boundary (Image I_{full});

- Display model with clipping plane, capture image;

- Extract pixels on boundary (Image I_{inters};

- Generate $I = I_{inters} - I_{full}$;

- Convert I to line segments.

The first step is completed by drawing the object in white on a black background. Fat diagonal lines can be removed in steps 2 and 4 by using only the 4-neighborhood of a pixel for pixel-to-pixel comparisons. Step 5 can be performed in the accumulation buffer if one is available. Deussen et al. then use a least squares fitting algorithm to convert the pixels to lines. The advantage is that steps 1, 3, and 5 are done in hardware and the pixel copy operations are fast on most graphics workstations.

Next, Deussen et al. capture a photorealistic image of the model and use halftoning to create the hatching curves. Each of the intersection curves has an associated tonal value which can be used to provide density control. Deussen et al. achieve density control by drawing lines of constant thickness across the image and controlling the number of lines. For example, if a region near an edge needs to have four times the density as the inside of the region, Deussen et al. start by drawing a fourth of the curves. They then draw the remaining sets of lines with a white halo, which partially overwrites some of the previously drawn lines. This effect is subtle, but can be seen in comparing the line segments in Figure 8.19.

For carefully chosen clipping planes and models, hatching effects generated by traditional illustrators can be generated for three-dimensional models, as shown in Figure 8.20. A drawback of Deussen et al.'s method is segmentation. For branching objects, the segments have to be chosen very carefully to create hatching as an artist would.

Figure 8.19. An example of prioritized drawing. A single set of lines is used in the image on the left. The middle image has two more line sets added. The right images has two more line sets than the middle image. Copyright 2000 Deussen et al. [Deussen et al. 99]. Used by permission.

Hatching Smooth Surfaces

Aaron Hertzmann and Denis Zorin [Hertzmann, Zorin 00] combined the techniques and ideas of several algorithms with hatching techniques used by several artists to create smooth hatching fields on smooth surfaces. They observe that artists generally use relatively straight hatch lines even when the surface has wrinkles. Artists convey smaller details by varying the density and number of hatch directions. Hertzmann and Zorin also note that principal curvature directions best define the shape of cylindrical surfaces. For cylindrical surfaces, one of the principal curvatures is zero, while the other principal curvature lines are all geodesics, i.e., the shortest line between two points on a surface. Based on these observations, Hertzmann and Zorin make the following requirements for their hatching fields:

Figure 8.20. Copyright 2000 Deussen et al. [Deussen et al. 99]. Used by permission.

- The fields should follow close to principal directions in areas where the surface is close to parabolic;

- Over the whole surface, the main curves of the field should be close to geodesic;

- If the surface has small details, the field should be generated based upon a smoothed version of the surface.

In order to render cross hatching, Hertzmann and Zorin define a *cross-field* that specifies an unordered pair of perpendicular directions at each point on the surface. Calculating the cross-field over a surface is accomplished using the following algorithm:

- Make a coarser copy of the original mesh, with regard to the smoothness of the original mesh and the detail desired for the current view.

- Find areas on the surface that are sufficiently close to parabolic (i.e., the ratio of minimal to maximal curvature is high), and where at least one curvature is large enough to be computed reliably. Mark vertices as unreliable if the average cross-field energy of its incident edges exceeds a threshold. This step will allow optimization of singularities (points with coinciding principal curvatures.)

- Compute principal directions over the whole surface in order to initialize the field.

- Keep the values of the field where the surface is close to parabolic and stable, optimizing individual hatch stroke directions over the rest of the vertices.

The last step involves an optimization function based on the requirement that the curves be close to geodesic. Hertzmann and Zorin try to keep the field as close to constant as possible. This is accomplished by establishing a correspondence between the tangent planes at nearby points on the surface. We leave it to the reader to review the paper by Hertzmann and Zorin for derivation details, and will skip to the resulting optimization function. As shown in Figure 8.21, finding one of the geodesics between vertices v_i and v_j for the cross field is described by a single angle θ_i for each vertex v_i. Let θ_i be the angle between a fixed tangent direction t_i and one of the directions of the cross field. Let φ_{ij} be the direction of the projection of the edge (v_i, v_j) onto the tangent plane at v_i. Then the function is:

$$E_{field} = - \sum_{\text{all edges}(v_i, v_j)} \cos 4((\theta_i - \varphi_{ij}) - (\theta_j - \varphi_{ji}))$$

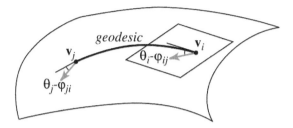

Figure 8.21. Moving vectors along geodesics. Copyright 2000 Hertzmann and Zorin [Hertzmann, Zorin 00] and ACM. Used by permission.

There are no constraints on θ_i and the values for φ_{ij} are constant. Hertzmann and Zorin use a variant of the BFGS conjugate gradient algorithm described by Zhu et al. [Zhu et al. 97] to perform the minimization. The results of the algorithm depend upon the threshold that determines which vertices are unreliable, as chosen in Step 2 of the algorithm. Figure 8.22 shows the results of the algorithm with different thresholds.

The final step of Hertzmann and Zorin's algorithm uses the cross-field to render the hatches. Users have control over the basic hatch density and the density of undercuts, which are specified in image space; thresholds that control highlights; thresholds for single versus cross hatched regions; maximum hatch length; and maximum deviation of hatches from initial direction in world space.

The surface of a three-dimensional model is divided into three regions for hatching: highlight and Mach bands, which receive no hatching; mid-tones (single hatching); and shadowed regions (cross-hatching). The algorithm proceeds by stepping along each silhouette and boundary curve in order to identify regions that should not be cross-hatched. Folded regions are identified through ray tests near each curve point. A Mach band is the area on the near side of a folded surface, near the silhouette. The other side of the fold is called an undercut, and these areas receive dense cross-hatching. The ray intersections with these areas are stored in a two-dimensional grid of the image plane. The next step creates evenly-spaced cross-hatches across all regions of the surface that should receive hatching, with a single pass over the surface using Jobard and Lefers' method for evenly-spaced streamlines of a two-dimensional vector field [Jobard, Lefer 97]. Surface regions that should have only a single layer of hatching are cleaned up later. The hatching algorithm is based on two user-chosen parameters: d_{sep} (a desired hatch separation distance) and d_{test} (how close the hatches get to each other before they are terminated; the authors used $d_{test}=0.75$). The algorithm creates a queue of surface curves, initially containing crit-

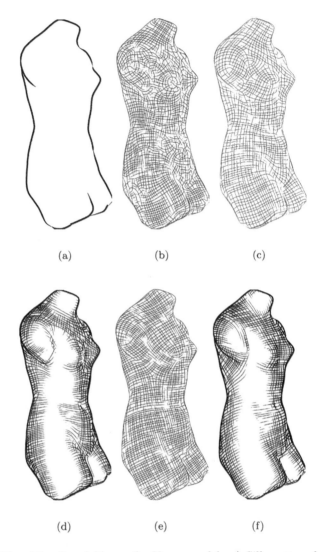

(a)   (b)   (c)

(d)   (e)   (f)

Figure 8.22.   Direction fields on the Venus model. a) Silhouettes alone do not convey the interior shape of the surface. b) Raw principle directions produce an overly-complex hatching pattern. c) Smooth cross-field produced by optimization. d) Hatching with the smooth cross-field. e) Very smooth cross-field produced by optimizing all directions. f) Hatching from the very smooth field. Copyright 2000 Hertzmann and Zorin [Hertzmann, Zorin 00] and ACM. Used by permission.

Figure 8.23. Hatching smooth surfaces. Copyright 2000 Hertzmann and Zorin [Hertzmann, Zorin 00] and ACM. Used by permission.

ical curves such as silhouettes, boundaries, creases, and self-intersections. While the queue is not empty, the first curve is removed from the queue and used to seed new hatches perpendicular to the curve at evenly spaced points in image space. At each step, the hatch lines follow one of the directions of the cross-field that has the smallest angle deviation from the previous direction. A hatch curve continues until:

- The hatch terminates in a critical curve;

- World-space hatch direction deviates from initial hatch direction by more than a constant;

- The hatch comes near a parallel hatch; i.e., endpoint of hatch p_1 is near a point p_2 on another hatch if $||p_1 - p_2|| < d_{test}d_{sep}$ in image space;

  - A line drawn between the two points in image space does not intersect the projection of any visible silhouettes, boundaries, creases, and self-intersection curves. (This test is to see that the curves are nearby on the surface.)

  - The world-space tangents of the two hatch curves are parallel.

By placing all of the hatches in a two-dimensional grid with grid spacing equal to d_{sep}, the search for nearby hatches is limited to at most nine grid cells.

The algorithm then removes hatches from the regions that should only have single hatching. Hatches are deleted if they contain a point p_1 near another hatch point p_2, such that:

- p_1 and p_2 lie within the single hatched region

- $\|p_1 - p_2\| < 2d_{sep}$ in image space;

- A line drawn between the two points in image space does not intersect the projection of any visible silhouettes, boundaries, creases, and self-intersections curves;

- The world-space tangents of the two hatch curves are perpendicular.

Hertzmann and Zorin stress that the order in which the hatches are traversed is important for maintaining evenness and consistency. They start with one hatch, then check all of its parallel neighbors in the hatched region. Then they iterate this check over all unchecked curves, if any, in the hatched region.

This method automatically generates smoothly hatched surfaces based on user-set thresholds. Although the silhouettes can be computed interactively and the field optimization may be fast, generating the hatching is time consuming and may take from seconds to minutes depending on the model and the hatch density. Hertzmann and Zorin also warn that the thresholds, hatching densities, and light sources have to be chosen carefully.

However, as with the other hatching algorithms, the imagery (shown in Figure 8.23 and Figure 8.22) may have more to offer to the viewer, especially in terms of surface information, than traditional computer graphics shading.

8.2.2   Cartoon Shading

One of the critical simplifications that made traditional cel animation possible and practical is that objects and characters are represented by line drawings filled with areas of solid color [Williams 91]. Details have to be used sparingly and consistently in order to generate 24 frames per second of film. This economy forces the artist to convey the optimal amount of information, emphasizing specific features while omitting extraneous information. For example, to give a two-dimensional line drawing of a fish shading, Lance Williams [Williams 91] used a simple graduated color defined by the bounding box of the fish, shown in Figure 8.24. This shaded region then moves, rotates, and scales with the drawing.

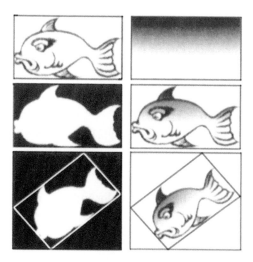

Figure 8.24. A two-dimensional line drawing of a fish with a simple graduated shading which moves, rotates, and scales with the drawing. Copyright 1991 Williams [Williams 91]. Used by permission.

Lake et al. developed a *hard-shading* algorithm that is similar to the cel animator's process of painting an already inked cel.

The lighting equation to calculate the diffuse lighting at the vertices for both smooth shading and Lake et al.'s cartoon shading is $C_v = a_g \times a_m + a_l \times a_m + (\max(\vec{L} \cdot \vec{n}, 0) \times d_l \times d_m)$,

where:
$$
\begin{aligned}
C_v &= \text{vertex color} \\
a_g &= \text{coefficient of global ambient light} \\
a_l &= \text{ambient coefficient of light source} \\
d_l &= \text{diffuse coefficient of light source} \\
a_m &= \text{ambient coefficient of object's material} \\
d_m &= \text{diffuse coefficient of object's material} \\
\vec{L} &= \text{unit vector from the light source to the vertex} \\
\vec{n} &= \text{unit vector normal to the surface vertex.}
\end{aligned}
$$

$\vec{L} \cdot \vec{n}$ computes the cosine of the angle between $\vec{L}$ and $\vec{n}$. The illuminated color for cartoon shading is achieved when $\vec{L} \cdot \vec{n} = 1$, or the light is directed straight at the vertex and the angle between the two vectors is zero. The shadowed color of the cartoon shading occurs when $\vec{L} \cdot \vec{n} = 0$, i.e., the color is only made of the ambient terms.

Instead of calculating the color per vertex, Lake et al. generate a texture map of the colors. In most cases the number of colors is two, one for the illuminated color, C_i, and one for the shadowed color, C_s. These colors can be stored in a one-dimensional texture map, and computed as a preprocess. At each frame, $\max(\vec{L}\cdot\vec{n}, 0)$ needs to be calculated for each vertex. Then the per vertex values can be used as texture coordinates for the precomputed one-dimensional texture map.

Cartoon Shading Algorithm

Figure 8.25 shows the cartoon shading algorithm applied to an image.

Preprocess:

- Calculate the illuminated diffuse color for each material: $C_i = a_g \times a_m + a_l \times a_m + d_l \times d_m$.

- Calculate the shadowed diffuse color:
  $C_s = a_g \times a_m + a_l \times a_m$.

- For each material create a one-dimensional texture map with two texels using the texture functionality provided by standard three-dimensional graphics APIs. Color the texel at $u = 1$ with C_i and the texel at $u = 0$ with C_s.

Runtime:

- Calculate the one-dimensional texture coordinate at each vertex using $Max(\vec{L} \cdot \vec{n}, 0)$.

- Render the model using standard graphics API with lighting disabled and one-dimensional texture maps enabled.

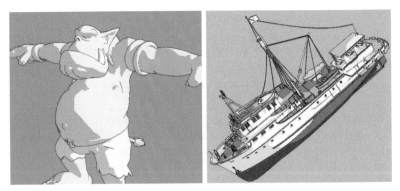

Figure 8.25. Cartoon shading. See Color Plate XXXIV. Reprinted by permission of Intel Corporation. Copyright 2000 Intel Corporation [Lake et al. 00] and ACM.

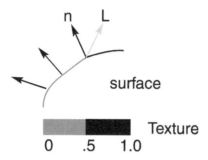

Figure 8.26. Generation of one-dimensional texture and the corresponding texture coordinates from $\vec{L}\cdot\vec{n}$. In this case, the shadow boundary occurs at the point where $\vec{L}\cdot\vec{n}$ equals 0.5. Reprinted by permission of Intel Corporation. Copyright 2000 Intel Corporation [Lake et al. 00] and ACM.

When this algorithm is used, the shadow boundary occurs at the point where $\vec{L}\cdot\vec{n} = 0.5$, illustrated in Figure 8.26. Simple changes to the resolution of the one-dimensional texture map can be used to create different effects. If an eight-texel texture, for example, is used with seven of the eight texels set to the shadow color and one to the illuminated color, the model will appear to be mostly in shadow with small portions illuminated, similar to the dark imagery in some comic books. Another approach is to use three colors and a higher resolution (such as 8 or 16 texels) instead of just two when building the one-dimensional texture map. At the illuminated end one or two of the texels can be set to a highlight color.

Lake et al. note that the transition between the illuminated and shadowed regions may appear jagged if viewed closely. They mention that using the three-dimensional graphics API texture filtering option of "nearest" will produce acceptable results, while using "linear" filtering will smooth the transition. The "linear" option may be too wide if the polygons on which the transitions occur are too large relative to screen space.

8.2.3 Pencil Shading

Extending the techniques for cartoon shading discussed in the previous section, Adam Lake, Carl Marshall, Mark Harris, and Marc Blackstein [Lake et al. 00] provide a method for creating pencil sketch shading with two-dimensional textures. Instead of selecting texels in a one-dimensional texture, their algorithm uses $\vec{L}\cdot\vec{n}$ to select a texture with the appropriate density, where $\vec{L}$ is a unit vector from the light source to the vertex and $\vec{n}$ is a unit vector normal to the surface vertex. The algorithm starts with a preprocess that reads in a pencil stroke texture and a paper texture,

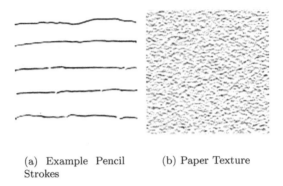

(a) Example Pencil   (b) Paper Texture
Strokes

Figure 8.27.   The pencil strokes and paper texture are combined to generate
various pencil sketch textures, shown in Figure 8.28. Reprinted by permission of
Intel Corporation. Copyright 2000 Intel Corporation [Lake et al. 00] and ACM.

as shown in Figure 8.27. Next, a set of N two-dimensional textures are
generated by randomly selecting pencil strokes and placing them uniformly
along the v direction with u spacing inversely proportional to the desired
density, producing textures as shown in Figure 8.28. They also subdivide
and group all polygons that need the same texture in order to minimize
the texturing overhead.

At runtime the process is as follows:

1. Draw the background (a polygon texture-mapped with the paper texture).

2. For each vertex, calculate $\vec{L} \cdot \vec{n}$ and use this value to index into one
   of N textures.

3. Build N lists of polygons. For each polygon, if all of its vertices have
   the same value for indexing one of the textures, put the polygon in

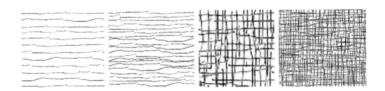

Figure 8.28.   Various levels of textures used for pencil sketching shader.
Reprinted by permission of Intel Corporation. Copyright 2000 Intel Corporation [Lake et al. 00] and ACM.

that texture's polygon list. Otherwise subdivide the polygon using linear interpolation.

4. Determine the (u, v) coordinates for the polygon if necessary (explained below)

5. For each list of polygons, render the polygons with multi-texturing using the appropriate texture.

Lake et al. suggest that the texture mapping of the polygons can be approached in two ways. One method associates a screen-space (u, v) mapping, which preserves the hand-drawn feel of the textures and works well for static images as shown in Figure 8.29. However, in animations, the images seem to crawl or swim. In the case of animations, it would be more desirable to fix the texture coordinates to the polygons, trading a flat appearance for frame-to-frame coherence.

8.2.4 Cool-to-Warm Shading

When shading is added, in addition to feature-edge lines, shape information can be maximized if the shading uses colors and intensities that are visually distinct from both the black edge lines and the white highlights. This means the dynamic range available for shading may be limited. Amy Gooch, Bruce Gooch, Peter Shirley, and Elaine Cohen [Gooch et al. 98] looked to technical illustrators and other artists to define a new kind of shading that would work alongside feature-edge lines.

Shading in technical illustration brings out subtle shape attributes, and provides information about material properties. Most illustrators use a single light source and technical illustrations rarely include shadows. In most technical illustrations, hue changes are used to indicate surface orientation rather than reflectance, because shape information is valued above precise reflectance information. Adding a hue shift to the shading model allows a

Figure 8.29.   Applying pencil-sketching shader to a model. Reprinted by permission of Intel Corporation. Copyright 2000 Intel Corporation [Lake et al. 00] and ACM.

reduction in the dynamic range of the shading, to ensure that highlights and edge lines remain distinct. A simple low-dynamic-range shading model is consistent with several of the principles from Tufte's *Visual Explanations* book [Tufte 97]. He cites a case study of improving a computer-graphics animation by lowering the contrast of the shading and adding black lines to indicate direction. Tufte states that this is an example of the strategy of *the smallest effective difference*: "Make all visual distinctions as subtle as possible, but still clear and effective."

Tufte feels that this principle is so important that he devotes an entire chapter to it in his book. Tufte's principle provides a possible explanation of why cross-hatching is common in black and white drawings and rare in colored drawings: colored shading provides a more subtle, but adequately effective, difference to communicate surface orientation. Based on observing several illustrations, surfaces with little or no curvature are generally flat or Phong-shaded in technical illustrations. Surfaces that have high curvature are shaded similar to the Phong shading model or are cool-to-warm–shaded as in Gooch et al. [Gooch et al. 98], unless the surface has a material property such as metal. Illustrators apply different conventions to convey metallic surface properties, especially if the object has regions of high curvature like an ellipsoid. We discuss shading algorithms to represent metal in Section 8.2.7.

Traditional Shading of Matte Objects

Traditional diffuse shading sets luminance to be proportional to the cosine of the angle between the light direction and the surface normal:

$$I = k_d k_a + k_d \, \max\left(0, \hat{\mathbf{l}} \cdot \hat{\mathbf{n}}\right), \qquad\qquad (8.2)$$

where I is the RGB color to be displayed for a given point on the surface, k_d is the RGB diffuse reflectance at the point, k_a is the RGB ambient illumination, $\hat{\mathbf{l}}$ is the unit vector in the direction of the light source, and $\hat{\mathbf{n}}$ is the unit surface normal vector at the point. This model is shown for $k_d = 1$ and $k_a = 0$ in Figure 8.30. This unsatisfactory image hides shape and material information in the dark regions. Both highlights and edge lines can provide additional information about the object. These are shown alone in Figure 8.31 with no shading. Edge lines and highlights could not be effectively added to Figure 8.30 because the highlights would be lost in the light regions, and the edge lines would be lost in the dark regions.

To add edge lines to the shading in Equation 8.2, either of two standard heuristics can be used. First k_a could be raised until it is large enough that

Figure 8.30. Diffuse shaded image using Equation 8.2 with $k_d = 1$ and $k_a = 0$. Black shaded regions hide details, especially in the small claws; edge lines could not be seen if added. Highlights and fine details are lost in the white shaded regions. Copyright 1998 Gooch et al. [Gooch et al. 98] and ACM. Used by permission.

the dim shading is visually distinct from the black edge lines, but this would result in loss of fine details. Alternatively, a second light source could be added, which would add conflicting highlights and shading. To make the highlights visible on top of the shading, k_d could be lowered until it is visually distinct from white. An image with hand-tuned k_a and k_d is shown in Figure 8.32. This is the best achromatic image using one light

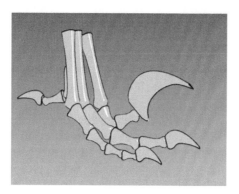

Figure 8.31. Image with only highlights and edges. The edge lines provide divisions between object pieces, and the highlights convey the direction of the light. Some shape information is lost, especially in the regions of high curvature of the object pieces. However, these highlights and edges could not be added to Figure 8.30 because the highlights would be invisible in the light regions and the silhouettes would be invisible in the dark regions. Copyright 1998 Gooch et al. [Gooch et al. 98] and ACM. Used by permission.

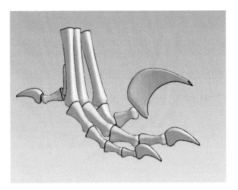

Figure 8.32.   Phong-shaded image with edge lines and $k_d = 0.5$ and $k_a = 0.1$. Like Figure 8.30, details are lost in the dark gray regions, especially in the small claws, where they are colored the constant shade of $k_d k_a$ regardless of surface orientation. However, edge lines and highlights provide shape information that was gained in Figure 8.31, but could not be added to Figure 8.30. Copyright 1998 Gooch et al. [Gooch et al. 98] and ACM. Used by permission.

source and traditional shading. This image is poor at communicating shape information, such as details in the claw nearest the bottom of the image, where it is colored the constant shade $k_d k_a$ regardless of surface orientation.

Tone-Based Shading of Matte Objects

In a colored medium such as air-brush and pen, artists often use both hue and luminance (grayscale intensity) shifts.   Adding black and white to a given color results in what artists call *shades* in the case of black and *tints* in the case of white. When color scales are created by adding gray to a certain color they are called *tones* [Birren 76]. Such tones vary in hue but do not typically vary much in luminance. Adding the complement of a color can also create tones. Tones are considered a crucial concept to illustrators and are especially useful when the illustrator is restricted to a small luminance range [Lambert 91]. Another quality of color used by artists is the *temperature* of the color. The temperature of a color is defined as being warm (red, orange, and yellow), cool (blue, violet, and green), or temperate (red-violets and yellow-greens). The depth cue comes from the perception that cool colors recede whereas warm colors advance. In addition, object colors change temperature in sunlit scenes, because cool skylight and warm sunlight vary in relative contribution across the surface, so there may be ecological reasons to expect humans to be sensitive to color temperature variation. Not only does the temperature of a hue depend upon the hue itself, but this advancing and receding relationship is affected by proximity [Browning 94]. Gooch et al. used these techniques and the psychophysical relationship of cool and warm colors as the basis for their shading model.

The classic computer-graphics shading model can be generalized to experiment with tones by using the cosine term $(\hat{\mathbf{l}} \cdot \hat{\mathbf{n}})$ of Equation 8.2 to blend between two RGB colors, k_{cool} and k_{warm}:

$$I = \left(1 - \frac{1 + \hat{\mathbf{l}} \cdot \hat{\mathbf{n}}}{2}\right) k_{cool} + \left(\frac{1 + \hat{\mathbf{l}} \cdot \hat{\mathbf{n}}}{2}\right) k_{warm}. \tag{8.3}$$

Note that the quantity $\hat{\mathbf{l}} \cdot \hat{\mathbf{n}}$ varies over the interval $[-1, 1]$. To ensure the image shows this full variation, the light vector $\hat{\mathbf{l}}$ should be perpendicular to the gaze direction. Because the human vision system assumes illumination comes from above [Goldstein 80], it is best to position the light up and to the right and to keep this position constant.

An image that uses a color scale with little luminance variation is shown in Figure 8.33. This image shows that a sense of depth can be communicated at least partially by a hue shift. However, the lack of a strong cool-to-warm hue shift and the lack of a luminance shift make the shape information subtle. The unnatural colors may also be a problem. The colors chosen for this hue shift must be picked with care. A red-green hue shift would be undesirable because of red-green color blindness. A blue-yellow hue shift is most common in many art forms and may be most natural because of yellow sunlight and shadows lit by the ambient blue sky. Blue and yellow, having a very large intensity shift, will also provide the desired luminance shift.

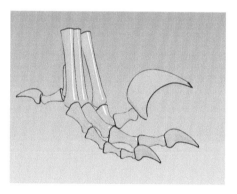

Figure 8.33. Approximately constant luminance tone rendering. Edge lines and highlights are clearly noticeable. Unlike Figures 8.30 and 8.32 some details in shaded regions, like the small claws, are visible. The lack of luminance shift makes these changes subtle. See Color Plate XXXV. Copyright 1998 Gooch et al. [Gooch et al. 98] and ACM. Used by permission.

In order to automate this hue shift technique, and to add some luminance variation to the use of tones, Gooch et al. examined two extreme possibilities for color scale generation: blue-to-yellow tones and scaled object-color shades. The final model is a linear combination of these techniques. Blue and yellow tones are chosen to insure a cool-to-warm color transition, regardless of the diffuse color of the object.

The blue-to-yellow tones range from a fully saturated blue: $k_{blue} = (0, 0, b), b \in [0, 1]$ in RGB space to a fully saturated yellow: $k_{yellow} = (y, y, 0), y \in [0, 1]$. This produces a very sculpted but unnatural image, and is independent of the object's diffuse reflectance k_d. The extreme tone related to k_d is a variation of diffuse shading where k_{cool} is pure black and $k_{warm} = k_d$. This would look much like traditional diffuse shading, but the entire object would vary in luminance, including where $\hat{\mathbf{I}} \cdot \hat{\mathbf{n}} < 0$. A compromise between these strategies will result in a combination of tone-scaled object color and a cool-to-warm undertone, an effect which artists achieve by combining pigments. The undertones can be simulated by a linear blend between the blue/yellow and black/object-color tones:

$$\begin{aligned} k_{cool} &= k_{blue} + \alpha k_d, \\ k_{warm} &= k_{yellow} + \beta k_d. \end{aligned} \tag{8.4}$$

Plugging these values into Equation 8.3 leaves four free parameters: b, y, α, and β. The values for b and y will determine the strength of the overall temperature shift, and the values of α and β will determine the prominence of the object color and the strength of the luminance shift. In order to stay away from shading that will visually interfere with black and white, intermediate values should be supplied for these constants. An example of a resulting tone for a pure red object is shown in Figure 8.34.

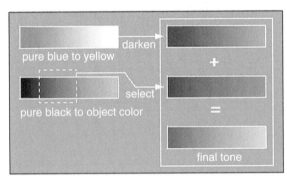

Figure 8.34.   How the tone is created for a pure red object by summing a blue-to-yellow and a dark-red-to-red tone. See Color Plate XXXVI. Copyright 1998 Gooch et al. [Gooch et al. 98] and ACM. Used by permission.

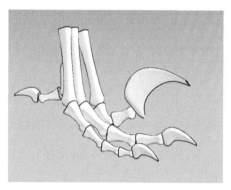

Figure 8.35. Luminance/hue tone rendering. This image combines the luminance shift of Figure 8.30 and the hue shift of Figure 8.33. Edge lines, highlights, fine details in the dark shaded regions such as the small claws, and details in the high luminance regions are all visible. In addition, shape details are apparent, unlike Figure 8.31 where the object appears flat. In this figure, the variables of Equation 8.3 and Equation 8.4 are: $b = 0.4$, $y = 0.4$, $\alpha = 0.2$, $\beta = 0.6$. See Color Plate XXXVII. Copyright 1998 Gooch et al. [Gooch et al. 98] and ACM. Used by permission.

Substituting the values for k_{cool} and k_{warm} from Equation 8.4 into the tone from Equation 8.3 results in shading with values within the middle luminance range, as desired. Figure 8.35 is shown with $b = 0.4$, $y = 0.4$, $\alpha = 0.2$, and $\beta = 0.6$. To show that the exact values are not crucial to appropriate appearance, the same model is shown in Figure 8.36 with

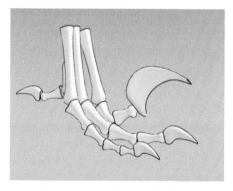

Figure 8.36. Luminance/hue tone rendering, similar to Figure 8.35 except $b = 0.55$, $y = 0.3$, $\alpha = 0.25$, $\beta = 0.5$. The different values of b and y determine the strength of the overall temperature shift, whereas α and β determine the prominence of the object color and the strength of the luminance shift. See Color Plate XXXVIII. Copyright 1998 Gooch et al. [Gooch et al. 98] and ACM. Used by permission.

Figure 8.37.   Comparing shaded, colored spheres. Top: colored Phong-shaded
spheres with edge lines and highlights. Bottom: colored spheres shaded with
hue and luminance shift, including edge lines and highlights. Note: In the first
Phong-shaded sphere (violet), the edge lines disappear, but are visible in the
corresponding hue and luminance shaded violet sphere. In the last Phong-shaded
sphere (white), the highlight vanishes, but is noticed in the corresponding hue
and luminance shaded white sphere below it. The spheres in the second row also
retain their "color name." See Color Plate XXXIX. Copyright 1998 Gooch et
al. [Gooch et al. 98] and ACM. Used by permission.

$b = 0.55$, $y = 0.3$, $\alpha = 0.25$, and $\beta = 0.5$. Unlike Figure 8.32, subtleties of
shape in the claws are visible in Figures 8.35 and 8.36.

The model is appropriate for a range of object colors. Both traditional
shading and tone-based shading are applied to a set of spheres in Figure 8.37. Note that with the new shading method, objects retain their
"color names," so colors can still be used to differentiate objects like coun-
tries on a political map, but the intensities used do not interfere with the
clear perception of black edge lines and white highlights. One issue that
is mentioned as people study these sphere comparisons is that the spheres
look more like buttons, or appear flattened. We hypothesize a few reasons
why this may be so. The linear ramp of the shading may be too uniform
and cause the spheres to flatten. The shading presented here is just a

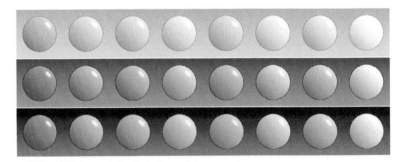

Figure 8.38.   Tone: and undertone-shaded spheres with backgrounds getting
darker. See Color Plate XL. Copyright 1998 Gooch [Gooch 98]. Used by permission.

Figure 8.39. Shaded spheres without edge lines. Top: colored Phong-shaded spheres without edge lines. Bottom: colored spheres shaded with hue and luminance shift, without edge lines. See Color Plate XLI. Copyright 1998 Gooch [Gooch 98]. Used by permission.

first-pass approximation to the shading artists use, and much improvement could be made. Another problem may be that the dark silhouettes around the object may tie the spheres to the background. Figure 8.38 shows three sets of spheres, shaded the same but put against different gradations of background. The edge lines of the spheres on the darkest background fade a little bit and even seem to thin towards the light, owing to the gradation of the background. In our opinion, the spheres set against the darkest background, where the edge lines lose some emphasis, seem to be a little more three-dimensional than the spheres with edge lines.

Figure 8.39 shows both the Phong-shaded spheres and the spheres with new shading without edge lines. Without the edge lines, the spheres stand out more. Spheres are not the best model to test the new shading and edge lines. Edge lines are not necessary on a sphere, since edge lines are used by illustrators to differentiate parts and discontinuities in a model. However, it is a computer-graphics tradition to test a shading model on spheres.

Approximation to New Model

This cool-to-warm model cannot be implemented directly in high-level graphics packages that use Phong shading. However, we can use the Phong lighting model as a basis for approximating our model. This is in the spirit of the nonlinear approximation to global illumination used by Walter et al. [Walter et al. 97]. In most graphics systems (e.g., OpenGL), we can use negative colors for the lights. We can approximate Equation 8.3 by two lights in directions $\hat{\mathbf{l}}$ and $-\hat{\mathbf{l}}$ with intensities $(k_{warm} - k_{cool})/2$ and $(k_{cool} - k_{warm})/2$ respectively, and an ambient term of $(k_{cool} + k_{warm})/2$. This assumes the object color is set to white. We turn off the Phong highlight because the negative blue light causes jarring artifacts. Highlights could be added on systems with accumulation buffers [Haeberli, Akeley 90].

C++ code fragment for generating the two lights, using the OpenGL API:

```
GLfloat R_warm, G_warm, B_warm,R_cool, G_cool, B_cool;
R_warm=207/255.0; G_warm=207/255.0; B_warm=145/255.0;
R_cool=80/255.0;  G_cool=80/255.0;  B_cool=145/255.0;

GLfloat hi_diffuse[] = { (R_warm-R_cool)/2.0,
                         (G_warm-G_cool)/2.0,
                         (B_warm-B_cool)/2.0 };
GLfloat lo_diffuse[] = { (R_cool-R_warm)/2.0,
                         (G_cool-G_warm)/2.0,
                         (B_cool-B_warm)/2.0 };
GLfloat hi_position[] = {  1,  1, EYE, 1 };
GLfloat lo_position[] = { -1, -1, EYE, 1 };

GLfloat ambient[] = { 0.5, 0.5, 0.5 };

glLightModelfv(GL_LIGHT_MODEL_AMBIENT, ambient);

glLightfv(GL_LIGHT0, GL_DIFFUSE, hi_diffuse);
glLightfv(GL_LIGHT0, GL_POSITION, hi_position);
glEnable( GL_LIGHT0 );

glLightfv(GL_LIGHT1, GL_DIFFUSE, lo_diffuse);
glLightfv(GL_LIGHT1, GL_POSITION, lo_position);
glEnable( GL_LIGHT1 );
```

This approximation is shown compared to traditional Phong shading and to the exact model in Figure 8.40. Like Walter et al., we need different light colors for each object. We could avoid these artifacts by using accumulation techniques, which are available in many graphics libraries.

8.2.5   Modifying the Cool-to-Warm Shader

Paul Rademacher [Rademacher 99] modified the cool-to-warm shader, allowing more control over how much the color of the object was modified by the cool and warm colors, using the following equation:

$$
\begin{aligned}
C_{final} = k_a C_{base} \quad &+ \quad (l_1 \cdot N)\,(C_{warm} - (C_{base} * k_1)) * k_2 \\
&+ \quad (l_2 \cdot N)\,(C_{cool} - (C_{base} * k_3)) * k_4,
\end{aligned}
$$

where l_1 and l_2 are the positions of the two lights, N is the surface normal, C_{final} is the final color of the surface, C_{base} is the base or diffuse color of the object, C_{warm} and C_{cool} are the warm and cool colors, respectively. The parameter k_a controls the amount of ambient light the surface receives.

(a) Phong-shading model for colored object.

(b) New shading model without edge lines.

(c) New shading model: edge lines, highlights, and cool-to-warm hue shift.

(d) Approximation: Phong shading, two colored lights, and edge lines.

Figure 8.40. Comparison of traditional computer-graphics techniques and techniques for creating technical illustrations. See Color Plate XLII. Copyright 1998 Gooch et al. [Gooch et al. 98] and ACM. Used by permission.

Parameters k_1 and k_3 prevent the lights from oversaturating the surface, and k_2 and k_4 control the intensity of the warm and cool lights.

With this method, the lighting for each surface (or each different colored region) can be more easily controlled with the parameters k_1, k_2, k_3, and k_4. For example, Rademacher disabled the warm light when rendering white-ish surfaces. For purple surfaces, he set k_4 to 2.0 (intensifying the cool light component), whereas for red surfaces he increased the cool light and decreased the warm light.

8.2.6 Additive Shader

Kaplan et al. [Kaplan et al. 00] created an algorithm similar to the cool-to-warm shading method. This method can be precalculated and stored with vertices of a model. This lighting model is occlusion-free, and simulates shadows with sources of negative light. They use the following non-standard equation to describe the surface color, C, at any point:

$$C = O_c + \sum \left(L_c N \cdot L_d \right),$$

where O_c is the object color, L_C is the light color, N is the surface normal at the vertex, and L_d is the light direction. This is a very simple light shader that maintains the object color and is only sensitive to the normal at the point on the surface and its relationship to the light sources.

Figure 8.41.   An anisotropic reflection can be seen in the metal objects in this photograph.

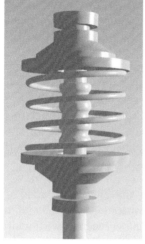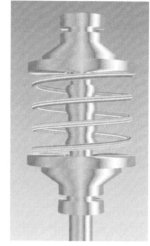

(a) Phong-shaded object.   (b) New metal-shaded
                                  object without edge lines.

(c) New metal-shaded   (d) Metal-shaded object
object with edge lines.   with a cool-to-warm
                                 shift.

Figure 8.42.   Representing metallic material properties. See Color Plate XLIII.
Copyright 1998 Gooch et al. [Gooch et al. 98] and ACM. Used by permission.

8.2.7   Metal Shading

Illustrators use a different technique to communicate the surface properties of metallic objects, as shown in the photograph in Figure 8.41. In practice, illustrators represent a metallic surface by alternating dark and light bands. This technique is the artistic representation of real effects that can be seen on milled metal parts, such as those found on cars or appliances. Milling creates what is known as "anisotropic reflection." Lines are streaked in the direction of the axis of minimum curvature, parallel to the milling axis. Interestingly, this visual convention is used even for smooth metal objects [Martin 89b][Ruppel 95]. This convention emphasizes that realism is not the primary goal of technical illustration.

To simulate a milled object, Gooch et al. [Gooch et al. 98] map a set of 20 stripes of varying intensity along the parametric axis of maximum curvature. The stripes are random intensities between 0.0 and 0.5, with the stripe closest to the light-source direction overwritten with white. Between the stripe centers, the colors are linearly interpolated. An object is shown Phong-shaded, metal-shaded (without and with edge lines), and metal-shaded with a cool-warm hue shift in Figure 8.42. The metal-shaded object is more obviously metal than the Phong-shaded image, and the metal-shaded object with edge lines provides more shape information. The cool-warm–hue metal-shaded object is not quite as convincing as the achromatic image, but it is more visually consistent with the cool-warm matte-shaded model of Chapter 8, Section 2, so it is useful when both metal and matte objects are shown together.

Chapter 9

Automatic Systems: Painting

Two basic approaches to digital painting and drawing are used in computer graphics. The first simulates the characteristics of an artistic medium such as canvas and paint, and is covered in Chapter 3. The second attempts to create drawings or paintings automatically by simulating the artistic process. Researchers who attempt to simulate the artistic process can also be divided into two groups: those who simulate paintings, and those who simulate painting techniques using standard computer-graphics rendering. In this chapter, we cover four systems for automatically generating digital paintings from source images. In addition, we include a section on artistic halftoning methods. We feel that halftoning and painting systems are similar because they are both describe methods for distributing marks on the image plane to convey information.

9.1 Background

Michael T. Wong, Douglas Zongker, and David Salesin [Wong et al. 98] explore methods for creating ornamental floral designs algorithmically. Their "adaptive clip art" uses open L-systems to define growth rules that describe how a set of geometric elements are structured in relation to one another. This procedural definition allows floral ornamentation to be "grown" into any user-defined area, and allows the area to be resized. An example of this type of automatic and adaptive floral ornamentation is shown in Figure 9.1.

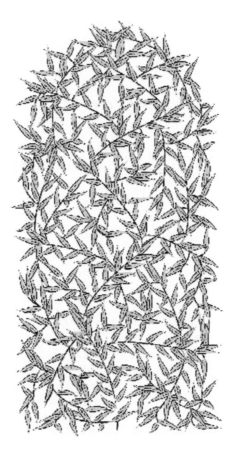

Figure 9.1. Wong et al.'s willow leaf pattern. Copyright 1998 Wong et al. [Wong et al. 98] and ACM. Used by permission.

Craig S. Kaplan and David H. Salesin present a system that produces "Escherized" images. That is, their images simulate the tiled images of the artist M. C. Escher. An example of an image created with their system is shown in Figure 9.2. The system tiles a plane with closed figures that are geometrically similar to a closed figure chosen by a user. Their solution works using a simulated annealing algorithim to optimize over a parameterization of the "isohedral" tilings, a class of tilings that is flexible enough to encompass nearly all of Escher's own tilings of the plane.

Tanaka and Ohnishi [Tanaka, Ohnishi 97] propose a method that generates painting-like artifacts, which can improve the perception of visual elements displayed in an image. Their technique works by reducing the intensity on illuminated surfaces, and expanding contrast at intensity edges.

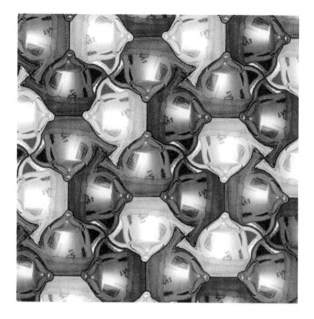

Figure 9.2.   Kaplan's "Tea-sselation" image. An example of a tile created from an image of a tea pot, and the tiling produced. See Color Plate XLIV. Copyright 2000 Kaplan and Salesin [Kaplan, Salesin 00] and ACM. Used by permission.

Litwinowicz [Litwinowicz 97] created a system that takes as input video or digital photos and generates impressionistic images and animations for commercial use. Hertzmann [Hertzmann 98] presented a method for creating images with a hand-painted appearance from a source photograph. Curtis et al. [Curtis et al. 97] presented a method for automatically generating watercolor images from three-dimensional models. Shiraishi et al. [Shiraishi, Yamaguchi 00] created a system for automatic painterly rendering, which uses image moments to generate rectangular brushstrokes that approximate local regions of the source image. Treavett and Chen [Treavett, Chen 97] use statistical techniques to automatically generate non-photorealistic images reminiscent of portrait paintings.

9.2   Processing Images and Video for An Impressionist Effect

Peter Litwinowicz [Litwinowicz 97] describes techniques for producing painterly animations from video clips automatically. Litwinowicz's system allows a software user to set parameters that will guide the painted output using the first image of a video sequence. These same parameters are then used to create a video sequence with a hand-painted look. The most significant result of his work is the use of optical flow fields to move brushstrokes from frame to frame in the same direction as pixel movement in the source video.

Litwinowicz's system consists of three key algorithms:

- An algorithm for rendering and clipping strokes.

- An algorithm for producing brushstroke orientations.

- An algorithm for frame-to-frame moving, adding, and deleting of brushstrokes.

Brushstrokes are first distributed over an input image, then rendered with anti-aliased lines or user-supplied textures. An image is initialized with one brushstroke for every other pixel in both the horizontal and vertical directions. Each stroke has the following parameters:

- Center—the x and y coordinates of the brushstroke center.

- Length—the length of the brushstroke.

- Radius—the width of the brushstroke.

- Theta—the orientation of the brushstroke.

- Color—(r, g, b) integer triple, each in the range [0, 255].

Every stroke is subjected to random perturbations to achieve a hand-crafted appearance in the final rendered image. Maximum and minimum values for the length and radius are supplied by a software user. Random values for length and radius are assigned to each stroke from within this specified range. All three color values are randomly perturbed in the range ±15, and the intensity of the perturbed color is further modified in the range [.85, 1.15]. Color values are then clamped to the range [0, 255]. The orientation of each stroke is perturbed in the range ±15 degrees. Note that parameter values for each stroke are perturbed only when the stroke is created. Perturbing the parameter values of the strokes on a frame-to-frame basis results in animations with too much frame-to-frame noise.

To preserve silhouette edges that occur in the source image in the painted image, brushstrokes are clipped, based on edge lines extracted from the source image. The line-clipping and drawing algorithm proceeds in the following steps:

- An intensity image is derived from the source image.

- The intensity image is blurred with a Gaussian kernel.

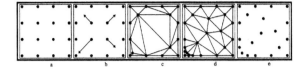

Figure 9.3. (a) Initial brushstroke positioning. (b) The four middle strokes are to be moved as shown. (c) Delaunay triangulation of the moved strokes. (d) Red points show new vertices introduced as a result of satisfying the maximal area constraint. (e) The updated list of brushstrokes. The original lower left corner brushstroke has been deleted because the distance between it and another original stroke satisfies the closeness test. Two of the potentially added new brushstrokes have also been removed form the list. Copyright 1997 Apple Computer, Inc. [Litwinowicz 97] and ACM. Used by permission.

- The blurred intensity image is Sobel filtered.

- Endpoints are found for each stroke.

- Strokes are rendered to the screen.

An intensity image is computed from the source image using the standard formula $(30*r + 59*g + 11*b)/100$ [Foley, van Dam 82] for each (r,g,b) pixel value. The intensity image is then blurred with a Gaussian kernel in order to reduce noise in the source image. The software user sets the size of the blur kernel. The image shown in Figure 9.4 was blurred with a kernel size of 11. The intensity image is then Sobel filtered to find edge lines in the source image. Sobel filtering [Jain et al. 95] is covered in Chapter 7, in the section on image space algorithms.

Given the center and orientation of a stroke, as well as the Sobel filtered image, endpoints for the stroke are computed. Endpoints are computed by "growing" the stroke out from its center in both directions along the orientation direction, until the maximum length for the stroke is reached or an edge in the source image is found. An edge is considered to be found if the Sobel value decreases in the direction the stroke is being grown. Litwinowicz [Litwinowicz 97] provides pseudocode for the clipping algorithm in his paper.

Strokes can be rendered using anti-aliased lines or brush textures. The color for a stroke is found by sampling the source image at the center point of the stroke. Strokes are rendered with a slight falloff and in random order to simulate a hand-painted image. The images in Figures 9.5, 9.6, and 9.7 are drawn using anti-aliased lines while the images in Figure 9.8 use brush textures.

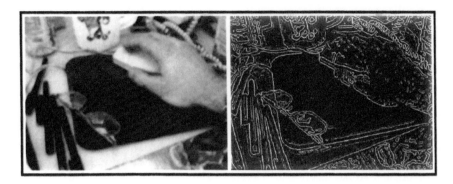

Figure 9.4.   Blurred image and the corresponding Sobel-filtered image. Copyright
1997 Apple Computer, Inc. [Litwinowicz 97] and ACM. Used by permission.

Litwinowicz provides the software user with a method of rendering
brush strokes in the direction of constant color in the source image. This
type of rendering is accomplished by making the assumption that an image
can be approximated locally with a short stroke in the gradient-normal
direction. Figure 9.6 shows an example of the gradient-normal technique.
The problem with this technique is that no gradient information is available in areas with constant or near-constant intensity in the source image.
Litwinowicz solves this problem by interpolating gradient values across the
Sobel-filtered image using a thin plate spline [Franke 79].

Litwinowicz's system as described thus far will generate the initial image
for a video sequence. In order to generate subsequent images, optical-
flow algorithms are used to track pixel positions and move brushstrokes to
new positions. Optical flow methods are a subclass of motion-estimation
techniques. A simple definition of optical flow is the movement of pixels
from one image to a subsequent image as shown in Figure 9.3.

When the pixel flow between a destination and target image is computed, for a pixel in the target image, one of three possibilities can occur:
exactly one pixel flowed to this pixel, no pixel flowed to this pixel, many
pixels flowed to this pixel. In the case where exactly one pixel flowed to the
current position, the brushstroke that represented the previous position is
rendered at the new position. In the case where no pixels flowed to the current position, Delaunay triangulation is used to generate new brushstroke
positions as shown in Figure 9.3. In the case where many pixel values flow
to a single pixel in the target image, brushstrokes are removed if they are
within a user-defined distance from each other. A display list of strokes is
maintained throughout the process, with a front-to-back rendering order.
The stroke that is furthest back in the display list is removed.

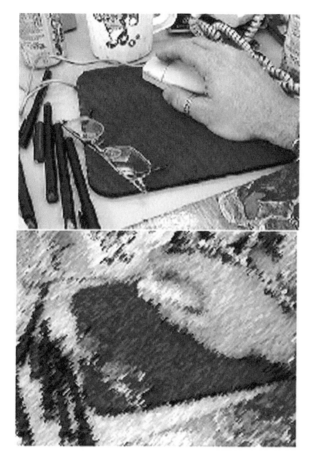

Figure 9.5.   The source image and all painted images are 640 × 480 pixels. Top: source image. Bottom: processed image using no brushstroke clipping and a constant base stroke orientation of 45 degrees. Copyright 1997 Apple Computer, Inc. [Litwinowicz 97] and ACM. Used by permission.

9.3 Painterly Rendering with Curved Brushstrokes of Multiple Sizes

Aaron Hertzmann [Hertzmann 98] presented a method for automatically creating an image with a hand-painted appearance from a photograph. Hertzmann's system renders brushstrokes onto a blurred copy of the source image. Brushstrokes are represented by B-spline curves, and are rendered by drawing filled circles along the path traced by the B-spline curve. Images are built up in a series of layers, with each layer composed of smaller

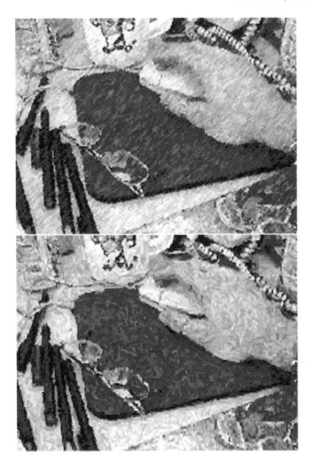

Figure 9.6.   Top: the technique is modified so that brushstrokes are clipped to edges detected in the original image. Bottom: the technique is modified to orient strokes using a gradient-based method. Copyright 1997 Apple Computer, Inc. [Litwinowicz 97] and ACM. Used by permission.

brushstrokes than the previous, built up on a jittered grid. This multi-layer technique allows the final painted images to have roughly the same spatial energy as the source image. An example of Hertzmann's method is shown in Figure 9.9.

Hertzmann computes a list of brushstrokes for each layer of the painting. The software user provides a list of brushstroke radii, and an individual layer is made for each size of brush. Brushstrokes are limited to a constant color, and image gradients are used to guide stroke placement. Each layer

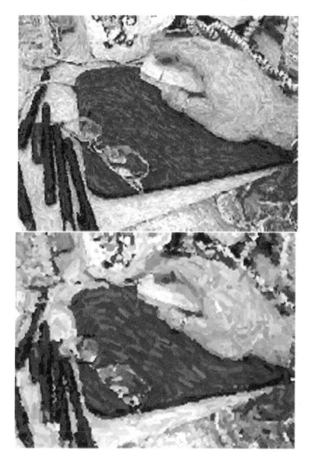

Figure 9.7. Top: in this image the technique is further modified, such that regions with vanishing gradient magnitude are interpolated from surrounding regions. Bottom: image produced using larger brushstroke lengths and radii. Copyright 1997 Apple Computer, Inc. [Litwinowicz 97] and ACM. Used by permission.

is made up of brushstrokes of only a single size. Layers are painted on top of one another in a simple four-step algorithm:

1. Create a reference image for the layer by blurring the source image, using a Gaussian blur with a kernel size based on the brush radius for that layer.

2. Compute a per-pixel difference image between the blurred reference image and the current painted image.

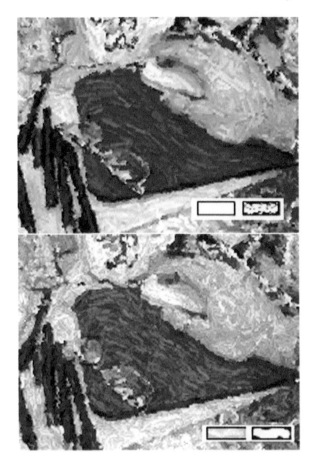

Figure 9.8.   Top: brushstroke textures are used. Lower right corner shows basic brush intensity and alpha. Bottom: another brushstroke texture is demonstrated. Copyright 1997 Apple Computer, Inc. [Litwinowicz 97] and ACM. Used by permission.

3. Grid off the painted image, and for each cell compute the average error in that cell from the difference image.

4. If the error in the cell is higher than a user set tolerance, compute a stroke starting in the current cell.

For each layer, the source image is blurred based on the radius of the brush size used for that layer. Hertzmann uses a Gaussian blur, but notes that nonlinear diffusion may be used instead to produce painted images

Figure 9.9.   An example of Hertzmann's system in its "impressionist" mode. See Color Plate XLVII. Copyright 1998 Hertzmann [Hertzmann 98] and ACM. Used by permission. Source photograph courtesy of Jonathan Meyer.

with more detailed edges. A per-pixel distance image is computed using $||(r_1, g_1, b_1) - (r_2, g_2, b_2)|| = \sqrt{(r_1 - r_2)^2 + (g_1 - g_2)^2 + (b_1 - b_2)^2}$. The difference image is used to speed the computation of the per-area error between the blurred reference image and the current painting. For each cell of a painted layer, if the error in that cell is below a user-set tolerance, no stroke is made for that cell. Examples of Hertzmann's painting process are shown in Figures 9.10, 9.11, 9.12, and 9.13.

Brushstrokes are represented as a color, a brush radius, and a list of control points. The color for a stroke is computed by finding the pixel with

Figure 9.10.   Painting with three brushes: the source image. See Color Plate XLVIII. Copyright 1998 Hertzmann [Hertzmann 98] and ACM. Used by permission.

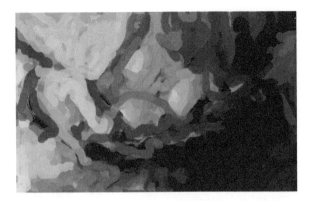

Figure 9.11.   Painting with three brushes: the first layer of the painting, after painting with a circular brush of radius 8. See Color Plate XLVIII. Copyright 1998 Hertzmann [Hertzmann 98] and ACM. Used by permission.

the maximum color distance from the corresponding pixel in the source image, and then setting the stroke color to be the color of the pixel in the source image. The brush radius is specified by the software user. Control points are computed by first computing the average error in the starting cell of a stroke. If the average error is above a user-set threshold, a stroke is started in the current cell; otherwise no stroke is created for that cell. When a starting point for a stroke is established, additional control points are found by first computing the image gradient at the current control

Figure 9.12.   Painting with three brushes: the image after painting with a brush of radius 4. See Color Plate XLVIII. Copyright 1998 Hertzmann [Hertzmann 98] and ACM. Used by permission.

Figure 9.13. Painting with three brushes: the final image, after painting with a brush of size 2. Note that brushstrokes from earlier layers are still visible in the painting. See Color Plate XLVIII. Copyright 1998 Hertzmann [Hertzmann 98] and ACM. Used by permission.

point using the Sobel-filtered luminance of the reference image. The next point is placed normal to the gradient at a distance equal to the radius of the current stroke. The next control point is placed at a distance equal to the radius, because the stroke radius represents the level of detail to be captured with the current brush size. This means that large brushes create loose sketches of the source image, which are later refined by smaller brushes.

By adjusting the following parameters, Hertzmann's method can be used to produce a variety of painted effects.

- *Approximation threshold*—How closely the painting must approximate the source image. Higher values of this threshold produce "rougher" paintings.

- *Brush sizes*—Hertzmann found it more useful to use two parameters to specify brush sizes: Smallest brush radius, and Number of Brushes. He then uses the brush ratio $R_{i+1}/R_i = 2$.

- *Curvature filter*—Used to limit or exaggerate stroke curvature.

- *Blur factor*—Controls the size of the blurring kernel. A small blur factor allows more noise in the image, and thus produces a more "impressionistic" image.

- *Minimum and maximum stroke lengths*—Used to restrict the possible stroke lengths. Very short strokes would be used in a "pointillistic" image; long strokes would be used in a more "expressionistic" image.

- *Opacity or alpha value*—Specifies the paint opacity, between 0 and 1. Lower opacity produces a wash-like effect.

- *Grid size*—Controls the spacing of brush strokes.

- *Color jitter*—Factors to add random jitter to hue, saturation, value, red, green, or blue color components.

The following is pseudo code for an implimentation of Hertzmann's method.

```
Color{

Data:

   int Red;
   int Green;
   int Blue;

Methods:

   int colorDifference(C2, C1); // least squares distance
      // between the colors in RGB space
}

int colorDifference(C1, C2){
   int value;

   value = (C1.Red - C2.Red) * (C1.Red - C2.Red);
   value += (C1.Green - C2.Green) * (C1.Green - C2.Green);
   value += (C1.Blue - C2.Blue) * (C1.Blue - C2.Blue);
   value = SquareRoot(value);

   return value;
}

Pair{ // an ordered pair class

Data:

  float x, y

Methods:

  void add(Pair); // adds the contents of a Pair to this Pair
```

```
   void subtract(Pair);  // subtracts the contents of a Pair from
                         // this Pair

   void scale(int);  // multiplies the contents of this pair by
                     // a constant

   void divide(int);  // divides the contents of this pair by
                      // a constant

   void normalize();  // normalizes the contents of this Pair

   Pair NormalPlus(Pair1, Pair2, width);  // returns a Pair in the
                                          // positive direction normal
                                          // to Pair1 and Pair2,
                                          // width units away

   Pair NormalMinus(Pair1, Pair2, width);  // returns a Pair in the
                                           // negative direction normal
                                           // to Pair1 and Pair2,
                                           // width units away
}


Image{

Data:

   int width;   // width and height of the image
   int height;

   Color pixels[width][height];

Methods:

   int getHeight();  // returns height

   int getWidth();   // returns width

   Color getColor(x,y);  // returns the color at the given coordinates

   Color getColor(Pair);  // returns the color at the given coordinates

   int gradientMagnitude(Pair);   // computes the magnitude of the
                                  // image gradient
```

```
    Pair gradientDirection(Pair); // computes a unit vector in the
                                  // direction of the image gradient
                                  // at the given coordinates

    Image newImage(); // returns a newly created image

    Image GaussianBlur(Image1, int); // applies a Gausian blur with
                                     // a given kernel to an image

    int[][] difference(Image1, Image2); // returns a 2d integer array
                                        // that represents a
                                        // difference image

    int SumError(int, int, int, int[][]); // returns the sum of
                                          // the difference terms
                                          // in a region of a
                                          // difference image

    Pair MaxError(int, int, int, int[][]); // returns the pixel
                                           //coordinates of the pixel
                                           // with the max error in
                                           // a region
}


Painting{ // a class that represents a painting

Data:

  int numberBrushes;                 // number of brushes used
                                     // for this painting
  int BrushRadii[numberBrushes]; // radius of each brush used
  Image Source_Image;
  Image referenceImage;

Methods:

  Image PaintCanvas(); // makes a painting on a canvas

  void PaintLayer(Image1, Image2, int); // paints a single layer of a
                                        // painting onto the first
                                        // image using the second image
                                        // as a reference, with brush
                                        // radius given by the int value
}
```

```
Stroke{ // a class that represents a single stroke

Data:

   int radius;

   Color StrokeColor;

   Pair{} StrokePoints; // a java array or a linked list of pairs

Methods:

   addPoint(Pair);   // adds an (x, y) pair of points to this stroke

Stroke makeStroke(int, int, int, Image, Image); // builds a stroke
}
```

```
Image PaintCanvas(){

   Image Canvas = newImage(Image1.getHeight, Image1.getWidth);

   for (int i = 0; i < numberBrushes; i++) {
referenceImage = GaussianBlur(Source_Image, i);
PaintLayer(Canvas, referenceImage, BrushRadii[i]);
   }

   return Canvas;

}
```

```
void PaintLayer(Canvas, refImage, R){

   StrokeSet{}; // a java array or linked list of strokes
   Stroke tempStroke;
   DiffImage[][]  = difference(Canvas,refImage); // create a
                                         // pointwise
                                         // difference image
   Pair Coords;
   int areaError;
   int ErrorTolerance;   // Set by user

    for (int x = R/2; x < referenceImage.getWidth(); x+=R) {
      for (int y = R/2; y < referenceImage.getHeight(); y+=R) {
```

```
      // Sum the error in a neighborhood of (x,y)
      areaError = SumError(x, y, R, DiffImage);
      areaError /= (R*R);
      if(areaError > ErrorTolerance) then {
        // find the largest error point
        Coords = MaxError(x, y, R, DiffImage);
 tempStroke = makeStroke(Coords.x, Coords.y, R, refImage, Canvas);
 StrokeSet.add(tempStroke); // add stroke to stroke list
      }
    }
  }
  StrokeSet.Paint();   // paints all strokes in this list
                       // in a random order
}


Stroke makeStroke(x, y, R, refImage){

  int maxStrokeLength; // set by user
  int minStrokeLength; // set by user
  int curvyFactor;     // set by user on the interval [1, 100]

  Pair Gradient;
  Pair GradientNormal;
  Pair LastPosition;
  Pair ThisPosition = new Pair(x, y);

  Stroke newStroke = new Stroke();
  newStroke.StrokeColor = refImage.getColor(x, y);

  newStroke.add(ThisPosition);

  for(int i = 0; i < maxStrokeLength; i++) {

    if((i > minStrokeLength) &&
       (colorDistance(refImage.getColor(ThisPosition),
        Canvas.getColor(ThisPosition))
        < colorDistance(refImage.getColor(ThisPosition),
        newStroke.StrokeColor))){
      return newStroke;
    }

    // detect vanishing gradient
    if(refImage.refImage.gradientMagnitude(ThisPosition) == 0){
      return newStroke;
    }
```

```
// compute unit vector of image gradient
Gradient = refImage.gradientDirection(ThisPosition);

// compute gradient normal direction
GradientNormal = new Pair(-Gradient.y, Gradient.x);

// if necessary, reverse direction
if((LastPosition.x * GradientNormal.x)
  + (LastPosition.x * GradientNormal.x) < 0)){
  GradientNormal.scale(-1);
}

// filter the stroke direction,
//used to make strokes more wavy between control points
GradientNormal.scale(curvyFactor);
GradientNormal.divide(100);
LastPosition.scale(1 - curvyFactor);
LastPosition.divide(100);
GradientNormal.add(LastPosition);
GradientNormal.normalise();
GradientNormal.scale(R);
ThisPosition.add(GradientNormal);


newStroke.add(ThisPosition);
LastPosition = ThisPosition;

 }
 return newStroke;
}
```

9.4 Statistical Techniques for the Automated Synthesis of Non-Photorealistic Images

Treavett and Chen [Treavett, Chen 97] present an approach to generating non-photorealistic images reminiscent of paintings automatically, using statistical techniques. Their techniques may also be used to generate animations or produce special effects from source video. Treavett and Chen observed that a human artist places brushstrokes in an ordered manner. However, the final image appears as a semi-random distribution of strokes across the canvas. They created distributions of computer-generated strokes across a digital image to simulate this effect.

Figure 9.14.   Abstract models of an artist's brush. Left: an image produced using a square "stamp." Right: an image produced using a circular "stamp." Copyright 1997 Treavett and Chen [Treavett, Chen 97]. Used by permission.

Treavett and Chen's system consists of three parts:

- Simulating brushstrokes.

- Computing a size and orientation for the brushstrokes.

- Positioning brushstrokes.

Brushes are simulated by sampling the source image, computing a color value, and "stamping" the corresponding area in the painted image by drawing either a circle or a square of the computed color. Examples of images drawn with this "stamping" technique are shown in Figure 9.14. In order to simulate the type of mark made by a paint brush more realistically, Treavett and Chen used alpha blending, guided by perturbed normal statistical distributions, along the width and length of the strokes. To aid in brushstroke simulation, separate distributions are used for the length and width. An example of an image created using this technique is shown in Figure 9.15. The stamping method produces symmetric strokes, while the normally-distributed alpha-blending method produces strokes that are longer in one direction.

Treavett and Chen use the standard deviation of pixel intensity in the source image to compute the size and orientation of brush strokes. Standard

Figure 9.15.   Normally-distributed and controlled strokes.   Copyright 1997 Treavett and Chen [Treavett, Chen 97]. Used by permission.

deviation is used because it gives a reasonable estimation of the amount of detail in the pixel's local neighborhood. The size of the stroke is calculated using the following formula:

$$\text{strokeSize}_{(x,y)} = \begin{cases} \frac{\text{maxSize}-\text{minSize}}{\sigma_{max}} \cdot (\sigma_{max} - \sigma_{(x,y)}) + \text{minSize} & \text{if } \sigma_{(x,y)} \leq \sigma_{max} \\ \text{minSize} & \text{if } \sigma_{(x,y)} > \sigma_{max} \end{cases}$$

where σ is the standard deviation of the pixel intensity in the source image, and maxSize and minSize are user-defined variables.

Stroke orientation is found for nonsymmetric strokes by computing the standard deviation of the intensity of points in each direction from the source pixel. The line with the smallest deviation is chosen as the direction of the stroke. Orientation does not need to be computed for symmetric strokes.

9.5   Automatic Painterly Rendering Based on Local Source-Image Approximation

Michio Shiraishi and Yasushi Yamaguchi [Shiraishi, Yamaguchi 00] present a method for automatic painterly rendering that synthesizes an image with a hand-crafted painted look from a source image such as a photograph. Their method generates rectangular textured brushstrokes that approximate local regions of the source image. Brushstrokes are generated using image moments computed for small subsections of the source image. Image moments result from the the statisical analysis of an image and yield an oval with the same rotational charateristics as the image. Shiraishi and Yamaguchi use image moments to compute brushstroke orientation. Brushstroke distribution is determined using a dithering method based on space-filling curves and the size of the brushstrokes.

Shiraishi's process proceeds in two steps:

1. Preparation—The system first determines the distribution of strokes, their attributes, and painting order.

2. Composition—Strokes are rendered onto a background image with alpha blending.

The preparation phase of Shiraishi's algorithm consists of three independent steps: computing a stroke distribution, computing individual stroke attributes, and computing an overall stroke painting order.

The stroke distribution is determined using a two-step process. First, an intensity image is computed based on the zeroth-order image moment at each pixel. R. Mukundan and K. R. Ramakrishnan's book [Mukundan, Ramakrishnan 98] is an excellent resource for a reader who would like to implement image moments. This intensity image is then used to drive a dithering process that distributes dots over an image. The positions of the dots are then used as stroke positions for the final image.

Once a stroke distribution has been found, attributes for individual strokes can be computed. All of the attributes for a stroke are computed in a four-step process as shown in Figure 9.16. Stroke attributes include color, location, orientation, and size. Orientation is the angle between the major axis of the stroke and the x axis of the canvas. Size has two parameters, length and width.

The computation of the strokes is then accomplished in the following steps:

- Color sampling—The color attribute of a stroke is determined by sampling the source image at the stroke's position.

- Source image cropping—The source image is cropped based on a stroke-size parameter set by the software user.

- Color-difference image generation—A color difference image is calculated using the cropped source image and the computed stroke color.

- Equivalent-rectangle calculation—Image moments are used to find an equivalent rectangle for the color difference image. The stroke location is moved to the center of the equivalent rectangle.

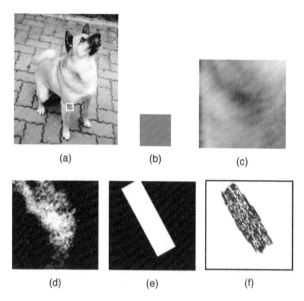

Figure 9.16. The process of stroke-attribute computation. (a) The source image. (b) The computed stroke color. (c) The cropped source image. (d) The color difference image. (e) An image of the equivalent rectangle. (f) The resulting brushstroke. Copyright 2000 Shiraishi and Yamaguchi [Shiraishi, Yamaguchi 00] and ACM. Used by permission.

When the attributes of all of the strokes for a given image have been computed, the strokes are sorted by the area of their equivalent rectangles. This assures that no small brushstrokes are obscured by larger brushstrokes. An example of a painting being built up is shown in Figure 9.17.

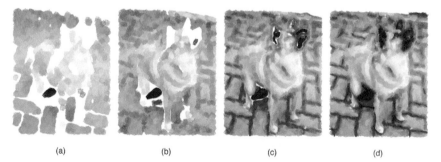

Figure 9.17. An example of a canvas image being built up. (a) 2500 strokes, (b) 5000 strokes, (c) 7500 strokes, and (d) 10000 strokes. See Color Plate XLIX. Copyright 2000 Shiraishi and Yamaguchi [Shiraishi, Yamaguchi 00] and ACM. Used by permission.

9.6   Artistically Motivated Halftoning

The process of halftoning approximates grayscale images with a distribution of black dots on white paper, or in the case of digital images, black pixels on a white background. Halftoning works because our eyes perceive a local average of the distribution. In photorealistic halftoning, the introduction of artifacts of any kind is undesirable. However, for applications such as book illustrations or currency, images with noticeable artifacts are desired. In this section, we list resources for implementing digital halftoning, then cover research in artistic halftoning.

Robert Ulichney's book "Digital Halftoning" [Ulichney 87] provides a comprehensive catalog of halftoning techniques, allowing the reader to evaluate halftoning algorithms easily. In "Graphics Gems II," Dale Schu-

Figure 9.18.   Approximations of: (a) Peano, (b) Hilbert, (c) Sierpinski space filling curves. Copyright 1991 Velho and Gomes [Velho, Gomes 91] and ACM. Used by permission.

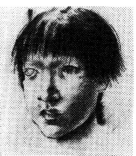

Figure 9.19. (a) Digitized test image: A drawing by the Brazilian artist Candido Portinari (1938). (b) Space-filling curve algorithm using a Hilbert curve. (c) Floyd-Steinberg algorithm (d) Clustered-dot ordered-dither algorithm using a matrix of order 8. Copyright 1991 Velho and Gomes [Velho, Gomes 91] and ACM. Used by permission.

macher gives a practical introduction and comparative guide to halftoning methods. Schumacher's article provides pseudocode and many examples. Adaptive clustering and selective precipitation adapted to halftoning in order to reduce blurring are the subject of Tien-Tsin Wong's "Graphics Gems V" [Wong 95] article.

Luiz Velho and Jonas de Miranda Gomes [Velho, Gomes 91] introduced a digital halftoning technique that uses space-filling curves to generate aperiodic clustered-dot patterns. An example of space-filling curves is shown in Figure 9.18. Their method leverages properties of space filling curves that allow the subdivision of a raster image into regions with desirable characteristics such as self-similarity. Clustered patterns of dots are then generated based on this type of subdivision, which results in the perception of an image with intensity equivalent to the original image. Examples of Velho and Gomes' images are shown in Figure 9.19.

Gershon Elber [Elber 95] presented a non-photorealistic halftoning scheme for scenes composed of isoparametric curves. The three-dimensional geometry of the scene is leveraged to create a coverage along the general stream lines of the models in the scene. The norm of the density coverage is tuned to become a function of simple lighting and shading models. Some examples of this technique are shown in Figure 9.20.

John Buchanan [Buchanan 96] discusses methods for introducing artifacts to images to create a stylized halftone of the source image. Buchanan demonstrates that these stylized artifacts are easy and intuitive to control. He also demonstrates a method for generating grayscale textures with artistic artifacts included.

Figure 9.20.   Two views of a B-58 airplane, halftoned using isoparametric curves, in two different specular powers and two different light sources. Copyright 1995 Elber [Elber 95] and © 1995 IEEE. Used by permission.

Lisa Streit and John Buchanan [Streit, Buchanan 98] introduced a new halftoning technique in which an importance function guides the halftoning algorithm. The importance function is defined by the user, and can be tuned to highlight areas of the source image with high variance, or to produce standard halftone images. Streit also demonstrates how line segments can be used instead of single pixels to provide edge enhancement and sketched effects in the halftone image. Examples of importance-driven halftoning are shown in Figure 9.21.

Oleg Veryovka and John Buchanan [Veryovka, Buchanan 99] demonstrate a method for controlling the halftoning texture artifacts introduced when using the ordered-dither algorithm. The ordered-dither algorithm approximates grayscale values in a source image, using a threshold matrix. Veryovka's algorithm uses histogram equalization on arbitrary images to

Figure 9.21.   Examples of images created with the method of Streit and Buchanan using relative intensity as the importance function and line segments as the drawing primitive. Copyright 1991 Streit and Buchanan [Streit, Buchanan 98]. Used by permission.

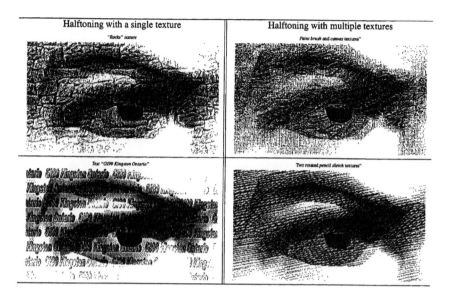

Figure 9.22. Non-photorealistic effects are introduced by a variation of dither screens. The possible sources for a dither screen are a complete image, a texture sample, or scanned text. A dither screen may also contain more than a single texture. In the images on the right, different textures were used for the dark and light ends of the grayscale range. Copyright 1999 Veryovka and Buchanan [Veryovka, Buchanan 99]. Used by permission.

generate threshold matrices that result in similar pixel distributions. This allows artistic effects to be introduced into the resulting halftone image. Examples are shown in Figure 9.22.

Victor Ostromoukhov and Roger Hersch [Ostromoukhov, Hersch 95] [Ostromoukhov, Hersch 99] proposed algorithms that allow the shape of the halftone dots to be tuned. Halftone screens created in this manner can be used to convey additional layers of information in an image, or in the case of currency, to prevent counterfeiting. Ostromoukhov and Hersch present additional algorithms to address the problem of color printing. An example image created with their system is shown in Figure 9.23.

9.7 Summary

We have discussed four methods for automatically deriving digital simulations of paintings from source images in this chapter. All of these systems can be implemented in less than a week by a good programmer. All of the

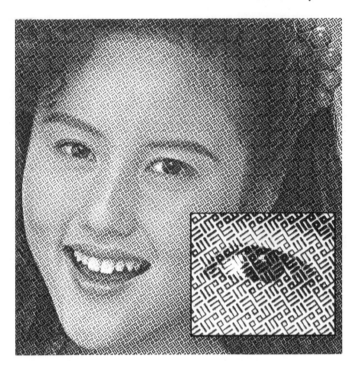

Figure 9.23. An example of the process of Ostromoukhov and Hersch. See Color Plate L. Copyright 1999 Ostromoukhov [Ostromoukhov 99] and ACM. Used by permission.

researchers involved admit that their systems are simple and naive. Yet, in all cases, striking results are possible. Another trait all these systems share is failure for certain input images, for example human portraits. We therefore believe that automatic painting is a rich area for future investigation. In addition, user-assisted methods built up from automatic painting techniques would be very interesting. Another area for future research is the adaptation of digital halftoning algorithms to an automatic painting process.

Bibliography

[Appel 67] APPEL, A. "The notion of quantitative invisibility and the machine rendering of solids." In *Proc. ACM Natl. Mtg.*, p. 387, Thompson Books, 1967.

[Appel et al. 79] APPEL, A., ROHLF, F. J., AND STEIN, A. J. "The haloed line effect for hidden line elimination." *Computer Graphics (Proc. SIGGRAPH 79)* 13(3): 151–157 (August 1979).

[Baecker 69] BAECKER, R. "Picture-Driven Animation." In SJCC 34, pp. 273-288, AFIPS, 1969.

[Badler, Glassner 97] BADLER, N. I., AND GLASSNER, A. S. "3D object modeling." In *Introduction to Computer Graphics (SIGGRAPH '97 Course Notes 18)*, August 1997.

[Banks 94] BANKS, D. C. "Illumination in diverse codimensions." In *Proceedings of SIGGRAPH 94, Computer Graphics Proceedings, Annual Conference Series*, edited by Andrew Glassner, pp. 327–334, New York: ACM Press, 1994.

[Barequet et al. 99] BAREQUET, G., DUNCAN, C. A., GOODRICH, M. T., KUMAR, S., AND POP, M. "Efficient perspective-accurate silhouette computation." In *Proceedings of the Fifteenth Annual Symposium on Computational Geometry*, pp. 417–418, New York: ACM Press, 1999.

[Berman et al. 94] BERMAN, D. F., BARTELL, J. T., AND SALESIN, D. H. "Multiresolution painting and compositing." In *Proceedings of SIGGRAPH 94, Computer Graphics Proceedings, Annual Conference Series*, edited By Andrew Glassner, pp. 85–90, New York: ACM Press, 1994.

[Biederman, Ju 88] BIEDERMAN, I., AND JU, G. "Surface versus edge-based determinants of visual recognition." *Cognitive Psychology* 20: 38–64 (1988).

[Birren 76] BIRREN, F. *Color Perception in Art.* New York: Van Nostrand Reinhold Company, 1976.

[Blythe et al. 99] BLYTHE, D., GRANTHAM, B., MCREYNOLDS, T., AND NELSON, S. R. *Advanced Graphics Programming Techniques Using OpenGL (SIGGRAPH '99 Course Notes)*, 1999.

[Braje et al. 95] BRAJE, W. L., TJAN, B. S., AND LEGGE, G. E. "Human efficiency for recognizing and detecting low-pass filtered objects." *Vision Research* 35(21): 2955–2966 (1995).

[Bremer, Hughes 98] BREMER, D. J., AND HUGHES, J. F. "Rapid approximate silhouette rendering of implicit surfaces." In *Proceedings of Implicit Surfaces '98*, pp. 155-164, June 1998.

[Browning 94] BROWNING, T. *Timeless Techniques for Better Oil Paintings.* New York: North Light Books, 1994.

[Brunner 84] BRUNNER, F. *A Handbook of Graphic Reproduction Process.* New York: Hasting House Publ., 1984.

[Buchanan 96] BUCHANAN, J. W. "Special effects with half-toning." *Computer Graphics Forum* 15(3): 97–108 (August 1996).

[Buchanan, Sousa 00] BUCHANAN, J. W., AND SOUSA, M. C. "The edge buffer: A data structure for easy silhouette rendering." In *NPAR 2000: First International Symposium on Non-Photorealistic Animation and Rendering*, edited by Jean-Daniel Fekete and David H. Salesin, pp. 39–42, New York: ACM SIGGRAPH, 2000.

[Buck et al. 00] BUCK, I., FINKELSTEIN, A., JACOBS, C., KLEIN, A., SALESIN, D. H., SEIMS, J., SZELISKI, R., AND TOYAMA, K. "Performance-driven hand-drawn animation." In *NPAR 2000: First International Symposium on Non-Photorealistic Animation and Rendering*, edited by Jean-Daniel Fekete and David H. Salesin, pp. 101–108, New York: ACM SIGGRAPH, 2000.

[Burtnyk, Wein 71] BURTNYK, N., AND WEIN, M. "Computer-generated key frame animation." *J. Society Motion Picture and Television Engineers* 80(3): 149–153 (1971).

[Cabral, Leedom 93] CABRAL, B., AND LEEDOM, L. C. "Imaging vector fields using line integral convolution." In *Proceedings of SIGGRAPH 93, Computer Graphics Proceedings, Annual Conference Series*, edited by James T. Kajiya, pp. 263–272, New York: ACM Press, 1993.

[Callen 82] CALLEN, A. *Techniques of the Impressionists*, 1982.

[Camhy 97] CAMHY, S. *Art of the Pencil: A Revolutionary Look at Drawing, Painting, and the Pencil.* New York: Watson-Guptill Publications, 1997.

[Catmull 83] CATMULL, E. *Tween Users' Manual.* New York: CGL Inc., 1983.

[Christou et al. 96] CHRISTOU, C., KOENDERINK, J. J., AND VAN DOORN, A. J. "Surface gradients, contours and the perception of surface attitude in images of complex scenes." *Perception* 25: 701–713 (1996).

[Claes et al. 97] CLAES, J., MONSIEURS, P., REETH, F. V., AND FLERACKERS, E. "Rendering Pen-drawings of 3D scenes on Network Processors." In *Fifth International Conference in Central Europe on Computer Graphics and Visualization (Winter School on Computer Graphics)*, 1997.

[Cockshott 91] COCKSHOTT, T. *Wet and Sticky: A Novel Model for Computer-Based Painting.* PhD thesis, University of Glasgow, 1991.

[Cockshott, England 91] COCKSHOTT, T., AND ENGLAND, D. "Wet and Sticky: Supporting interaction with wet paint." In *People and Computers VI: Proceedings of the HCI '91 Conference*, edited by D. Diaper and H. Hammond, pp. 199-208, 1991.

[Cockshott et al. 92] COCKSHOTT, T., PATTERSON, J., AND ENGLAND, D. "Modelling the Texture of Paint." *Computer Graphics Forum* 11: 217–226 (1992).

[Cohen et al. 00] COHEN, J. M., HUGHES, J. F., AND ZELEZNIK, R. C. "Harold: A world made of drawings." In *NPAR 2000: First International Symposium on Non-Photorealistic Animation and Rendering*, edited by Jean-Daniel Fekete and David H. Salesin, pp. 83–90, New York: ACM SIGGRAPH, 2000.

[Corrêa et al. 98] CORRÊA, W. T., JENSEN, R. J., THAYER, S. E., AND FINKELSTEIN, A. "Texture mapping for cel animation." In *Proceedings of SIGGRAPH 98, Computer Graphics Proceedings, Annual Conference Series*, edited by Michael Cohen, pp. 435–446, Reading, MA: Addison-Wesley, 1998.

[Coutts, Greenberg 97] COUTTS, R., AND GREENBERG, D. P. "Rendering with streamlines." Unpublished, (1997).

[Coutts 98] COUTTS, R. M. *Conceptual modeling and rendering techniques for architectural design.* Master's thesis, Cornell University, 1998.

[Crow 97] CROW, F. C. "Shadow algorithms for computer graphics." *Computer Graphics (Proc. SIGGRAPH 77)* 11(2): 242–248 (July 1977).

[Curtis et al. 97] CURTIS, C. J., ANDERSON, S. E., SEIMS, J. E., FLEISCHER, K. W., AND SALESIN, D. H. "Computer-generated watercolor." In *Proceedings of SIGGRAPH 97, Computer Graphics Proceedings, Annual Conference Series*, edited by Turner Whitted, pp. 421–430, Reading, MA: Addison-Wesley, 1997.

[Curtis 98] CURTIS, C. "Loose and Sketchy Animation." In *Conference Abstracts and Applications, SIGGRAPH 98*, pp. 317, New York: ACM SIGGRAPH, 1998.

[Decaudin 96a] DECAUDIN, P. *Cartoon-looking rendering of 3D-scenes.* Tech. Rep. INRIA 2919, Universite de Technologie de Compiegne, France, June 1996.

[Decaudin 96b] DECAUDIN, P. *Modeling using Fusion of 3D Shapes for Computer Graphics—Cartoon-Looking Rendering of 3D Scenes.* PhD thesis, Universite de Technologie de Compiegne, France, Dec. 1996.

[Deussen et al. 99] DEUSSEN, O., HARNEL, J., RAAB, A., SCHLECHTWEG, S., AND STROTHOTTE, T. "An illustration technique using hardware-based intersections." In *Graphics Interface Proceedings 1999*, edited by Scott MacKenzie and James Stewart, pp. 175–182, San Francisco, CA: Morgan-Kaufmann Publishers, 1999.

[Deussen, Strothotte 00a] DEUSSEN, O., AND STROTHOTTE, T. "Computer-generated pen-and-ink illustration of trees." In *Proceedings of SIGGRAPH 2000, Computer Graphics Proceedings, Annual Conference Series*, edited by Kurt Akeley, pp. 13–18, Reading, MA: Addison-Wesley, 2000.

[Dobie 86] DOBIE, J. *Making Color Sing*. New York: Watson-Guptill Publications, 1986.

[Dooley, Cohen 90] DOOLEY, D., AND COHEN, M. F. "Automatic illustration of 3D geometric models: Surfaces." *IEEE Computer Graphics and Applications* 13(2): 307–314 (1990).

[Douglas, van Wyk 93] DOUGLAS, D., AND VAN WYK, D. *The Drawing Process: Rendering*. Englewood Cliffs, NJ: Prentice Hall, Inc., 1993.

[Driskill 96] DRISKILL, E. *Towards the Design, Analysis, and Illustration of Assemblies*. PhD thesis, University of Utah, Department of Computer Science, Salt Lake City, Utah, Sept. 1996.

[Edwards 89] EDWARDS, B. *Drawing on the Right Side of the Brain*. New York: J. P. Tarcher, 1989.

[Hodges 89] ELAINE HODGES, E. *The Guide Handbook of Scientific Illustration*. New York: Van Nostrand Reinhold, 1989.

[Elber 95] ELBER, G. *Gridless halftoning of freeform surfaces via a coverage of isoparametric curves*. Tech. Rep. 9507, Center for Intelligent Systems Report, Israel Institute of Technology, Mar. 1995.

[Elber 95] ELBER, G. "Line art rendering via a coverage of isoparametric curves." *IEEE Transactions on Visualization and Computer Graphics* 1(3): 231–239 (Sept. 1995).

[Elber 98] ELBER, G. "Line Art Illustrations of Parametric and Implicit Forms." *IEEE Transactions on Visualization and Computer Graphics* 4(1): 71–81 (Jan.–Mar. 1998).

[Elber, Cohen 90] ELBER, G., AND COHEN, E. "Hidden Curve Removal for Free Form Surfaces." *Computer Graphics (Proc. SIGGRAPH '90)* 24(4): 95–104 (Aug. 1990).

[Evans 96] EVANS, L. *The New Complete Illustration Guide: The Ultimate Trace File for Architects, Designers, Artists, and Students*. New York: Van Nostrand Reinhold, 1996.

[Fekete et al. 95] FEKETE, J., BIZOUARN, É., COURNARIE, É., GALAS, T., AND TAILLEFER, F. "TicTacToon: A Paperless System for Professional 2-D animation." In *Proceedings of SIGGRAPH 95, Computer Graphics Proceedings, Annual Conference Series*, edited by Robert Cook, pp. 79–90, Reading, MA: Addison-Wesley, 1995.

[Finkelstein, Salesin 94] FINKELSTEIN, A., AND SALESIN, D. H. "Multiresolution curves." In *Proceedings of SIGGRAPH 94, Computer Graphics Proceedings, Annual Conference Series*, edited by Andrew Glassner, pp. 261–268, New York: ACM Press, 1994.

[Foley, van Dam 82] FOLEY, J. D., AND VAN DAM, A. *Fundamentals of Interactive Computer Graphics*. Reading, MA: Addison-Wesley, 1982.

[Franke 79] FRANKE, R. *A critical comparison of some methods for interpolation of scattered data*. Naval Postgraduate School, Report NPS-53-79-003 (1979).

[Franks 88] FRANKS, G. *Pencil Drawing*. Laguna Hills, CA: Walter Foster Publishing Inc., 1988.

[Geisel 71] GEISEL, T. *The Lorax*. New York: Random House, 1971.

[Geisel 88] GEISEL, T. *The Foot Book*. New York: Random House, 1988.

[Giesecke et al. 36] GIESECKE, F., MITCHELL, A., AND SPENCER, H. *Technical Drawing*. New York: The Macmillan Co., 1936.

[Girshick et al. 00] GIRSHICK, A., INTERRANTE, V., HAKER, S., AND LEMOINE, T. "Line direction matters: An argument for the use of principal directions in 3D line drawings." In *NPAR 2000: First International Symposium on Non-Photorealistic Animation and Rendering*, edited by Jean-Daniel Fekete and David H. Salesin, pp. 43–52, New York: ACM SIGGRAPH, 2000.

[Goldstein 80] GOLDSTEIN, E. B. *Sensation and perception*. Belmont, CA: Wadsworth Publishing Co., 1980.

[Gombrich 60] GOMBRICH, E. "Formula and Experience". In *Art and Illusion* (1960).

[Gooch et al. 98] GOOCH, A., GOOCH, B., SHIRLEY, P., AND COHEN, E. "A non-photorealistic lighting model for automatic technical illustration." *Proceedings of SIGGRAPH 98, Computer Graphics Proceedings, Annual Conference Series*, edited by Michael Cohen, pp. 447–452, Reading, MA: Addison-Wesley, 1998.

[Gooch 98] GOOCH, A. A. *Interactive non-photorealistic technical illustration*. Master's thesis, University of Utah, December 1998.

[Gooch et al. 99] GOOCH, B., SLOAN, P.-P., GOOCH, A., SHIRLEY, P., AND RIESENFELD, R. "Interactive Technical Illustration." In *ACM*

Symposium on Interactive 3D Graphics, edited by Jessica Hodgins and James D. Foley, pp. 31–38, New York: ACM Press, 1999.

[Green et al. 99] GREEN, S., SALESIN, D., SCHOFIELD, S., HERTZMANN, A., LITWINOWICZ, P., GOOCH, A., CURTIS, C., AND GOOCH., B. *Non-Photorealistic Rendering (SIGGRAPH '99 Course Notes)*. New York: ACM Press, 1999.

[Guo 95] GUO, Q. "Generating Realistic Calligraphy Words." *IEEE Trans. Fundamentals E78-A* 11: 1556–1558 (Nov. 1995).

[Guo, Kunii 91] GUO, Q., AND KUNII, T. L. "Modeling the diffuse painting of Sumi-e." In *IFIP Modeling in Computer Graphics*, edited by T. L. Kunii, 1991.

[Guptill 76] GUPTILL, A. L. *Rendering in Pen and Ink*. New York: Watson-Guptill Publications, 1976.

[Guptill 97] GUPTILL, A. *Rendering in Pencil*. New York: Watson-Guptill Publications, 1997.

[Haeberli 90] HAEBERLI, P. "Paint By Numbers: Abstract Image Representation." In *Computer Graphics (Proc. SIGGRAPH 90)* 24(4): 207–214 (Aug. 1990).

[Haeberli, Akeley 90] HAEBERLI, P. AND AKELEY, K. "The Accumulation Buffer: Hardware Support for High-Quality Rendering." In *Computer Graphics (Proc. SIGGRAPH 90)* 24(4): 309–318 (Aug. 1990).

[Hall 95] HALL, P. "Non-photorealistic shape cues for visualization." In *Winter School of Computer Graphics 1995*, February 1995.

[Hamel, Strothotte, 99] HAMEL, J., AND STROTHOTTE, T. "Capturing and re-using rendition styles for non-photorealistic rendering." *Computer Graphics Forum* 18(3): 173–182 (September 1999).

[Hanrahan, Haeberli 90] HANRAHAN, P., AND HAEBERLI, P. E. "Direct WYSIWYG Painting and Texturing on 3D Shapes." *Computer Graphics (Proc. SIGGRAPH '90)* 24(4): 215–223 (Aug. 1990).

[Hertzmann 98] HERTZMANN, A. "Painterly rendering with curved brush strokes of multiple sizes." In *Proceedings of SIGGRAPH 98, Computer Graphics Proceedings, Annual Conference Series*, edited by Michael Cohen, pp. 453–460, Reading, MA: Addison-Wesley, 1998.

[Hertzmann, Perlin 00] HERTZMANN, A., AND PERLIN, K. "Painterly rendering for video and interaction." In *NPAR 2000: First International Symposium on Non-Photorealistic Animation and Rendering*, edited by Jean-Daniel Fekete and David H. Salesin, pp. 7–12, New York: ACM SIGGRAPH, 2000.

[Hertzmann, Zorin 00] HERTZMANN, A., AND ZORIN, D. "Illustrating smooth surfaces." In *Proceedings of SIGGRAPH 2000, Computer Graphics Proceedings, Annual Conference Series*, edited by Kurt Akeley, pp. 517–526, Reading, MA: Addison-Wesley, 2000.

[Hoppe 96] HOPPE, H. "Progressive meshes." In *Proceedings of SIGGRAPH 96, Computer Graphics Proceedings, Annual Conference Series*, edited by Holly Rushmeier, pp. 99-108, Reading, MA: Addison-Wesley, 1996.

[Horton 94] HORTON, J. *An Introduction to Drawing*. London: Dorling Kindersley Limited, 1994.

[Hough 62] HOUGH, P. *A method and means for recognizing complex patterns. U. S. Patent 3,069,654*, 1962.

[Hsu et al. 94] HSU, S. C., AND LEE, I. H. H. "Drawing and animation using skeletal strokes." In *Proceedings of SIGGRAPH 94, Computer Graphics Proceedings, Annual Conference Series*, edited by Andrew Glassner, pp. 109–118, New York: ACM Press, 1994.

[Hutton-Jamieson 86] HUTTON-JAMIESON, I. *Colored Pencil Drawing Techniques*. Cincinnati, OH: North Light Books, 1986.

[Igarashi et al. 99] IGARASHI, T., MATSUOKA, S., AND TANAKA, H. "Teddy: A sketching interface for 3D freeform design." In *Proceedings of SIGGRAPH 99, Computer Graphics Proceedings, Annual Conference Series*, edited by Alyn Rockwood, pp. 409–416, Reading, MA: Addison-Wesley, 1999.

[Interrante et al. 95] INTERRANTE, V., FUCHS, H., AND PIZER, S. "Enhancing transparent skin surfaces with ridge and valley lines." In *IEEE Visualization '95*, pp. 221–228, Los Alamitos: IEEE, 1995.

[Interrante et al. 96] INTERRANTE, V., FUCHS, H., AND PIZER, S. "Illustrating transparent surfaces with curvature-directed strokes." In *IEEE Visualization '96*, pp. 211–218, Los Alamitos: IEEE, 1996.

[Interrante 97] INTERRANTE, V. L. "Illustrating surface shape in volume data via principal direction-driven 3D line integral convolution." In *Proceedings of SIGGRAPH 97, Computer Graphics Proceedings, Annual Conference Series*, edited by Turner Whitted, pp. 109–116, Reading, MA: Addison-Wesley, 1997.

[Ivins 88] IVINS, JR., W. M. *How Prints Look.* London: John Murray Publ. 1988.

[Jain et al. 95] JAIN, R., KASTURI, R., AND SCHUNCK, B. *Machine Vision.* New York: McGraw-Hill, 1995.

[Jobard, Lefer 97] JOBARD, B., AND LEFER, W. "Creating evenly-spaced streamlines of arbitrary density." In *Proc. of 8th Eurographics Workshop on Visualization in Scientific Computing*, pp. 45-55, Eurographics, 1997.

[Johnson 77] JOHNSON, C. *Harold and the Purple Crayon.* New York: Harper-Collins Juvenile Books, 1977.

[Kamada, Kawai 87] KAMADA, T., AND KAWAI, S. "An enhanced treatment of hidden lines." *ACM Transactions on Graphics* 6(4): 308–323 (October 1987).

[Kaplan, Salesin 00] KAPLAN, C. S., AND SALESIN, D. H. "Escherization." In *Proceedings of SIGGRAPH 2000, Computer Graphics Proceedings, Annual Conference Series*, edited by Kurt Akeley, pp. 499–510, Reading, MA: Addison-Wesley, 2000.

[Kaplan et al. 00] KAPLAN, M., GOOCH, B., AND COHEN, E. "Interactive artistic rendering." In *NPAR 2000: First International Symposium on Non-Photorealistic Animation and Rendering*, edited by Jean-Daniel Fekete and David H. Salesin, pp. 67–74, New York: ACM SIGGRAPH, 2000.

[Katchen 90] KATCHEN, C. *Creative Painting with Pastel.* Cincinnati, OH: North Light Books, 1990.

[Klein et al. 00] KLEIN, A. W., LI, W., KAZHDAN, M., CORR A, W. T., FINKELSTEIN, A., AND FUNKHOUSER, T. "Non-photorealistic virtual environments." In *Proceedings of SIGGRAPH 2000, Computer Graphics Proceedings, Annual Conference Series*, edited by Kurt Akeley, pp. 527–534, Reading, MA: Addison-Wesley, 2000.

[Kowalski et al. 99] KOWALSKI, M. A., MARKOSIAN, L., NORTHRUP, J. D., BOURDEV, L., BARZEL, R., HOLDEN, L. S., AND HUGHES, J. "Art-based rendering of fur, grass, and trees." In *Proceedings of SIGGRAPH 99, Computer Graphics Proceedings, Annual Conference Series*, edited by Alyn Rockwood, pp. 433–438, Reading, MA: Addison-Wesley, 1999.

[Kreutz 86] KREUTZ, G. *Problem Solving for Oil Painters.* New York: Watson-Guptill Publications 1986.

[Kruger, Rist 95] KRUGER, A., AND RIST, T. "Since less is often more: Methods for stylistic abstractions in 3D-graphics." In *Electronic Proceedings of the ACM Workshop on Effect Abstractions in Multimedia*, 4: (Nov. 1995).

[Lake et al. 00] LAKE, A., MARSHALL, C., HARRIS, M., AND BLACKSTEIN, M. "Stylized rendering techniques for scalable real-time 3D animation." In *NPAR 2000: First International Symposium on Non-Photorealistic Animation and Rendering*, edited by Jean-Daniel Fekete and David H. Salesin, pp. 13–20, New York: ACM SIGGRAPH, 2000.

[Lambert 91] LAMBERT, P. *Controlling color: a practical introduction for designers and artists*, Vol. 1. Hong Kong: Everbest Printing Company Ltd., 1991.

[Lansdown, Schofield 95] LANSDOWN, J., AND SCHOFIELD, S. "Expressive Rendering: A Review of Nonphotorealistic Techniques." *IEEE Computer Graphics and Applications* 15(3): 29–37 (May 1995).

[Lavallee et al. 95] LAVALLEE, S., SZELISKI, R., AND BRUNIE, L. "Anatomy-based registration of three-dimensional medial images, range images, x-ray projections, and three-dimensional models using octree-splines." *Computer Integrated Surgery*: 115–143 (1995).

[Lebaredian 96] LEBAREDIAN, R. "Traditional Cel Animation Look with 3D Renderers." In *Siggraph 96 Visual Proceedings*, New York: ACM Press, 1996.

[Lewis 84a] LEWIS, D. *Pencil Drawing Techniques.* New York: Watson-Guptill Publications, 1984.

[Lewis 84b] LEWIS, J. P. "Texture synthesis for digital painting." *Computer Graphics (Proc. SIGGRAPH 84)* 18(3) 245–252 (July 1984).

[Litwinowicz 91] LITWINOWICZ, P. C. "Inkwell: A 2D animation system." *Computer Graphics (Proc. SIGGRAPH 91)* 25(4): 113-122 (July 1991).

[Litwinowicz 97] LITWINOWICZ, P. "Processing images and video for an impressionist effect." In *Proceedings of SIGGRAPH 97, Computer Graphics Proceedings, Annual Conference Series*, edited by Turner Whitted, pp. 407–414, Reading, MA: Addison-Wesley, 1997.

[Lohan 78a] LOHAN, F. *The Drawing Handbook.* Chicago: Contemporary Books, Inc., 1978.

[Lohan 78b] LOHAN, F. *Pen and Ink Techniques.* Chicago: Contemporary Books, Inc., 1978.

[Luebke, Erikson 97] LUEBKE, D., AND ERIKSON, C. "View-dependent simplification of arbitrary polygonal environments." In *Proceedings of SIGGRAPH 97, Computer Graphics Proceedings, Annual Conference Series*, edited by Turner Whitted, pp. 199-208, Reading, MA: Addison-Wesley, 1997.

[Magnan 70] MAGNAN, G.. *Using Technical Art: An Industry Guide.* New York: John Wiley and Sons, Inc., 1970.

[Manyyla 88] MANTYLA, M. *An Introduction to Solid Modeling.* New York: Computer Science Press, 1988.

[Markosian, et al. 97] MARKOSIAN, L., KOWALSKI, M. A., TRYCHIN, S. J., BOURDEV, L. D., GOLDSTEIN, D., AND HUGHES, J. F. "Real-time nonphotorealistic rendering." In *Proceedings of SIGGRAPH 97, Computer Graphics Proceedings, Annual Conference Series*, edited by Turner Whitted, pp. 415–420, Reading, MA: Addison-Wesley, 1997.

[Markosian, et al. 99] MARKOSIAN, L., COHEN, J. M., CRULLI, T., AND HUGHES, J. F. "Skin: A constructive approach to modeling free-form shapes." In *Proceedings of SIGGRAPH 99, Computer Graphics Proceedings, Annual Conference Series*, edited by Alyn Rockwood, pp. 393–400, Reading, MA: Addison-Wesley, 1999.

[Markosian, et al. 00] MARKOSIAN, L., MEIER, B. J., KOWALSKI, M. A., HOLDEN, L. S., NORTHRUP, J., AND HUGHES, J. F. "Art-based rendering with continuous levels of detail." In *NPAR 2000: First International Symposium on Non-Photorealistic Animation and Rendering*, edited by Jean-Daniel Fekete and David H. Salesin, pp. 59–66, New York: ACM SIGGRAPH, 2000.

[Martin et al. 00] MARTIN, D., GARCIA, S., AND TORRES, J. C. "Observer dependent deformations in illustration." In *NPAR 2000: First International Symposium on Non-Photorealistic Animation and Rendering*, edited by Jean-Daniel Fekete and David H. Salesin, pp. 75–82, New York: ACM SIGGRAPH, 2000.

[Martin 89a] MARTIN, J. *High Tech Illustration*. Cincinnati, OH: North Light Books 1989.

[Martin 89b] MARTIN, J. *Technical Illustration: Materials, Methods, and Techniques*. MacDonald and Co. Publishers, 1989.

[Martin 97] MARTIN, J. *The Encyclopedia of Colored Pencil Techniques*. Philadelphia, PA: Running Press, 1997.

[Masuch et al. 97] MASUCH, M., SCHLECHTWEG, S., AND SCHÖNWÄLDER, B. "DALI! – Drawing Animated Lines!" In *Simulation und Animation '97*, edited by O. Deussen and P. Lorenz, pp. 87–96, SCS Europe, 1997.

[Masuch et al. 98] MASUCH, M., SCHUMANN, L., AND SCHLECHTWEG, S. "Animating Frame-to-Frame Consistent Line Drawings for Illustrative Purposes." In *Simulation und Animation '98*, edited by P. Lorenz and B. Preim, pp. 101–112, SCS Europe, 1998.

[Meier 96] MEIER, B. J. "Painterly rendering for animation." In *Proceedings of SIGGRAPH 96, Computer Graphics Proceedings, Annual Conference Series*, edited by Holly Rushmeier, pp. 477–484, Reading, MA: Addison-Wesley, 1996.

[Mestetskii 00] MESTETSKII, L. "Fat curves and representation of planar figures." *Computers & Graphics* 24(1): 9–21 (February 2000).

[Miller 94] MILLER, G. "Efficient algorithms for local and global accessibility shading." In *Proceedings of SIGGRAPH 94, Computer Graphics Proceedings, Annual Conference Series*, edited by Andrew Glassner, pp. 319–326, New York: ACM Press, 1994.

[Misawa 93] MISAWA, H. *An Introduction to Pencil Techniques: Easy Start Guide*. Los Angeles, CA: Books Nippan, 1993.

[Mukundan, Ramakrishnan 98] MUKUNDAN, R., AND RAMAKRISHNAN, K. R. *Moment Functions in Image Analysis—Theory and Applications*. Singapore: World Scientific Pub Co., 1998.

[Noot, Ruttkay 00] NOOT, H., AND RUTTKAY, Z. "Animated char-toon faces." In *NPAR 2000: First International Symposium on Non-Photorealistic Animation and Rendering*, edited by Jean-Daniel Fekete and David H. Salesin, pp. 91–100, New York: ACM SIG-GRAPH, 2000.

[Northrup, Markosian 00] NORTHRUP, J., AND MARKOSIAN, L. "Artistic silhouettes: A hybrid approach." In *NPAR 2000: First International Symposium on Non-Photorealistic Animation and Rendering*, edited by Jean-Daniel Fekete and David H. Salesin, pp. 31–38, New York: ACM SIGGRAPH, 2000.

[Ostromoukhov 99] OSTROMOUKHOV, V. "Digital facial engraving." In *Proceedings of SIGGRAPH 99, Computer Graphics Proceedings, Annual Conference Series*, edited by Alyn Rockwood, pp. 417–424, Reading, MA: Addison-Wesley, 1999.

[Ostromoukhov, Hersch 95] OSTROMOUKHOV, V., AND HERSCH, R. D. "Artistic screening." In *Proceedings of SIGGRAPH 95, Computer Graphics Proceedings, Annual Conference Series*, edited by Robert Cook, pp. 219–228, Reading, MA: Addison-Wesley, 1995.

[Ostromoukhov, Hersch 99] OSTROMOUKHOV, V., AND HERSCH, R. D. "Multi-color and artistic dithering." In *Proceedings of SIGGRAPH 99, Computer Graphics Proceedings, Annual Conference Series*, edited by Alyn Rockwood, pp. 425–432, Reading, MA: Addison-Wesley, 1999.

[Packard 00] PACKARD, H. *HP PEX texture mapping*. Technical Report, 2000. www.hp.com/mhm/WhitePapers/PEXtureMapping/ newline PEXtureMapping.html

[Paeth 94] PAETH, A. W. "Ideal tiles for shading and halftoning." In *Graphics Gems IV*, edited by Paul S. Heckbert, pp. 486–492, Boston: Academic Press, 1994.

[Parramon 97] PARRAMON'S EDITORIAL TEAM *Drawing (Barron's Art Handbook)*. New York: Barron's Educational Series, Inc., 1997.

[Perlin, Velho 95] PERLIN, K., AND VELHO, L. "Live paint: Painting with procedural multiscale textures." In *Proceedings of SIGGRAPH 95, Computer Graphics Proceedings, Annual Conference Series*, edited by Robert Cook, pp. 153–160, Reading, MA: Addison-Wesley, 1995.

[Petrovic et al. 00] PETROVIC, L., FUJITO, B., FINKELSTEIN, A., AND
    WILLIAMS, L. "Shadows for cel animation." In *Proceedings of SIG-
    GRAPH 2000, Computer Graphics Proceedings, Annual Conference
    Series*, edited by Kurt Akeley, pp. 511–516, Reading, MA: Addison-
    Wesley, 2000.

[Pham 91] PHAM, B. "Expressive brush strokes." *Computer Vision,
    Graphics, and Image Processing. Graphical Models and Image Pro-
    cessing* 53(1): 1–6 (Jan. 1991).

[Phong 75] PHONG, B.-T. "Illumination for Computer Generated Im-
    ages." *Communications of the ACM* 18(6): 311–317 (June 1975).

[Pitz 57] PITZ, H. C. *Ink Drawing Techniques.* New York: Watson-Guptill
    Publications, 1957.

[Pnueli, Bruckstein 94] PNUELI, Y., AND BRUCKSTEIN, A. M.
    "Digdurer—a digital engraving system." *The Visual Computer*
    10: 277–292 (Aug. 1994).

[Preparata, Shamos 85] PREPARATA, F. P., AND SHAMOS, M. I. *Com-
    putational Geometry.* New York: Springer-Verlag, 1985.

[Price 93] PRICE, G. *Pencil Drawing (from the Art is... Video Series).*
    Crystal Productions, 1993.

[Pudet 94] PUDET, T. "Real time fitting of hand-sketched pressure brush-
    strokes." *Computer Graphics Forum, (Proc. Eurographics 1994)*
    13(3): 205–220 (Aug. 1994).

[Rabb 98] RABB, A. *Techniques for Interacting with and Visualization
    of Geometric Models.* PhD thesis, Otto-von-Guericke University of
    Magdeburg, 1998.

[Rademacher 99] RADEMACHER, P. "View-dependent geometry." In *Pro-
    ceedings of SIGGRAPH 99, Computer Graphics Proceedings, Annual
    Conference Series*, edited by Alyn Rockwood, pp. 439–446, Reading,
    MA: Addison-Wesley Longman, 1999.

[Rankin 86] RANKIN, D. *Mastering Glazing Techniques in Watercolor.*
    New York: Watson-Guptill Publications, 1986.

[Raskar, Cohen 99] RASKAR, R., AND COHEN, M. "Image Precision Sil-
    houette Edges." In *Proc. 1999 ACM Symposium on Interactive 3D
    Graphics*, edited by Jessica Hodgins and James D. Foley, pp. 135–140,
    New York: ACM Press, 1999.

[Robertson 94a] ROBERTSON, B. "Digital toons." *Computer Graphics World*: 40–46 (June 1994).

[Robertson 94b] ROBERTSON, B. "Disney lets caps out of the bag." *Computer Graphics World*: 58–64 (July 1994).

[Rossignac, van Emmerik 92] ROSSIGNAC, J., AND VAN EMMERIK, M. "Hidden contours on a frame-buffer." In *Proceedings of the 7th Eurographics Workshop on Computer Graphics Hardware*, pp. 188–204, 1992.

[Ruppel 95] RUPPEL, T., Ed. *The way science works*, Vol. 1. New York: MacMillan, 1995.

[Saito, Takahashi 90] SAITO, T., AND TAKAHASHI, T. "Comprehensible Rendering of 3-D Shapes." *Computer Graphics (Proc. SIGGRAPH '90)* 24(4): 197–206 (Aug. 1990).,

[Salisbury et al. 94] SALISBURY, M. P., ANDERSON, S. E., BARZEL, R., AND SALESIN, D. H. "Interactive pen-and-ink illustration." In *Proceedings of SIGGRAPH 94, Computer Graphics Proceedings, Annual Conference Series*, edited by Andrew Glassner, pp. 101–108, New York: ACM Press, August 1994.

[Salisbury et al. 96] SALISBURY, M., ANDERSON, C., LISCHINSKI, D., AND SALESIN, D. H. "Scale-dependent reproduction of pen-and-ink illustrations." In *Proceedings of SIGGRAPH 96, Computer Graphics Proceedings, Annual Conference Series*, edited by Holly Rushmeier, pp. 461–468, Reading, MA: Addison-Wesley, 1996.

[Salisbury et al. 97] SALISBURY, M. P., WONG, M. T., HUGHES, J. F., AND SALESIN, D. H. "Orientable textures for image-based pen-and-ink illustration." In *Proceedings of SIGGRAPH 97, Computer Graphics Proceedings, Annual Conference Series*, edited by Turner Whitted, pp. 401–406, Reading, MA: Addison-Wesley, 1997.

[Salwey 25] SALWEY, J. *The Art of Drawing in Lead Pencil.* London: B. T. Batsford, Ltd., 1925.

[Sander et al. 00] SANDER, P. V., GU, X., GORTLER, S. J., HOPPE, H., AND SNYDER, J. "Silhouette clipping." In *Proceedings of SIGGRAPH 2000, Computer Graphics Proceedings, Annual Conference Series*, edited by Kurt Akeley, pp. 327-334, Reading, MA: Addison-Wesley Longman, 2000.

[Sato 84] SATO, S. *The Art of Sumi-e.* Tokyo: Kodansha International, 1984.

[Schaeffer 91] SCHAEFFER, S. A. *The Big Book of Painting Nature in Oil.* New York: Watson-Guptill Publications, 1991.

[Schlechtweg 97] SCHLECHTWEG, S. "Lines and how to draw them." *Norsk samarbeid inner grafisk databehandling* 4–6 (February 1997).

[Schofield 94] SCHOFIELD, S. *Non-photorealistic Rendering.* PhD thesis, Middlesex University, England, 1994.

[Schofield 96] SCHOFIELD, S. Piranesi: A 3-D Paint System. *Proceedings Eurographics UK 96,* (1996).

[Schumacher 91] SCHUMACHER, D. A. "A comparison of digital halftoning techniques." In *Graphics Gems II,* edited by James Arvo, pp. 57–71, 502–508, San Diego: Academic Press, 1991.

[Schumann 96] SCHUMANN, J., STROTHOTTE, T., RAAB, A., AND LASER, S. "Assessing the Effect of Non-Photorealistic Rendered Images in CAD." In *CHI 96 Electronic Proceedings,* New York: ACM, 1996.

[Schumann et al. 96] SCHUMANN, J., STROTHOTTE, T., RAAB, A., AND LASER, S. "Assessing the effect of NonPhoto-realistic rendered images in CAD." In *Proceedings of the Conference on Human Factors in Computing Systems : Commun Ground,* edited by M. J. Tauber, V. Bellotti, R. Jeffries, J. D. Mackinlay, and J. Nielsen, pp. 34–41, New York: ACM Press, 1996.

[Seligmann, Feiner 91] SELIGMANN, D. D., AND FEINER, S. "Automated generation of intent-based 3d illustrations." *Computer Graphics (Proc. SIGGRAPH 91)* 25(4): 123–132 (July 1991).

[Shiraishi, Yamaguchi 99] SHIRAISHI, M., AND YAMAGUCHI, Y. *Image moment-based stroke placement* Tech. Rep. skapps3794, University of Tokyo, Tokyo, Japan, May 1999.

[Shiraishi, Yamaguchi 00] SHIRAISHI, M., AND YAMAGUCHI, Y. "An algorithm for automatic painterly rendering based on local source image approximation." In *NPAR 2000: First International Symposium on Non-Photorealistic Animation and Rendering,* edited by Jean-Daniel Fekete and David H. Salesin, pp. 53–58, New York: ACM SIGGRAPH, 2000.

[Simmons 92] SIMMONS, G. *The Technical Pen*. New York: Watson-Guptill Publications, 1992.

[Small 91] SMALL, D. "Simulating watercolor by modeling diffusion, pigment, and paper fibers." In *Proceedings of SPIE '91*, February 1991.

[Smith 82] SMITH, A. R. "Paint." In *IEEE Tutorial: Computer Graphics*, 2nd edition, edited by K. S. Booth, pp. 501–515, Los Alamitos: IEEE Computer Society Press, 1982.

[Smith 84] SMITH, A. R. "Plants, fractals and formal languages." *Computer Graphics (Proc. SIGGRAPH 84)* 18(3): 1–10 (July 1984).

[Smith 95] SMITH, A. R. *Varieties of digital painting*. Tech. Rep., Microsoft Research, August 1995.

[Smith 97] SMITH, A. R. *Digital Paint Systems Historical Overview*. Redmond, WA: Microsoft Corporation, May 1997.

[Smith 87] SMITH, R. *The Artist's Handbook*. New York: Alfred A. Knopf, 1987.

[Snibbe, Levin 00] SNIBBE, S. S., AND LEVIN, G. "Interactive dynamic abstraction." In *NPAR 2000: First International Symposium on Non-Photorealistic Animation and Rendering*, edited by Jean-Daniel Fekete and David H. Salesin, pp. 21–30, New York: ACM SIGGRAPH, 2000.

[Snyder, Barlow 98] SNYDER, A. W., AND BARLOW, H. B. "Revealing the artist's touch." *Nature* 331(14): 117–118 (1998).

[Solso 99] SOLSO, R. L. *Cognition and the Visual Arts*. Cambridge, MA: MIT Press, 1999.

[Sousa, Buchanan 99a] SOUSA, M. C., AND BUCHANAN, J. W. "Observational model of blenders and erasers in computer-generated pencil rendering." In *Graphics Interface Proceedings 1999*, edited by I. Scott MacKenzie and James Stewart, pp. 157–166, San Francisco: Morgan Kaufmann Publishers, 1999.

[Sousa, Buchanan 99b] SOUSA, M. C., AND BUCHANAN, J. W. "Computer-generated graphite pencil rendering of 3d polygonal models." *Computer Graphics Forum* 18(3): 195–208 (September 1999).

[Sousa, Buchanan 00] SOUSA, M. C., AND BUCHANAN, J. W. "Observational models of graphite pencil materials." *Computer Graphics Forum* 19(1): 27–49 (March 2000).

[Strassmann 86] STRASSMANN, S. "Hairy brushes." *Computer Graphics (Proc. SIGGRAPH 86)* 20(4): 225–232 (August 1986).

[Streit, Buchanan 98] STREIT, L. M., AND BUCHANAN, J. W. "Importance driven halftoning." *Computer Graphics Forum* 17(3): 207–218 (1998).

[Strothotte, Strothotte 97] STROTHOTTE, C., AND STROTHOTTE, T. *Seeing Between the Pixels: Pictures in Interactive Systems.* Berlin: Springer-Verlag, 1997.

[Strothotte et al. 94] STROTHOTTE, T., PREIM, B., RAAB, A., SCHUMANN, J., AND FORSEY, D. R. "How to render frames and influence people." *Computer Graphics Forum* 13(3): 455–466 (1994).

[Sullivan 22] SULLIVAN, E. J. *Line: an Art Study.* London: Chapman and Hall, 1922.

[Sutherland 63] SUTHERLAND, I. "Sketchpad: A man-machine graphical communication system." In *Proc. AFIPS Spring Joint Computer Conference*, pp. 329–346, Spartan Books, 1963.

[Szabo 74] SZABO, Z. *Creative Watercolor Techniques.* New York: Watson-Guptill Publications, 1974.

[Takagi et al. 99] TAKAGI, S., NAKAJIMA, M., AND FUJISHIRO, I. "Volumetric modeling of colored pencil drawing." In *Pacific Graphics '99* (October 1999).

[Tanaka, Ohnishi 97] TANAKA, T., AND OHNISHI, N. "Painting-like image emphasis based on human vision systems." *Computer Graphics Forum* 16(3): 253–260 (August 1997).

[Teece 98a] TEECE, D. "3D Painting for Non-Photorealistic Rendering." In *SIGGRAPH 98: Conference Abstracts and Applications*, p. 248, New York: ACM SIGGRAPH, 1998.

[Teece 98b] TEECE, D. *Three Dimensional Interactive Non-Photorealistic Rendering.* PhD thesis, University of Sheffield, England, 1998.

[Thomas, Johnston 81] THOMAS, F., AND JOHNSTON, O. *Disney Animation—The Illusion of Life.* New York: Abbeville Press, 1981.

[Thomas 68] THOMAS, T. *Technical Illustration*, 2nd. Edition. New York: McGraw-Hill, New York, 1968.

[Tjan et al. 95] TJAN, B. S., BRAJE, W. L., LEGGE, G. E., AND KERSTEN, D. "Human efficiency for recognizing 3-D objects in luminance noise." *Vision Research* 35(21): 3053–3069 (1995).

[Treavett, Chen 97] TREAVETT, S. M. F., AND CHEN, M. "Statistical Techniques for the Automated Synthesis of Non-Photorealistic Images." In *Proc. 15th Eurographics UK Conference*, Mar. 1997.

[Tufte 97] TUFTE, E. *Visual explanations*. Cheshire, CT: Graphics Press, 1997.

[Tumblin, Turk 99] TUMBLIN, J., AND TURK, G. "LCIS: A boundary hierarchy for detail-preserving contrast reduction." *Proceedings of SIGGRAPH 99, Computer Graphics Proceedings, Annual Conference Series*, edited by Alyn Rockwood, pp. 83–90, Reading, MA: Addison-Wesley, 1999.

[Turk 96] TURK, G., AND BANKS, D. "Image-guided streamline placement." In *Proceedings of SIGGRAPH 96, Computer Graphics Proceedings, Annual Conference Series*, edited by Holly Rushmeier, pp. 453–460, Reading, MA: Addison-Wesley, 1996.

[Ulichney 87] ULICHNEY, R. *Digital Halftoning*. Cambridge, MA: The MIT Press, 1987.

[Velho, Gomes 91] VELHO, L., AND DE MIRANDA GOMES, J. "Digital Halftoning with Space Filling Curves." *Computer Graphics (Proc. Siggraph 91)* 25(4): 81–90, 1991.

[Vermeulen, Tanner 89] VERMEULEN, A. H., AND TANNER, P. P. "Pencilsketch—a pencil-based paint system." In *Graphics Interface Proceedings 1989*, pp. 138–143, San Francisco: Morgan Kaufmann Publishers, 1989.

[Veryovka, Buchanan 99] VERYOVKA, O., AND BUCHANAN, J. W. "Halftoning with image-based dither screens." In *Graphics Interface Proceedings 1999*, pp. 167–174, San Francisco: Morgan Kaufmann Publishers, 1999.

[Walter et al. 97] WALTER, B., ALPPAY, G., LAFORTUNE, E. P. F., FERNANDEZ, S., AND GREENBERG, D. P. "Fitting Virtual Lights for Non-Diffuse Walkthroughs." In *Proceedings of SIGGRAPH 97, Computer Graphics Proceedings, Annual Conference Series*, edited by Turner Whitted, pp. 45–48, Reading, MA: Addison-Wesley, 1997.

[Wang, Kaufman 95] WANG, S. W., AND KAUFMAN, A. E. "Volume sculpting." In *1995 Symposium on Interactive 3D Graphics: Proceedings*, pp. 151–156, New York: ACM, 1995.

[Ware 88] WARE, C. "Color Sequences for Univariate Maps: Theory, Experiments, and Principles." *IEEE Computer Graphics & Applications* 8(5): 41–49 (1988).

[Watson 78] WATSON, E. *Course in Pencil Sketching, Four Books in One.* New York: Van Nostrand Reinhold Company, 1978.

[Whitted 83] WHITTED, T. "Anti-aliased line drawing using brush extrusion." *Computer Graphics (Proc. SIGGRAPH '83)* 17(3): 151-156 (July 1983).

[Williams 83] WILLIAMS, L. "Pyramidal parametrics." *Computer Graphics (Proc. SIGGRAPH '83)* 17(3): 1–11 (July 1983).

[Williams 90] WILLIAMS, L. "3D paint." In *1990 Symposium on Interactive 3D Graphics*, edited by Rich Riesenfeld and Carlo Séquin, pp. 225-233, New York: ACM Press, 1990.

[Williams 91] WILLIAMS, L. "Shading in Two Dimensions." In *Graphics Interface '91*, pp. 143–151, San Francisco: Morgan Kaufmann Publishers, 1991.

[Winkenbach, Salesin 94] WINKENBACH, G., AND SALESIN, D. H. "Computer-generated pen-and-ink illustration." In *Proceedings of SIGGRAPH 94, Computer Graphics Proceedings, Annual Conference Series*, edited by Andrew Glassner, pp. 91–100, New York: ACM Press, August 1994.

[Winkenbach, Salesin 96] WINKENBACH, G., AND SALESIN, D. H. "Rendering Parametric Surfaces in Pen and Ink." In *Proceedings of SIGGRAPH 96, Computer Graphics Proceedings, Annual Conference Series*, edited by Holly Rushmeier, pp. 469–476, Reading, MA: Addison-Wesley, 1996.

[Winter 00] WINTER R.. "Art by the numbers." *UCLA Magazine* 26–31 (Spring 2000).

[Wong 95] WONG, T-T. "Halftoning with selective precipitation and adaptive clustering." In *Graphics Gems V*, edited by Alan W. Paeth, pp. 302-313, Boston: Academic Press, 1995.

[Wong 99] WONG, E. *Artistic rendering of portrait photographs.* Master's thesis, Cornell University, 1999.

[Wong et al. 98] WONG, M. T., ZONGKER, D. E., AND SALESIN, D. H. "Computer-Generated Floral Ornament." In *Proceedings of SIG-GRAPH 98, Computer Graphics Proceedings, Annual Conference Series*, edited by Michael Cohen, pp. 423–434, Reading, MA: Addison-Wesley, 1998.

[Wood et al. 97] WOOD, D. N., FINKELSTEIN, A., HUGHES, J. F., THAYER, S. E., AND SALESIN, D. H. "Multiperspective panoramas for cel animation." In *Proceedings of SIGGRAPH 97, Computer Graphics Proceedings, Annual Conference Series*, edited by Turner Whitted, pp. 243–250, Reading, MA: Addison-Wesley, 1997.

[Zeleznik et al. 96] ZELEZNIK, R. C., HERNDON, K. P., AND HUGHES, J. F. "Sketch: An interface for sketching 3D scenes." In *Proceedings of SIGGRAPH 96, Computer Graphics Proceedings, Annual Conference Series*, edited by Holly Rushmeier, pp. 163–170, Reading, MA: Addison-Wesley, 1996.

[Zhang, 97] ZHANG, H., AND HOFF, III, K. E. "Fast backface culling using normal masks." In *Proc. 1997 Symposium on Interactive 3D Graphics*, edited by Michael Cohen and David Zeltzer, pp. 103–106, New York: ACM SIGGRAPH, 1997.

[Zhang et al. 99] ZHANG, Q., SATO, Y., TAKAHASHI, J., MURAOKA, K., AND CHIBA, N. "Simple cellular automaton-based simulation of ink behaviour and its application to Suibokuga-like 3D rendering of trees." *The Journal of Visualization and Computer Animation* 10(1): 27–37 (1999).

[Zhu et al. 97] ZHU, C., BYRD, R. H., LU, P., AND NOCEDAL, J. "Algorithm 778: L-bfgs-b: Fortran subroutines for large-scale bound-constained optimization." *ACM Trans. Math. Software* 23(4) 550–560 (1997).

Index

Printed and bound by CPI Group (UK) Ltd, Croydon, CR0 4YY

23/10/2024

01777693-0002